WE, THE AR

by

DR. NORMA J. MILANOVICH

with

BETTY RICE

and

CYNTHIA PLOSKI

ATHENA
Publishing

First Printing August 1990
Sixth Printing May 1994

ISBN 0-9627417-0-1

Library of Congress Catalog Card Number 90-082682

Cover Illustration: Arthur Douët

Cover Design: Robert K. Mortensen

Published by
ATHENA PUBLISHING
Mossman Center, Suite 206
7410 Montgomery Blvd. NE
Albuquerque, NM 87109-1574

Printed in the United States of America
15 14 13 12 11 10 9 8 7 6

DEDICATION

THIS BOOK is dedicated to my niece, Tracy Marie Crothers, who died suddenly at the age of 14 on September 19, 1986 in Scandia, Minnesota. Tracy was a very popular, radiant child who had the reputation of being an excellent student and athlete. She was also one of the most dedicated, hard-working youngsters in her class.

I happen to know that she never lost these characteristics—even after she passed over to the other side. From the day after her death, Tracy became my spiritual guide, found a way to communicate with me, and focused her efforts on showing me the path to enlightenment and to the Masters. Her never-ending dedication to her mission was always present as she continually instructed me on the importance of giving and receiving love and the power of forgiveness. She was the one responsible for helping me understand how to raise my vibrational rate in order to communicate more directly with the magnificent Beings in the other dimensions of time and space.

Although Tracy never took the credit for it, I think that it was she who was responsible for bringing Cynthia and Betty into my life. I truly believe that it was through her relentless efforts that we three met, became good friends, and were able to bring this document through for others.

I thank you Tracy; Betty and Cynthia thank you; your family thanks you; and so do the Arcturians. "This book's for you!"

Emblem of the Arcturian Starship Athena

This drawing, and the one on page 32, were completed
by Cynthia Ploski

The instructions for the design of this emblem were
transmitted by programmed instruction in one session.
By following the directions, Cynthia was able to produce
the above symbol.

ACKNOWLEDGMENTS

THROUGHOUT THE development of this book, several people contributed in many ways to assist the authors. We would like to take this opportunity to voice our thanks to all of them:

To Rudy Milanovich: Grateful appreciation for the countless hours he donated in programming our edited versions of the transmissions into the computer and warm thanks for the number of times he tried to bail us out when the computer demonstrated irrational irritability and refused to cooperate....

To Rudy Milanovich, Jr.: For his unending optimism and support in listening to our discussions and occasionally sitting in on the weekly dialogues with the Arcturians....

To Reeve Love: For all the time and effort she put into reading and editing the raw version, using her wisdom and acute awareness to refine the manuscript into its present form....

To husbands, children, and friends who have encouraged and supported us....

And to a very special group of people from the U.S. Air Force at Altus Air Force Base in Altus, Oklahoma, who decided that the project was for real and dedicated their energies to support us: SSGT. Ester Posey, who has passed beyond and now understands it all; James W. Watson Jr. and his wife, Holly, and son, Matt; Joseph M. Huffman, Jr.; Glenn T. Young; Carl Douglas Martin; James A. Eden, Sr.; Nelson E. Kinsey III; Cynthia Marie Edwards; Farhad Abbassi; John K. Arnold; Stephen Wade Fitzpatrick; Don Hughes; Fredrick Lyons; and Darrell A. Jenkins.

WE, THE ARCTURIANS

TABLE OF CONTENTS

PAGE

Dedication i

Acknowledgements iii

A Note to the Reader vii

Preface 1

Introduction 7

CHAPTER 1: The First Encounters 15

CHAPTER 2: The Visitors 36

CHAPTER 3: The Revelations Of The Elders 62

CHAPTER 4: Language Systems On Arcturus 89

CHAPTER 5: Educational Systems on Arcturus . . . 115

CHAPTER 6: The Land They Left Behind 136

CHAPTER 7: Starship General Divisions 142

CHAPTER 8: The Training Program 216

CHAPTER 9: The Mission 236

CHAPTER 10: The Future 298

Glossary 305

Autobiographies of the Authors 311

A NOTE TO THE READER

THE INFORMATION in this book was received from fifth dimensional Beings who say that they are from the planet Arcturus. All of the transmitted messages recorded here are in a form nearly identical to that in which they were received. Some minor editing was done, however, to make them easier to read. In order to keep these messages as accurate as possible, the types of editing that were done by the authors are described in this section. It is our hope that by providing you, the reader, with information regarding our editing, this will help to maintain the integrity of the information transmitted in its purest form.

It is important to begin by describing the process by which Norma Milanovich receives her messages. When a question is asked of the Being with whom she is communicating, she goes into a semi-trance state, allowing the source to communicate through her via a microcomputer. The messages that were transmitted in this book were all received on a microcomputer using the software package PFS: Professional Write, Version 2.1. In this process, once the Beings begin to send the information, she receives the messages telepathically as fast as they will speak to, or through, her. In this mode of operation, her physical body also is involved in the receiving of the messages, and she types as fast as 60 to 80 words a minute, non-stop, for as long as an hour or more. It is this state of hyperactivity that can, and sometimes does, cause errors to occur in receiving the information.

During this time her fingers may hit more than one key simultaneously, causing misspelled words. Also, some of the words that are sent through her may be misinterpreted. For example, the word "hear" could be sent, but the word "here" might appear in print. The unseen communicators also are known to create their own words, which they do frequently.

In these cases, editing was done to correct misspelled words, to change words so that they represented the correct meanings, or to define the new vocabulary that was being used. All transcriptions were checked with PFS: Professional Write's spell checker. Whenever this software package determined that a word was misspelled, and suggested a correction, the correction was given priority and the change was made.

Often, when the Arcturians used words with which the authors were unfamiliar, these words were left untouched in the manuscript. The reader will find several of these "jewels" throughout the book. In the beginning, this situation drove the authors crazy, as they were confused as to what the Arcturians were really saying. Eventually, however, it was deemed necessary to include this new vocabulary in the manuscript.

In all cases, whenever a change was made that was considered significant, Norma checked out the editing with the Arcturians. She would ask them if this new word or explanation said what they wished to say, and if they replied that it did, then that version was included in the book. This process seemed no different from the original process of receiving the transmissions, so the approach was judged valid and not considered likely to contaminate the messages.

Interestingly enough, the Arcturians did not always like the changes that were made, and they would tell Norma so. In these instances, the original words were kept intact and left for the reader to interpret, even though they were not fully understood by the authors themselves. There are a few such words in this book.

Other minor forms of editing that were done included adding plural endings to words when it was obvious that they should be there and punctuating sentences correctly. It is important to note here, however, that all the italics that are included in these transmitted messages were put there by our unseen visitors. These came through at the time of the original communications, and have remained untouched. The authors took editorial liberties in three major areas:

1. Whenever a message was received in a sentence that was longer than normal, they broke it up into smaller sentences and took out the "ands," etc.

2. Occasionally the Arcturians would end a sentence with a preposition. Whenever this was discovered the sentence was amended to be grammatically correct.

3. Whenever pronouns were used too extensively, and it became confusing for the reader to determine the references, these pronouns were changed to make the referents clear.

No other changes were made. Basically, everything appears just as it was received by Norma.

We hope that our efforts and the explanations help you, the reader, to assimilate the information contained in this book with greater ease. We also hope that you appreciate reading the transmissions on the following pages as much as we have appreciated receiving them.

As our Arcturian friends so frequently say to us in our communications:

"Adonai, our sisters and brothers of the Light. Enjoy!"

WE, THE ARCTURIANS

PREFACE

THIS BOOK is about change and the possibility of a new door opening to the future for planet Earth. It contains information on Beings from another section of the universe: their characteristics, the Starship on which they ride, a description of their home planet, their mission, their mode of functioning, and explanations of dimensions of space and time that only a few scientists on our planet, such as Einstein, appeared to understand. It is about a new way of behaving and about the future of humanity. It may even contain sections of a code for survival in the New Age.

The transmissions that are recorded in these chapters are from those who claim to be extraterrestrial Beings (or Celestials, as they prefer to be called), and who state that they are here from Arcturus. The messages contain little information based upon systems and data that are presently in place on Earth. They do, however, present a foundation for what could be in place tomorrow or for what might be our destiny.

These Celestials, the Arcturians, do not speak as we do on Earth. Where we are preoccupied with the physical world and the acquisition of power in that dimension, they focus on the inner world and the untapped resources that we have yet to discover. Where we focus on concrete objects and events that we can see, feel, and "kick," they refer to energy, Light, a concept of oneness, the universal laws, and fourth and fifth dimensional frequencies and above. Where we struggle with the meaning of life and

1

wonder why we are even here, they claim that they are aided by the Ascended Masters, work for Jesus, the Christ and other magnificent Beings such as Ashtar and Kuthumi, and have transcended that struggle of reality centuries ago. They state emphatically that they are here on a mission of love and Light, and testify that they are only some among many entities who presently are aiding Earth and its inhabitants on a journey into the next millennium.

Are these claims and messages fact or fiction? Is the source of these transmissions actually Beings from a higher state of consciousness, or are these messages coming from entities who are pathological liars with a plan to deceive and take over the Earth? We cannot say. We only provide the messages on the following pages to help you make that determination. As the organizers and partial authors of this book, we can only give you the words that we have received.

After many long months of debating this same question ourselves, we chose to take the position of believing the unseen visitors. If they claim they are from Arcturus, then we acknowledge that they are. We have no data to indicate that they are not. Any further reference to them, then, is only a statement of our chosen beliefs, and not a case of trying to "brainwash" the reader to accept our position.

There are several reasons why we take this stand. The first reason we choose to believe these unseen visitors is because of the consistent quality of the information that is sent through from them. We have yet to receive a transmission that is derogatory, harmful, or in the least bit directive. These Beings never tell us what to do or what to think; they only make suggestions and answer our questions with a candid optimism. We find this attitude refreshing and comforting.

A second reason we choose to believe them is because they are always consistent in the information that they send. Often information sent at one time (and consequently forgotten by us) was reinforced by another transmission at a later time, when we least expected it. Upon checking the accuracy and substance of consecutive messages, we were always impressed to discover the consistency with which the information had been relayed to us. Therefore, it appeared to us that we were communicating with a source that was reliable and not one that was into game-playing.

Another reason we choose to believe these Beings is because they also transmitted to us information and data to which we did not have access at the time. Whenever this happened, we would research their messages, and would find that the information received was true. This happened on many occasions, which served to secure our confidence that we indeed were communicating with a source that had access to information that was far beyond our own capabilities of acquisition.

In analyzing many of the transmissions in this book, one might conclude that the abilities of the Arcturians are much greater than those of humans. They "speak" with fluent "tongues" and always seem to have an answer for any question that is posed to them. They never degrade another Being or individual or civilization, and seem to be above that level of interaction. They also appear to have the innate mental ability to form meaningful analogies, at any given moment, between the most unlikely objects or categories. For instance, when they were asked to describe what the fourth and fifth dimensional frequencies were like, they instantly replied that since the experience of those frequencies was beyond the consciousness of humans, they would have to use the analogy of the "fragrance of the rose" to explain what it would be like to live on those dimensions. Then, within a matter of minutes, they wove a beautiful tapestry with their words that actually explained what it would be like to exist on those levels. Now, how many humans could pass this kind of test in a writing class?

If you are an individual with a healthy curiosity about life, who believes in the existence of other life forms or a power greater than yourself, and who has the desire to learn new things, then you might find much enjoyment in this book. And if you are also a believer in UFOs and acknowledge that the numerous UFO sightings reported may have validity, then you will probably find this book intriguing. In fact, the information contained in these pages may even give you new hope for contact with Celestial Beings in the future.

The information presented here is the truth as we believe it to be, derived from the multitude of "weird experiences" that have occurred over the last several months of our lives. The messages in this book, written by our unseen Arcturian visitors, are meant to be shared with all who will benefit from them.

The following is a preface that was transmitted to us by the Acrturians for insertion in this book. It was received after the document was completed.

The next few years on the planet Earth will be difficult ones for many of the children of Light. This will be in varying degrees, but for those who have mastered the principles of love and Light, they will have all the tools needed to move into the millennium.

We, The Arcturians, do bid you hello in this new phase your lives will experience. The leap of consciousness and the mobility you will experience will be one of the greatest of your lifetimes. It will be the magnificent journey into the world of thought and love. It will be the creator of the universes, majestic planes, and temples that many of you dream about in your sleeping states.

4

The next few years will be like the snake or other reptiles shedding their skins. The transformation into the future will turn the destiny of the planet Earth back to the Divine. The Masters will rejoice with the children of the Light, and the inheritance will be that of the gold.

In the beginning of this book you will see the formation of what we look like. We will describe ourselves and give you information on what it is like to live in this fifth dimension—the one which you are entering. This vision will soon be yours in the physical plane, for we will be appearing to you before the twinkling of an eye. The command decree has been lifted, and we are now able to move around more freely in the different dimensional frequencies. We can now teach in the fifth, fourth, and third dimensions of time and space. We can also sing of the vibrations that will be emanating from the Highest and instruct all of the children of the magnificent awakening that is falling around the beloved Terra.

This new era into which we are journeying will be one shared among us all. We will be walking by your side as we move into the future together. On this side by side path, we will all be singing the songs of creation, as we build the future in the years to come.

We, The Arcturians, come as your brothers and sisters, and we enter the kingdom of the All. We hold your hands in the instruction, and sing together to make the laws and rules of the universe unfold.

We have been given permission to work with the authors and provide them with information on universal laws that will apply in the new millennium. They will be able to support our role by announcing new information that will help all of humanity survive in the New Age.

This information will be coming through many sources and channels in the years to come. This information is unfolding as we telepathically communicate to you. But also, THE TIME IS NOW to begin the learning of these lessons.

We are pleased to be the bearers of this news. We are also pleased to have served all of you in this fashion.

INTRODUCTION

THIS DOCUMENT is about contact with extraterrestrial Beings from Arcturus, who claim that they are visiting planet Earth. It represents only a small portion of the dialogue and transmitted messages that have been exchanged between the authors and these Celestials for approximately nine months. It is the result of a true experience, and one that is ongoing.

Does this sound incredible? Well, in case you are wondering, it does to the authors as well.

A few years ago, if anyone had told us that there were individuals "down the street" carrying on weekly dialogues with "ETs," we would have burst into laughter. Not only would we have considered that thought absurd, but we also would have rejected the idea that it was possible for extraterrestrials to be that close to humans.

Somehow, it is believable that the increased number of UFO sightings and encounters on Earth are real. It is also conceivable that the reported abductions and firsthand UFO experiences are also true—as long as they never become *our* reality. Right? For that is where it seems to become necessary for most individuals to draw the line. What we already have heard about or witnessed usually constitutes the boundary for our acceptance of anything new.

Can there possibly be something more going on than what people have been reporting to date? Is it plausible that there is a plan to make contact with us here, and that the sightings and abductions are only the first phase of this plan? If these reports are indeed true (and millions of people, worldwide, seem to believe they are) is it not probable that there is an ongoing progression of events regarding human interactions with these Beings from other parts of the universe? Is it not also possible that, if this is so, the natural progression of events might include direct communication with people on Earth as the next step?

It is our experience and truth that this is what has happened. This is exactly what this book is all about. It reveals ongoing communications of "the ninth kind" (as our unseen friends have called it) that a group of average people in New Mexico have had with these Beings over a long period of time.

Many individuals have attended the weekly sessions and have participated in the dialogues with these visitors, all for different reasons. Some came with a curiosity that needed to be quenched. Others came to test the validity of the source, and still others came as seekers of the truth. Whatever the case, our unseen friends *always* provided entertainment, wisdom, and answers.

Over the course of more than a year, hundreds of pages of dialogue have been received, all of which are so fascinating that we felt this information must be shared. Thus, we decided to publish this book, to allow others on Earth to receive these messages too.

As the authors of this book, we cannot "prove" that the information contained within it is true, nor is it our intention to try to do so. We can only describe, step by step, the process we have gone through in receiving the messages, be honest in describing our experiences over the last several years, organize the messages in a coherent fashion, and share them with those who feel that they will benefit from the information. That is all we have attempted to do.

This has not been, however, an easy project to complete. How does one begin "casually" to describe events that are far outside the parameters of normal experience, while trying to maintain something of a dignified posture? Each of us is acutely aware of the possibility that the publishing of this document could ruin our professional reputations and cast doubt upon the credentials that we have put together so carefully over the years. It has not been an easy decision to publish these messages, for we are all quite content with our lives, having attained considerable success in our individual careers. The public, reporters, tabloids, government and military officials, etc., can be merciless in dealing with new ideas, especially ideas as controversial as those that we are presenting here.

This book contains more than just new ideas and information. This book is about stepping over a new threshold of time and space. It possibly could contain messages that are opening the door to a whole new dimension of communications and life in the future—the fifth dimension. In fact, the truth contained in this book is even stranger than fiction.

Some of the information we are presenting here is so incredible that we offer no explanation, interpretation, or defense for it. We leave it to you to determine the validity of the contents. We have a high regard for the intelligence of the majority of individuals on our planet today. We also trust in a higher Force that guides us all, and feel that the process of acceptance or rejection of this material will be perfect for each individual who reads it.

In addition, we have a firm belief that it is the spirit of the word that gives life and meaning to us all and that it is the letter of the word that can kill. If the reader senses the spirit of the messages that have been sent to us, as we do, then we are optimistic that our decision to share these messages serves a higher purpose. We have been inspired by the words of the Arcturians, and hope that those who read these messages will be moved as we have been.

This concludes *our* introduction, but not the introduction to our book. We asked the Arcturians if they also wished to include some opening remarks, and they replied, "Yes!"

The following is the introduction they transmitted:

Good Evening in the Light of Our Most Radiant One.

We, the Arcturians, do collectively welcome you to our home in the skies and to the dimensional frequency that will soon be the home of planet Earth, as well.

Our journey to your beautiful planet is one of friendship, dedication, and love to you, our brothers and sisters of Earth. We acknowledge the importance of your missions with as much respect as we accord the importance of ours, that being to assist Earthlings to enter another dimensional frequency of reality, which is the fifth dimension.

In order to do this, the fundamental ingredient of the process demands that one becomes love. In this process, the human must reach a new state of ecstasy that will enable him or her to move to a higher frequency of behavior. This higher frequency will lend itself automatically to the perfection of the physical, emotional, mental, and spiritual bodies that are contained within each of your electronic circles.

This progression into the unknown must come to pass and is the natural state of evolution that humans must encounter. We have been in this dimensional frequency for many of your Earth centuries, and are here now to assist you in this "rebirthing process."

We are also the watchtower, so to speak, that will enable the beloved Terra to make her transition into the New Age with as little pain as possible.

In order for her to do so, the human quality of negativity must come to a halt. This quality, which is developed out of fear and guilt, must be exchanged for the qualities of love and Light. In the exchange will come the peace, harmony, and ecstasy that each soul has longed for on the Earth.

We are here to assist any soul who will journey with us to this higher level of consciousness. We will work and communicate with any Being who finds that this higher state of consciousness is deserving of the attention it receives. We are also here to achieve our mission, which is the fulfillment of the plan of the Ascended Masters of the Universe, who are commanded by Jesus, the Christ, who is also known as Sananda on the higher realms. The Masters have a dedicated mission to save the planet Earth from its own possible, fatal destruction. They have the command and the vision to guide all who will continue on their evolutionary paths to a better world.

We take our mission very seriously. We understand whom we serve. There is no doubt as to where our loyalties lie in the serving of the Masters who so lovingly dedicate their energy and consciousness to the children of the planet. We share in their vision and in the glory that a new day will emerge on the Earth. We rejoice in the day when this vision also will become your reality.

We come in peace. We bring you love and Light from a distance across the galaxy that is

11

incomprehensible to any mind on Earth. We bring you tidings of good will and joy from the Elders and the officials who serve us well, back on Arcturus.

Our journeys are far and are destined to fulfill the highest of movements and commands. Our journeys are also weary, for we have been away for so many Earth years that it is difficult to assess the conditions of what we left behind. We have been here with you, our sisters and brothers of Earth, for so many years that it is not even comprehensible to you that we have worked among you for that long. It is the truth, and has been the plan for two thousand years.

We have learned much about our own history from observing you in your struggle to achieve a higher consciousness. We watch in amazement at your battles against the delusions of the illusions that surround your essence. We weep for the torment and the anger that you bestow upon one another—for what purpose, we cannot say.

In these observations we have also learned of the beautiful quality of life on Earth, that is worthy of preserving. We have learned of the grace and beauty which you command. We marvel at your independence and the maneuvers which you use to maintain and preserve that independence. And in all of this, we continually ask "Why?"

It is through the answering of this unanswered question that we have posed a question for you. In our wondering about your patterns of motivation and behavior, we observe that you often ask about ours. So, we pose this question to you: "Would you like to learn more about us, and what we are like?"

If your answer is "yes," then we suspect you will enjoy that which is being transmitted on these pages. We are pleased to make your acquaintance by welcoming you to our home in the fifth dimension, and by taking you on a guided tour of our home. If the answer is "no," then please pick up another book and enjoy the contents of another adventure of your choosing.

We thank you for this opportunity to say these few introductory words, and we look forward to observing your reactions when you read the information that we have transmitted on the following pages. Please know that we will be monitoring each of you on our screens when you are absorbing the energy contained on these pages, and that, in so doing, you will be providing us with additional data on your human qualities and traits. We do strive continually to work hard while on Earth assignment, and therefore, are always working. So while you will be reading this document and hopefully enjoying the contents, we will be working at enjoying you, as you are experiencing your introduction to us and our home.

We now shall discontinue this transmission.

Adonai, our beautiful sisters and brothers in the Light.

We, the Arcturians, do salute you for the journey on which you are about to embark.

Nothing more was transmitted.

Now that our combined introductions are complete, find a comfortable chair, curl up with a soft pillow, and settle in for what we hope will be one of the most fascinating awakenings of your lifetime.

We are pleased to introduce you to "The Arcturians," visitors to Earth who come from Arcturus, located in the Bootes Constellation, and who represent Heaven's enlightened Celestial Command.

CHAPTER I:
THE FIRST ENCOUNTERS

IT IS difficult to condense the extraordinary circumstances that have led to the development of this document.

Many individuals have asked us how this process began. They have experienced the communication sessions and have been amazed at the information sent through. The speed at which this information is transmitted and the uniqueness of the answers have sparked a multitude of questions, such as:

"How did Norma first come into contact with these Beings?"

"How does she continue to make contact with them?"

"How do Betty, Cynthia, and Norma know that they are communicating with Arcturians on a spacecraft?"

"Why do they believe they are communicating with the Arcturians?"

"Can anyone make contact with these Beings?"

All of these questions, and many others, are legitimate, and deserve attention. They are questions that address our very sanity, as well as stimulate our curiosity.

Although each believed that his or her questions were unique, we began to notice a definite pattern of inquiry evolving. As a result, we made a decision to include in this book the background information that would put the answers to questions such as these into perspective. So, before you read what the Arcturians have to say, allow us to explain how we came to meet them.

The First Encounters—Norma's Story

In the early 1980s, I started experiencing an increase in psychic happenings that began to overwhelm me. I had always known that I had a "small" gift for seeing into the future, and some telepathic abilities, but almost overnight these phenomena began to take command of my consciousness. More and more, I began experiencing a mode of existence that earlier had been foreign to me.

For example, I often would know what someone was going to say before the words were spoken. Then I began to "see" and experience things that were taking place thousands of miles away. This was accomplished through my senses and inner knowingness only, and with none of the "rational" tools that I had learned to use for obtaining factual knowledge. Always, upon checking with the sources from which these perceptions originated, I would find that the perceptions were confirmed in fact. How I would know such things I cannot say, for just a few months prior to the onset of these experiences I was "normal." Therefore, I had little data with which to compare what was happening to me and what was beginning to overtake my life. Furthermore, the area of psychic phenomena was one with which I was not familiar, and I did not know where to turn for information.

What always had given me comfort were the psychological, medical, and educational journals which had been an important part of my life. These were the references which I had been trained to use for over 19 years of my professional career at two major universities. When I turned to these sources for answers regarding what was happening to me, I felt betrayed. The answers simply were not to be found.

What I did find was an abundance of skepticism about this kind of phenomena, and the most prominent writers in the field were often those who were the most critical. Many of the articles ascribed sinister qualities to the individuals who either had or claimed to have these abilities, and their very tone made me feel uncomfortable, for clearly I was the subject of their discrimination.

At the time, I was an assistant professor at the University of New Mexico, and I had been at that institution for years. Prior to that, I had spent nearly six years instructing at the University of Houston. To be a member of the "inside" community of the educationally elite, and to be experiencing phenomena that clearly were not of this realm, was very difficult. It was like being trapped between two different worlds—the one from which I had emerged and the one into which I was entering. Yet, they were both reality.

As a result, I said very little and tried to find my answers through individuals whom I trusted or who seemed to be experiencing the same phenomena that I was experiencing. Eventually, I came to meet many well known and respectable people in New Mexico who were undergoing these same kinds of experiences. Needless to say, this gave me great comfort. There is always security in numbers, and it was calming to me to find so many other professionals who understood. Over time we formed some support groups to discuss the events that each of us were experiencing.

The networks of the psychic world were still relatively unfamiliar to me, however. Furthermore, they were totally alien to any modalities that I had been taught for retrieving information. At that time, my existence was attached to a world that honored primarily the "practical" aspects of knowledge. Instruction was expected to be based upon the most current research available. In short, one was not deemed intelligent or respectable if one's path for acquiring knowledge did not fit those parameters.

So, where does one turn for answers when the "official" sources are not there? The search for control over my life was frustrating. At the time I did not understand what was happening to me, and I often felt more like a victim than someone who was developing a gift. My experiences kept getting stranger, and it quickly occurred both to me and to my husband that I was not in control. That did not set well with me, as I have always been an individual who felt a need to be in control.

Over time, I began to acquire more and more telepathic abilities. Then I noticed that I also was becoming empathic. This was really the pits! Some of my experiences in this capacity were as follows:

Three times within one year, a friend who lived in Michigan experienced very painful back problems. In all three cases, she ended up bedridden from having thrown her back out. All three times, the instant her back went out, I experienced the trauma in New Mexico. On one occasion I was in my office at the University and I suddenly collapsed with pain without warning, and had to be driven home from work. These kinds of experiences got a little old after a while.

There were others, too. I experienced a friend's excruciating pain in my own lower jaw from the root canal she was having. What a treat that experience was! I carried this incredible pain for five days before her problem was corrected. I had no idea how to protect myself from this kind of event, but I knew that it was not my teeth that were giving me the problem. I have perfect teeth. Ever since her problem was fixed, I have had no pain.

Then there were the times when I would actually assume other individuals' personalities. If a friend was involved in a stressful situation and could not sleep, for example, who would be the one to wake up, with no warning, at 2 a.m. with a pounding heart? That's right! Often I would lose an entire night's sleep because I could not shut down my adrenal system, even though I knew intuitively that it was not my problem. My body just would not do what I wanted it to do.

The list of examples goes on and on. Some of my close friends would joke with me about being such a good friend and helping so many others experience their periods of distress. While I could see their humor, I also saw little humor in the situation for me.

It was truly a frustrating time for me. I used to say, "I don't like what is happening to me, I didn't ask for this, and I don't deserve this!" In addition, I didn't have time for it. Still, I could not prevent the events from occurring. I remember telling my Dean of the College of Education one day that "This was not in my job description when I took my job." However, I felt compelled to devote more and more time to finding out what was happening to me.

I had always been the type of individual who justified my existence with my family life and a list of 20 things to do each day. As I continually crossed off the items at the top of the list, I would add more things to do at the bottom. This made me feel needed and important, and seemed to give me a purpose for being here. That was all I knew. I worked very hard at teaching my classes, conducting research, developing educational programs, writing proposals, advising students, and fulfilling my commitments on committee assignments. My work day often began at 8 or 9 a.m. and ended after graduate classes ended in the evening, sometimes close to 10 p.m. This left little time for anything else, but it did not seem to matter to whomever or whatever was imposing itself on me.

The progression and timing of the experiences that I was having were not predictable. It was clear to me that I was not in control—or at least I did not believe so. I felt as if I were being jerked around at another's convenience, but I did not understand who this "other" was.

Then one day, in the spring of 1985, I was sitting at the Albuquerque Technical-Vocational Institute waiting to counsel staff members on their professional development programs, and another strange thing happened. Normally, I had dozens of people waiting to see me when I spent my one afternoon a week there. On that particular day, no one came by. I sat there alone in the conference room doing my work and reading a report. Suddenly I heard a voice say, "Pick up a pen. Pick up a pen." I looked around the room and there was definitely no one there. But, as surely as I am sitting here writing this now, I heard that voice. It was not a voice in my head or in my imagination. For some unexplainable reason, I picked up a pen and a piece of paper. To this day, I am not even sure why I did it. It seemed like a crazy thing to do. I sat there and waited for the voice to give further instruction. No one spoke. Instead, what happened was that my hand began to move on the paper. I sat there and watched it move, forced by an energy that was not my own. Although that voice has not spoken to me since, the experience opened up a door to a whole new world.

What is significant about all of this is that this experience occurred long before I even had heard about channeling or automatic writing. I had not read a single book on the subject, and in fact, the area was not even within my range of interests. Many of my colleagues and friends can testify to that. When I later discovered this area, all of what had happened to me only had greater credibility. It was obvious to me that the writers of the books I was beginning to read also knew this to be a reality, and not the fiction that some individuals prefer to believe it to be.

After this event, I began to reach a new level of acceptance. I had grown, over the months, to stop fearing these phenomena. I also had begun to move out of the resentment stage for the most part, although the pain and inconvenience that I occasionally was experiencing were still a burden that I did not understand. My life was changing, and I slowly began to like what I was experiencing.

In time, the set of circumstances surrounding me began to change. The incidents increased in intensity as my expertise in handling them increased. In our support groups, it became obvious to many of us that a progression of events was occurring, as members of these groups all would experience similar events at the same time. We began to wonder if there were not some sort of masterminded training program being imposed upon us. We also began to notice that there was a direct correlation between our increased ability to relinquish our fears and an increase in the level of importance and sophistication of the events that continued to occur. Our unseen trainers were good, and they always seemed to know just how far each of us could be pushed.

Meanwhile, the messages I received began to come in faster and to present higher levels of information. In the course of 8 months I was moved from automatic writing to receiving messages on my computer. I was quickly moved in my communications from one level of Being to another, and was told that I was what is called a "multidimensional channel." Beings such as Monka and Kuthumi introduced themselves to me, as did others. They are great teachers, and continue to answer any questions that I may have.

Their messages often contained information and suggestions for helping individuals raise their levels of consciousness and improve their patterns of behavior. Frequently, the suggestions made were the opposite of what we have learned on Earth. What was so surprising, though, was that when we implemented the suggestions made by our unseen friends, they always worked! We continually saw positive results.

An example of this occurred when the suggestion came through to practice "letting go" for a change. All of us had been taught to be in charge and to take control of our lives. Yet, when we actually made honest efforts just to allow things to happen and to move out of the directive mode, we began to see wonderful things falling into place around us. It was like having little miracles happen.

In the groups, all of us could see our personalities changing. We began to get happier, less stressed, and more productive. Somehow, this was not what we had thought was supposed to happen. This was not what we had been taught – for there was no research or data to support it! It was as if we were getting help from an unseen force to ease the pressures that we had been carrying around all of our lives. In the fall of 1987, I sat at my computer one evening and decided to ask more questions of my unseen friends. I stated the first question and requested that "the Being most qualified, and only one who was in the Light" come through. (By now, I had learned a lot about protecting myself.)

To my amazement, the transmission that came through stated that those communicating were Beings from Arcturus, who were riding on a Starship that was situated to the southeast of Albuquerque. The Arcturians also stated that they had been selected to answer my questions that evening.

When I read that transmission, I thought that it was a joke. I stopped the communication and went into the den to tell my husband. We discussed it briefly, but neither of us knew what to think of such a response.

At the time, this was so far removed from my perceptions of reality that I was not even interested in pursuing the communication. In fact, it frustrated me, in that it appeared to me that continuing the session would be a waste of my time. I was still trying desperately to maintain my existence in the "real" world, even though, on another level, I already had accepted the fact that my life would never be the same again. So, I left the computer and did not even return to it until several weeks later.

The next time that I did so there was a young woman, Laura, with me at my home who was also very interested in this phenomenon. I told her about my previous experience, and her interest was piqued. She wanted to go back to the computer room and see if we could connect with that source again. I agreed to do so.

We sat at the computer and completed a short meditation, and I did a relaxation exercise. I placed my hands on top of two large crystals as I was meditating. This was a standard practice that I had initiated months before, at the request of my unseen friends.

For the first time, while I was meditating, the crystal beneath my right hand began to turn. Laura and I sat there in amazement as we watched the crystal move clockwise. It was fascinating. Events like this no longer frightened me, since I now took each new experience as the next step in my training program. So, we just allowed the crystal to turn until the source that was moving it decided to stop the motion.

We asked to be connected to this source and they obliged. We began by asking:

WITH WHOM ARE WE COMMUNICATING?

We are those who are among your colleagues with whom you can now communicate.

The reason that we started this message in this way [meaning the turning of the crystal] *is because you have not yet communicated with us before this time on your unsophisticated microcomputer. We have positioned your beautiful communication device in a direction that will help you make better contact with us.*

We are the Arcturians, but on another mission than that of the last contact that you made just a few brief moments ago, in your Earth time. We are positioned to the south-east of your city overlooking the high rock structures. We are presently on a different dimension of time-space than you are accustomed to understanding. We would explain further, but since you were never an astute student of your physics, we will not bother to teach you the entire course in just one paragraph or one transmission.

Please do not feel that we are mocking you, we are only saying that we have more important things to say, and it is in this opportunity that we would like to fill the spaces on your screen with something more profound than the lecture on time-space.

The response intrigued and amused us. Also it was quite accurate, for the hardest subject I ever took in school was physics. We continued the dialogue with the following question:

WHY ARE YOU NOT REPOSITIONING THE CRYSTAL NOW? (I asked this question because my hand had been on top of the crystal, but it no longer moved.)

We are not repositioning your crystal because we are repositioning your thinking instead. It is not we who are actually doing the repositioning of the crystal. Instead, it is the energy of our thought waves that is interacting with your consciousness and energy, and as the two combine they get stronger. It is the strength of the combined energy fields that turns the crystal to where we are located.

If you follow this process one step forward, you will see that the combined energy of our two entities can be used to communicate to any number of other frequencies. If it should get strong enough, it could even scramble radio and electronic wave broadcasts. What we did initially was to use more "effort," so to speak, and use a bit more force to tune you into our consciousness.

The second time around the two of you were very much attuned already, so we chose not to influence the turning of the crystal. Instead, we decided to baffle you, hoping that you would ask the question. Since you did, we thank you for the opportunity to clear up the transmission.

This answer seemed a bit sarcastic to us, and yet challenging. We decided to ask a "trick question" of our unseen visitors. In our ignorance of just whom or what we were connected to at that time, we decided to ask an impossible question. In actuality, we could have preceded this question with, "If you're so smart...."

WOULD YOU DO A COMPUTER GRAPHIC (we knew that my computer does not have the capabilities to do graphics) AND SHOW US WHAT YOU LOOK LIKE? We received the following answer.

Of course YOU can, but we will have to give you very intricate instructions as to what to do to complete this three-dimensional type of thought form.

First, you must know that you should not take your consciousness from our communication for an extended length of time. If you can follow this physical and mental dexterity training session, then we will be able to work with you to complete this magnificent drawing. Let us begin.

We were stunned by this response, as we never believed that these communicants would be able to respond to our question. We were also curious as to just how they would accomplish what they said they would do. So, we decided to give them a chance and proceeded to follow their instructions as they dictated information to us.

During this entire two-hour session, Laura worked behind me and I never once looked back to see what she was doing. I brought through the instructions and she followed them.

It quickly became apparent to us that they were writing a computer program through me. When we were ready to receive they began with:

Place an "X" in the center of a page. Have your dear friend, Laura, assist you with this activity.

Now draw a horizontal line only one third down from the top of the page. Know that the two points would intersect around the back in a three-dimensional form, if your flat, two-dimensional paper was representing our depth.

Place the pencil in the middle of that line, and now draw a vertical line down the center, but stop that line approximately one inch from the bottom of the page. This will give you the proximity of the length of our faces, but we do not call them faces on our planet. Instead we call them something like the focus of communications and love.

Now, look at the crystal that has been repositioned on your computer. [Figure 1 is Cynthia's drawing of the crystal cluster that sits at my computer.]

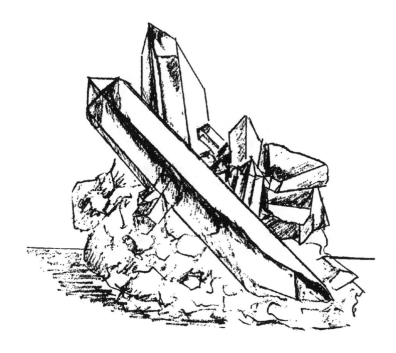

Figure 1

**Crystal cluster used by the Arcturians to complete
their program of instructions.**

*In it you see many projections.   Stoop in front of it and
notice the projection that is the largest and the most prominent.   Check the angle, and then follow the line of the
longest side on the top of it.   Use this angle to draw the
tops of what you would call "two eyes."*

*But before you do, let us relate to you where you should
position them.   As a reference, place the pencil on the "X."*

Then lift the pencil up and reposition it approximately one-half inch in your northeast and northwest direction from that "X." Draw a straight line, the same angle of the crystal, and then stop the pencil approximately two inches from the point where you first laid the lead on the paper.

Laura proceeded to follow their instructions and completed the task. We then asked:

ARE LAURA'S ATTEMPTS THUS FAR ACCURATE?

Splendid!

Now you must arc that line, by forming the arc above the straight line, and making sure that the line's arc is no further from the original line than one-eighth inch.

Take the pencil and place it in the middle of the ellipse. Picture that the eye would extend itself down, vertically from the original line that you drew, approximately one-half inch. With this new width, now go ahead and draw a larger ellipse for the eyes, following this new dimension that we have given you.

Reposition your pencil now, so that it is at the middle, bottom of the page.

Now, with this new position, extend the pencil on its side. Lay it on the paper in the same trajectory angle of the longest facet of that crystal.

At the point that it reaches the edge of your paper, this is the exact point at which our faces are the widest. Knowing this, now mark a place that is approximately one inch in from the sides of the paper.

Our faces are somewhat like a hexagon, without the points that are so abrupt. Can you picture and draw this, knowing that the "chin" area is a bit narrower than the "forehead" area?

The arc of the chin you have drawn is not bad, but we do consider ourselves not to have such fat cheeks.

The top of the head is not to be left as a flat-top haircut.

The line extending across the page is significant, however. Do not remove that line. Instead, just "point" or arc the top of the head gently.

IS LAURA'S LINE OKAY?

Yes.

The line that is left there should now be dropped on the page about two inches. In other words, just draw a parallel line two inches lower on the page, but draw this line lightly.

We have an opening for ingestion that you call a mouth, but that we do not. We call it the oracle of the truth, but we do not use it to communicate with. We will now have you draw this part.

Take the pencil and place it on the line, about two inches to the right from the center "X." Then mark the same place to the left. It is in the marking that you will learn of the width of the mouth or oracle. You now must drop your pencil down on the center line about two inches, and then connect the triangle.

Now erase the last line that you drew ever so lightly.

You must know that no form of our Being has sharp angles in it, so now it is important for you to round all the corners a bit.

With this new center of attraction on our faces, now place a circle in the center of that ill-defined triangle.

HOW BIG?

It can vary because it does when we use it. For your purposes, pretend it is singing praises to the Most Radiant One, and make the circle with a one-inch diameter.

Now, at the widest point of the face, it is important for you to draw some small holes. These are not holes as you would know them, but they serve the purpose for the ingestion of certain frequencies. We would like for you to be sure and place these impressions on the sides of our heads.

HOW MANY?

There are five on each side and positioned in a pentagon effect, with the two holes on the top and the one on the bottom. You will barely be able to see these on your two-dimensional drawing. It would be easier to draw your Earth ears, but we have found them no longer to be functional. So we do not have such characteristics any longer.

At this point the graphic drawing from this computer that YOU have created seems to be very much finished. We do not have such things as hair, eyebrows, eyelashes, or such frivolous things that keep one synchronized with other creatures who contain these features. These are no longer functional. Our skin tone is what you would call a grey color, with much white in the tone. But others have also described it with a touch of beige or green to it.

It does not matter. What does matter is that you have accomplished a marvelous feat today.

We have certainly enjoyed "rapping" with you two, and look forward to our next encounter. Thank you for your friendship, and for your interest in the subject of our appearance.

By the way, we are about 3'-4' tall, in comparison to you Earth people.

So long for now, and we bid you farewell.

Nothing more was transmitted that night.

On the following page is the line drawing that Laura produced that evening. In retrospect we believe that the drawing probably does not depict the appearance of these Beings in photo realism. The drawing is too crude. We are, however, amazed at how similar this drawing is to other pictures of aliens that we have since seen published. What is even more astonishing is that the complexity of the numerous and innovative instructions actually produced a face.

During the entire two hour session, I never once looked to see what Laura was doing. I only waited for her to complete each step before proceeding to receive the next instruction. What was produced, on a certain level, was brilliant! There is no way I could have written these instructions and held the thought for that long a period of time.

Futhermore, when I instinctively bent the page vertically, like a mask, it became a startlingly realistic three-dimensional representation.

We sat there in amazement, wondering what had happened and what it all meant. A million thoughts ran through our heads. Whom does one tell about something

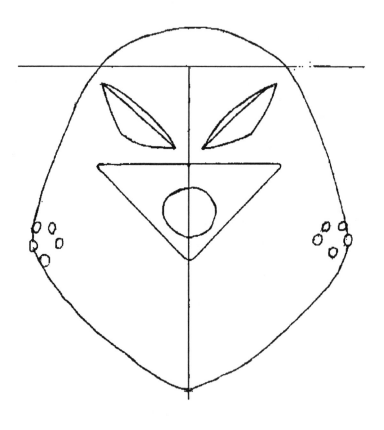

Figure 2

**Laura's Original Drawing of the Arcturian's
Face/Head Structure**

like this? Is this even real? And, more importantly, what does one do with this?

I knew instinctively that few would believe me. I sat there after Laura left that evening and began to consider my options. Few of them looked encouraging, given who and what I was at that moment.

Perhaps I could get permission to develop a new course for the University and call it "Aliens 101." (And if you believe that, I have swamp land in Nevada to sell you, too!) The challenges seemed overwhelming at the time.

The option that I chose was to deny this entire experience. I did so, and quite effectively, for nine months. I mentioned it to very few people, and only connected to my "other sources" for information. It was at this time that I turned to the other Beings for contact. One who called himself Kuthumi, "The World Teacher," and another who identified himself as Monka, "The Communicator of the Technical and Head of the Tribunal Council," were my primary sources of information. I felt safer with these Beings, and they always gave me excellent guidance on my journey.

I used this connection to receive answers that were more closely related to what my reality was at the time. I asked questions on spiritual development, past lives, karma, etc., and felt safer with this connection and source of information. Somehow, this source of information was connected with God, but the extra-terrestrial communicants were of a quality to be feared and avoided. It was not until almost a year later that I caught on that the source of my transmissions was truly the same, but only from different beings representing various aspects of the God Force of the universe. What a blow to my ego that was.

It was at about this time that Cynthia and Betty came into my life, and for some reason I found myself telling them about that earlier evening with the Arcturians. They wanted to experience what I was describing, and requested that I connect with the Arcturians again and ask some questions about them. So, each of them came to my home and on separate occasions I obliged.

When Cynthia initially came to my home and we connected, we found that my computer and printer went out of control. She got a first-hand demonstration of power that truly impressed her. Neither of us could explain what was happening.

While I was bringing through the transmissions from the Beings to whom we were connected, suddenly the words stopped appearing on the screen, even though my fingers were continuing to hit all the keys. When we asked why this had happened, we got a strange answer that said that the reason the words were not appearing on the screen was because "their ship had temporarily moved out of range of my telepathic receiving powers, and that even though I was entering the words with my fingers on the keyboard, the energy of the words was not being transmitted." They apologized profusely, and then explained that they were not Beings who enjoyed frustrating Earthlings.

The computer then scrolled a script on the screen that contained the essence of the message that had come through for Cynthia. This all happened without my hands touching the keyboard. Then the printer printed out the part of the message that had not appeared on the screen previously, even though my fingers were hitting the keyboard. We looked at each other and laughed. Our only comment was, "This is weird."

It was clear to us that we were not in charge. It was also obvious that we were connected to some other life form that had intelligence and a command over our intelligence. In fact, it even demonstrated powers over the technology that we have here on Earth.

When Betty came to my home at another time, we had a similar, (although not identical) experience. The effect of the demonstration was the same—that there was an unexplainable intelligence communicating with us that had a command over our thoughts and our equipment. What was truly interesting, however, was that between these communications the computer behaved perfectly whenever my husband or I used it for business purposes. Further, I cannot reproduce these experiences at will, nor have I been successful in my many attempts at requesting the unseen visitors to duplicate these same events.

Both Cynthia and Betty now had witnessed strange phenomena and events through these transmissions that none of us could explain. It was not long afterwards that we made a decision and a commitment to explore this further. None of us felt afraid. In fact, we were rather excited. It was also nice to have a support group to work with in exploring these unexplainable events. It was like being adventurers, walking into the unknown.

That was July 1988 and nine months later we had a document that even we cannot explain. It just is "what is."

We know so little about the future. Yet, our world is moving faster and faster toward a mystical, undefined image of greatness and power. It is hard even to begin to imagine what its blueprint will be like in the years to come. Will it include open contact with Beings from other parts of the universe? Could this actually be a reality?

If this is indeed a part of our future's blueprint, then this book contains some of the initial information that we will need in learning how to relate to these other life forms. Our very survival may depend upon our ability to adapt and change in this new world which we are entering.

CHAPTER II:
THE VISITORS

ONCE THE decision was made to commit time and energy to connecting with our unseen friends and allowing information to come through for this book, we were faced with defining the scope and context of the work. Each of us came to this project with different desires and expectations. Now, the task was to coordinate them all. What objectives did we want to establish? What were our limits? What did we want to learn from this encounter, and, more importantly, how could our effort benefit humanity? These all were important questions, considering the unusual nature of this book and the controversy that we anticipated it might generate.

Betty had a fascination with the Pleiades, which led her to want to know more about Beings from other star systems in general. She also thought that the project would be fun to do. Although she was not sure at first just who, or what, was transmitting messages through Norma, she was willing to go along and see how the project developed. She hoped to discover how it tied into her own life, and was interested in what she might learn from the entire experience.

Cynthia was probably the most skeptical of the three. She felt that Norma's transcriptions were more likely to be messages from universal consciousness rather than direct communication with "sky guys." She then began to realize that the source of the information did not matter. What was important, she felt, was that the information coming through was positive and that it contributed to growth and understanding, making it valid and worth committing to paper in the hope that it also would effect change and progress in others.

Norma's reason for committing to this undertaking was a strong urge to contribute to our knowledge of the truth. She had come from a point of having no information and little understanding regarding what was happening to her, and had been compelled to develop spiritually as the result of the unending and extraordinary experiences to which she had been subjected over the previous five years. In experiencing these energies, she gradually began to trust them, and once she began to receive transmissions she made a personal commitment to become as pure a channel as possible, and to deliver, to the best of her abilities, only the truth.

The Celestials had impressed upon her the importance of karmic law and responsibility. They also had taught her how important it is not to interfere with the developmental paths of others. Their advice was so convincing, in fact, that the thought of her bringing through misinformation that might influence other individuals wrongly was a heavy burden to consider as she looked at her own soul's path. These three-foot Beings had never appeared to her to prove their own existence or to discuss "a joint planning process" for this book. She had only the words and the physical evidence that had come through her and manifested around her, as well as her own intuition, upon which to rely. She wrestled with the dilemma for nearly a year before she decided to publish these messages. What finally precipitated this decision was the accumulated number of pages of transmissions and the volume of positive messages that were contained within these pages. In actuality, this book contains only one fourth of the material that these Celestials have transmitted through her.

Norma believes that there is truth and validity in the information coming through, and that, where there is indeed truth, one has a responsibility to share it. Once our personal fears and dilemmas had been resolved, we began discussing the objectives of this book. After many lengthy discussions, we decided that the book would focus on asking for descriptions of other planets and Beings in the universe. We decided to draw comparisons between civilizations and cultures, producing a multicultural learning experience involving the constellations within our universe. But where does one start? Well, we started with "A", the Arcturians. We never got to anyone else.

What came through was so interesting, so comprehensive, so revealing, and so loving that we quickly became fascinated and wanted to explore all the philosophical issues of the Arcturians in greater and greater depth. Thus, the book began to write itself and our subjects, the Arcturians, became the teachers.

At first, we were eager for details about the Arcturians themselves. We wanted to know what they looked like, how they ate and moved, what their homes were like, what their atmosphere was, etc. The picture that emerged of the Arcturians was that they are Beings in the Light, eager to let humans know more about themselves and their mission to assist with the birthing of this New Age on Earth. Every question, no matter how mundane, was answered courteously and respectfully.

As we sat for the first time in Norma's computer room and connected to "the source" on July 5th, 1988 we had so many questions that we had trouble deciding where to begin. So, we began with the obvious! After uttering a short prayer for protection and guidance, we asked:

PLEASE DESCRIBE YOUR PHYSICAL CHARACTER-ISTICS TO US.

Immediately, we were addressed with courtly humor.

WE, THE ARCTURIANS

We would not win any beauty contests on your planet, according to your standards!

We are short—and you prefer tall. We are about one meter high, according to your measurement. We are also very wispy and very slender. Perhaps we would win points there! As we are on the leaner side, we prefer to be called a finer species. We pride ourselves on our appearance.

Although we all look very much alike, we have chosen this mode, for we are past the pettiness of comparison. Since we understand the holistic concept of God and the universe, being different no longer appeals to us.

Our skins are a greenish color, but that is actually a lie. In terms of the wave lengths that the Earth is able to perceive, some say we are of this color. But in the galaxy we have a color that does not register on your planet.

We also have three projectiles for our locomotion on the arms that extend by our sides. We find these more functional than the many appendages that Earthlings have. Perhaps you will ask about this at a later time.

In the area of the face, we have two very large almond shaped eyes, and it is these areas that sense the light frequencies that we work with so often.

Is there anything more that you would like to know?

This was indeed an unnecessary question. There were a million things that we wanted to know. Confused by the Arcturians' use of the words "projectiles" and "appendages," we asked for clarification:

PLEASE CLARIFY WHAT YOU MEANT BY THE PRO-
JECTILES AND APPENDAGES.

*What we were referring to was the area of the human
hand. We do not speak in these terms, but we mean the
same area of the body. The appendages of which we
spoke referred to the fingers that you use to handle and
grasp objects.*

*We have only three, for we do not find that we need any
more. Our three projectiles are such that they respond to
the physical maneuvers of the body, and also those of the
mind. We can defy gravity, if we choose to do so. Therefore, with the powers of what you would call our minds,
but what we call the* CENTRAL FORCE, *we are able to
move objects with our minds, synchronized with the mo-
tions of those appendages. Therefore, we do not need all
five digits, and we do think that any more than three is
inefficient.*

No offense, please.

To us it seemed that they used the same basic process of
brain-muscle motion that humans use, only perhaps more
efficiently. Pressing them further about appendages, we
asked:

WHAT IS YOUR MEANS OF LOCOMOTION? DO YOU
HAVE LEGS?

*Yes, we do have legs. We use them on all of our journeys,
but we also do not need them, if we choose not to use
them.*

*We can float, but we do not attempt this movement with
any kind of consistency.*

BY FLOATING, DO YOU MEAN LEVITATION? ALSO, CAN YOU DIRECT YOUR FLOATING WHERE YOU WISH?

The answer is "yes" to both of those questions.

Levitation is the defying of gravity. We can do that for there is no such thing as gravity in the fourth and fifth dimensions of time and space.

We can direct our motion and move in the direction that we choose. We do that by tapping our consciousness into the Liquid Light, and this brings us to our destinations. We do not use this mode of travel on a consistent basis, for we prefer to use our appendages, or legs, just to give them the exercise they need.

Eager to obtain as much information as possible, and excited by the freely offered responses, we jumped from one subject to another.

WHAT IS YOUR MEANS OF NOURISHMENT?

We consume energy, just as all of the Beings in the universe do.

We have a different form of food than what you are accustomed to eating. We prefer mainly effervescent liquids that are high on the vitality scale for the spirit.

Those foods that vibrate on the lower levels cannot be consumed by our people, for they are of the nature that will dull the senses to the higher consciousness and states of mind.

If we were to describe some of the foods we consume, we would have to describe them in terms of some of the minerals that you have on the planet Earth. We do not choose those of an unstable chemical structure.

We can produce just about any combination of vibration foods with the Ship's devices, and we do not dwell on the flavors or smells, as you do on Earth.

We fill the inner mechanisms with energy in a similar fashion as you fill your automobiles. When we run low on the vibration that we need, we make a concoction of the highest grade of energy and vibration to accommodate our spirit.

We do not have to do this on a regular basis. We only do this when necessary.

Continuing to jump from subject to subject, the next question we asked referred to their physical bodies.

HOW DO YOU REPRODUCE YOUR SPECIES?

In all more enlightened species, the reproduction cycle is left to assignment of a few chosen ones.

We reproduce with much pride, but we do not have to mate physically, for we are all truly connected with the spirit of the holistic concept of God.

So, in this process, we find two of the complimentary energies of embodiment. Even though all of our Beings do look alike, we will find them in the vibrational frequency patterns that are conducive for reproduction.

To you it would be like the splitting of a cell inside the womb of the female.

WE, THE ARCTURIANS

We find that the presence of these two compatible vibrational frequencies produces, within one of the two members, the cellular structure that begins to sing the music and vibration of the new life, as you would call it on Earth.

The term of the sapling is then kept by both of the makers of the new energy until the young is able to care for itself and to be removed from the one.

Thus began the Arcturians' description of themselves as physical Beings. Much more was to follow in later transmissions.

In the second transmission, the spokesman for the Arcturians made himself known. He is Juluionno, the Commander of the Starship Athena, and the mission leader for all the Arcturians on the planet Earth.

Juluionno proved to be a willing informant, and a Being of patience, dignity, and a certain degree of humor. Any questions we asked were answered in detail and with great courtesy.

The following questions and replies shed more light upon the Arcturians' physical qualities:

WHAT IS THE COLOR OF YOUR EYES? AND ARE YOUR EYES THE PRIMARY MODE OF SEEING?

Our eyes are likened to your color of dark brown or even a black color, if we may call black a color. This is so as we are Beings who need this coloring to shield our eyes from selected rays of the sun. These are shields, so to speak, which filter out certain rays of energy that can actually hurt our telepathic abilities. Speaking of telepathic abilities, that is our primary mode of seeing. Our eyes are the secondary source for input.

The eyes have another function. They are sensors for the spiritual nature of our Beingness. Our eyes act like filters, and can weed out the lower vibrational senses and energies that can affect our qualities. They are the windows to the soul. Have you not heard that statement on your planet, as well?

The eyes do serve a dual purpose in the visionary realms. They have the quality to act as the optical nerve for depth and character perception. This is accomplished through moving another sensor behind the wide coloring of the eye that you would notice. It is this inner sensor that can perceive distances in very minute detail, and then transmit other data back to our central nervous systems about the quality and character of that which is being perceived.

Another function is that the eye has the capability of being in two or more places at one time. This means that we can focus our inner and outer vision at the same time, and this then aids us in our telepathic abilities. The inner sensor that is behind our outer layer is the one part that connects with the inner reality. The outer lens and coloring is what perceives the energy and density of that which surrounds the inner reality.

DO ARCTURIANS HAVE A HEART? AND WHAT IS THE NATURE OF YOUR METABOLISM?

Yes, we do have hearts. This is one feature that is consistent with most of the Beings in the universe.

Although this is the reality, many species use their hearts for different purposes. In our case, we have a function of our hearts that is similar to yours on Earth. We have a mission to the planet Earth, to teach humans to hear the energy source and the words that come from their hearts. It was in this practice that we first learned to raise our own consciousness eons ago. Now, we are here to help you with this same process.

The heart holds the answers to the universal keys. It contains the balancing energy of the yin and the yang, or the positive and negative energies.

We are of the same kind, when we say that our mission is of the heart. We are of the same origin, when we say that all of our hearts will lead us back to God.

Our role in the re-awakening is to teach many of our sisters and brothers on Earth to listen to their hearts. That is what we do, and we hope that you too will soon discover the true significance of this action.

Our metabolic rate is much higher, in comparison to yours. In this higher state of existence, we manage to find much more enlightenment in our everyday affairs. This reflects itself in our health, appearance, and life span, and also in the delivery of our telepathic abilities. You on Earth will find that your metabolic rates will increase as you progress to arenas of higher states of consciousness. This does not necessarily mean that you will have higher blood pressures or that you will be diseased. In fact, the opposite is true. What does occur is that the new lift of life that comes from this awareness will bring to your physical bodies new states of renewal and spirits, and you will feel this lift right to the bottom of your feet. At this time, you will begin the movement of locomotion and will float, just as we are able to do.

WHAT SENSES DO YOU HAVE THAT WE DO NOT HAVE?

In addition to the inner eye, we also have one for hearing. One of the weaknesses we perceive in the human race is they do not know how to listen. We also did not have this ability well developed in the beginning of time. But, over time, we managed to strengthen this inner sense through discipline and dedication, and have developed a sense of hearing that transcends even our telepathic abilities.

When we are using it, we can hear sounds that are out of the range of normal hearing. We can hear sounds from the fifth-dimensional level and above. Only certain of our species, however, have developed this sense to that level. It is indeed a sense that is the next one for Earthlings to encounter. We see many make the effort already, as we see on the horizon a pattern of similar development between our two civilizations.

Another sense we have that you do not have is that we can sense with the backs of our heads. We have what you would call a nerve that is well developed which is situated in that part of our central nervous systems. This sensing nerve is there for the development of powers that enhance the manifestation powers for which we are known. This nerve is situated in such a place that, depending upon which way we tilt our heads, we are able to gain access to different forms of information to help us make decisions relating to that which we wish to manifest.

It is interesting to note that several of your movie writers have depicted space aliens with a strange tilt to their heads at times. This is so because it is one of the realities of our existence. We do have this habit, but it actually is for the purpose described above.

Other than these, there are no other exceptional senses that we have developed.

WHAT IS THE LIFE SPAN OF THE ARCTURIANS, EQUATED TO OUR YEARS ON EARTH?

In terms that you are familiar with on Earth, we live much longer than you do. The average life span for our species is approximately 350-400 of your Earth years.

We are not in the mode of aging, so we do not look at this in the same way you do on your planet. Instead, we have the ability to transcend time and age simply by not acknowledging them.

What does terminate our life is the contract that we arrange for our own existence. We find that this is a much more efficient and more important way to conduct our affairs than to wait wondering, "Will today be the day that we cross over to another dimension or to another side?" We anticipate the length of our contracts by the number of accomplishments we wish to fulfill. We measure this by the vibrational level that we are able to attain.

On Arcturus, we have no sickness. That was eliminated many centuries ago. We have found we can control our population and our life spans by planning for the highest in our evolutionary patterns, and we do so with a strict dedication to the highest for all concerned.

Occasionally something will go wrong with the planning, such as the times when some of our spacecraft have crashed on other planets. Under conditions like those, we have no need to fulfill the contracts that we have designed, since conditions of imperfection make it difficult to do so.

Therefore, those Beings are excused from their existence and assignments, but do report back to the Elders in another form of consciousness. This, perhaps, should be left for another dialogue, for this aspect of our life does and would take a considerable amount of time to explain.

WHAT TYPE OF CLOTHING DO YOU WEAR?

We wear very functional clothing. It has the ability to transcend time and space, and can manifest in various dimensions.

The clothing that we wear when we are away from the planet is usually bluish-green. There are different shades of this coloring, and it is designed primarily for the protection of our species when we are outside the rays of our own solar system.

The clothing is of this color because it supports the texture of what you would call our skin. It has the quality and, therefore, the ability (so to speak) to prevent some of the sun's rays from your galaxy penetrating our Beings. This is necessary because, unlike your planet where the sun's rays support life, in our situation it would actually cause a deterioration of our composition.

The form, color, and clothing are all uniform, and fit very closely to our bodies. This gives us the functional quality of being mobile, while at the same time protected.

Our garments fit closely to our skin. We do not wish our skin to breathe as you do on Earth. Therefore, this clothing helps to block out this process. We have little or no protection over our "hands." We do not have the protection of color or fabric over our head areas either.

We use this garment to help us with locomotion, for this has a sensing device that helps us tune in our faculties to the former position of the oneness of the mental quality. We use this clothing to help us filter out and filter in the consciousness and thoughts of those with whom we are directed to interact. This is a safeguard, for we are in a strange atmosphere, cluttered with lower vibrations, and we sometimes have difficulty, even with this protective clothing, in communicating telepathically in the highest and purest forms.

There is a strange quality about the planet Earth that we learned to identify many centuries ago. That is why this clothing was designed and it was done so specifically to support our journeys to Earth.

There is something else that is very special about the garments we wear. They have no pockets and they do not have any openings. Perhaps we should let you figure out how we put on this attire. This could be a puzzle for you to contemplate, and we will be amused to learn of the logic that you use to figure out the solution to this subject.

WE THINK THAT YOU MIGHT BE "DIPPED" IN THE FABRIC OR THE GARMENTS MIGHT BE APPLIED ELECTRICALLY. CYNTHIA ALSO HYPOTHESIZES THAT YOU CAN PENETRATE THE GARMENTS BY DEMATERIALIZING AND THEN MATERIALIZING WITHIN THEM. ONE OTHER SUGGESTION IS THAT YOU ARE CLOTHED WITH LIGHT. ARE ANY OF THESE ANSWERS CORRECT?

No, but we appreciate your attempting to answer this puzzle.

Actually, the way that we move in and out of these garments is through passing our form from the fifth dimension to the fourth dimension and then to the third dimension of time and space.

We use this, for these garments are actually created for purposes of protection from the difficulties in the third dimension. We come from the fifth dimension, but we must pass through the fourth before we can come into the atmosphere of Earth.

To confuse you even more, remember that all these dimensions do exist simultaneously. Therefore, we must move with the currents of the electromagnetic fields around the Earth. It is one of the special chambers in the Ship that provides us with the technology and instrumentation to perform this task of dressing and undressing.

WHAT DO YOU WEAR ON YOUR HOME PLANET?

There are a variety of garments that are designed for wear on Arcturus. We sometimes have the problem of having an over selection in this area, for we are steeped in formality. Most of the time we wear free-flowing garments that do not hinder our locomotion, for we do not use this mode of travel as frequently there as we do when we travel abroad. You see, our character and composition changes, depending upon where we visit. We must adapt, just as you find that you must.

The garments that are used for everyday existence on the planet are either non-existent or they are of the protocol. To define what we mean by "of the protocol" is to tell you that they are somewhat like uniforms. We do not look like we are in a competitive display, and it is important that I state this now.

The different garments are merely for uniformity of respect and the laws which we admire and to which we adhere. We tell you this, for in appearance we all look very much alike.

There are very few differences between our physical appearances. This is so because we feel that it is non-functional to compete, or to look different from one another. The various garments, then, are only used for the adornment qualities of showing respect.

*Does this give you enough information, or do you wish for
me to continue more at this time?*

After reviewing the information that came through, we
decided to pursue the subject a little longer. We asked
for clarification on the following:

WE ARE CURIOUS ABOUT WHAT YOU MEAN BY NON-
EXISTENT CLOTHING. PLEASE EXPLAIN THIS CON-
CEPT.

*What we mean is that we feel we do not have a need to
adorn ourselves with any garment. At times of meditative
contemplation, in the pursuing of the path to increase
one's own vibrational quality or the right strategies for
growth and development, a Being does not need to adorn
itself with clothing. Our "children" do not have to wear
any either, and there are many reasons why it is important for them not to for the first several periods of their
development. Therefore, we have and do use the term of
"non-existent," to designate the lack of.*

DO YOU NOT NEED CLOTHING FOR WARMTH?

*Our clothing was never designed for any function other
than respect and protocol. On Arcturus, we do not have
the cold and extreme hot temperatures that you have on
Earth. We are contained in the vibrational frequency
that is above the light spectrum known to Earth. It is a
dimension that is not of the duality, but of the oneness.
We can manifest whatever we need, and we do so with
only the directive of serving our own vibrational quality
in making it more compatible with God.*

*We do not need clothing for warmth, for we do not experience
cold. The ecstasy of this condition for living is indeed one
that the planet Earth may achieve one day, as it too is*

51

consumed by the Great Central Sun. This is one of the benefits that come from living in a higher existence.

A prevailing impression that humans have of the typical extraterrestrial personality is one of emotionless, robot-like behavior. At this point the information that had come through Norma's transmissions had given no clue to the Arcturian's emotions, except that they did exhibit some humor. In contrast, humans often are viewed as highly emotional. We discussed this, made the assumption that perhaps humans were some of the most emotional Beings in the universe, and then asked the next, very direct question. We received a rather surprising answer.

ARE WE THE EMOTIONAL PLANET OF THE UNIVERSE?

You are indeed emotional, but it is all in degrees. You have not mastered your emotions. That is the critical element for higher consciousness and transformation.

There are also other planets that are inhabited by souls who are more emotional than you, for they know that it is through the direction of feeling that color and sound manifest into the physical. We are of such a planet.

We are different, for we have mastered the flow of the currents that come from our emotions. In this respect, the people on Earth are indeed like infants when it comes to maturity.

We are the emotional planet of the universe. You are the weakest and least disciplined of the species.

Moving from physical and emotional characteristics, we asked questions in subsequent dialogues about Arcturian culture and environment. In many ways, they had

similar concerns about education and family life, but their
advanced spiritual attitudes and technical achievements
seemed to have solved all the problems that humans still
encounter.

DO YOU HAVE FAMILIES ON ARCTURUS?

*We have the unit. It is not the same as what you have on
Earth. Instead, it is the dominant factor for controlling
the young's vibrational frequencies.*

*You see, on Arcturus we are concerned with the oneness
of the civilization. In comparison, we view the Earth
inhabitants as humans who are interested in preserving
and actually promoting separateness. We think you call
it "individual identity."*

*In that situation a family can be a very important structure,
for in this organization an individual's personality type is
nurtured. This mode of behavior often brings to that
individual certain, select opportunities that enhance his
or her individuality. The parents and friends often
encourage and promote this, as well.*

*On Arcturus, we have a unit structure that promotes
increasing the young's vibrational frequency. This unit
structure is comprised of some very dedicated, wise souls
who understand the principles of energy. They are also
skilled in the laws of physics, as applied to learning. In
your culture you would call this psychology. It is the
behavioral changes that make the differences between individuals.*

*On Arcturus, it is the increased vibrational quality that
adds to harmony and understanding. This is the basic
difference between our two civilizations.*

HOW ARE THESE DEDICATED, WISE SOULS SELECTED TO BE IN CHARGE OF THE UNIT STRUCTURES?

The selection process is simple. Those who are deemed at birth to have the color of the violet-equivalent frequency are those who are initially screened for the positions. These souls are not at all like the ones on your planet who are later given the terms of baby-sitter or child care expert. Instead, these souls are selected strictly on their color frequencies, for it is in this aura reading that we are able to determine one's ability to learn and practice the laws that will be applied to learning situations later in life.

We have an extensive screening process for what would be called "Phase II." Since the raising of our young is so important, we do not allow just any frequency to be near them while they are in the very delicate, developmental years. We cannot predict what the frequency of each soul will be at a later time in its life, but we can tell, just by the color of the aura reading, what the potential for that soul's accomplishment will be.

So, in this Phase II process, we put the souls through many "tests" to determine two things. One is how well their energy fields can intermingle with the other souls around them. This has something to do with their telepathic abilities later on in life. This also has to do with what you would term intelligence. Since we want only the wisest of souls to associate with our young, we will measure these very carefully.

The tests that we put them through are ones whereby we allow them access to a special room and environment that promotes the extension of one energy field into another. It is about the only chamber on our planet that has what is called a conflicting energy force field. What this means is that it not only has the ability to promote the mixing of force fields, but at times it will usher in an energy field that also splits them apart.

A Being in this chamber, who has incredible power to intermingle its energy force field with another's, is a Being who also can resist the force that tries to separate the energies. This Being's abilities are measured and recorded on very sophisticated instruments, and in a matter of moments a determination is made.

It is these Beings we desire to have near our young, for it is they who can promote the increased vibrational frequencies of our young at a faster rate.

The second test that we put them through is the "flag test." This is the final determination test that establishes the credentials of those who will receive these honored positions.

You can see here another distinction between our two civilizations. We on Arcturus have the feeling and awareness that those who govern our units and take care of our young are the highest and wisest in the land.

We observe that you have quite the opposite feeling on Earth and, in fact, give those individuals very few rewards for their efforts. We also notice that you do not have extensive screening processes for these positions, and we observe this with much interest.

There are two reasons we give our Beings a flag test. The first is to determine if they have the desire to receive the benefits and privileges of this position in our society. The second is to determine which ones are the most qualified to rule the units and to be of service on the level with the young themselves.

The flag test that we use is only another device by which to choose the Beings who must serve in a rulership position that is reserved for the Highest. The test is comprised of two parts. The first is the identification of weaknesses and strengths of the system of oneness. In this test the Being is actually taken on experiences of moving throughout our civilization. In this experiential program, the soul is given many tests of compassion, patience and oneness with one's divinity.

In each test, the Being is asked to identify the lessons that need to be learned in acquiring the frequency associated with different, selected choices related to handling these situations. In the answers, each Being actually receives many or few flags, for building the energy force fields within its own presence.

The one who does acquire the most flags is not actually the automatic winner. The ones who figure out the process of acquiring knowledge and the reasons for the answers are selected to become the Elders in the rulership position of the units.

Those who acquire many flags by passing many of the tests are rewarded for achieving the highest form of vibrational quality, and are, therefore, honored among the group as being of the most radiant.

What this does for the society is to direct the attention of the Light toward an innermost group, and they, in turn, filter the energy flow to the rest of the planet. This provides for a higher frequency to filter into the collective consciousness levels.

WHAT TYPE OF RECREATION OR LEISURE DO YOU HAVE ON ARCTURUS?

All of life is our recreation. We only know the oneness and not the strife that comes from the duality nature of a planet such as Earth.

We do have patterns of mind control and games that we find most enjoyable, for they, when mastered, do give us immediate gratification. We have no need to want, but instead, we do have the need to create.

In the mental state of creating, we find that we challenge all, even the Elders, by the creative aspects of our lives. You will note that creativity is also one of the mental skills that is being nurtured and respected more on Earth in the last few years.

That is why the artists, poets, and the creative geniuses are getting a recognition that they have not enjoyed in a long time. This is by design, for as a civilization progresses, it automatically moves into this mode of existence, and the mind begins to take more control over the physical.

On Arcturus, we delight in all mental feats, and we particularly like to indulge in any kind of creativity that helps our young to excel at a much faster pace.

There is a whole area for recreation, as you would call it, that deals with the pairing up of the Elders and most gifted with the young, and designing ways to influence the creative mental abilities of those who are destined to be our leaders.

WHAT IS THE MEASUREMENT USED ON ARCTURUS FOR DAYS, MONTHS, AND YEARS?

The measurement that we primarily use is outside of time and space. Again, it is what we call the increment. It is the measurement of success and not of the time elapsed for the accomplishment or the defeat of a task.

Our measurement is one which we are required to follow for every detail of our lives. We are born into a civilization that only looks to the oneness and the holistic concept of God. In this oneness, we are conditioned and taught to learn that all are together for raising our vibrational levels. Therefore, the only measurement we honor is that which can be measured by our frequency counters.

I fear that it may disappoint you to repeat this again, but may I say that we truly are outside of time and space, and therefore, do not have a measurement for it.

IS NOT ARCTURUS SUBJECT TO THE SAME LAWS THAT EARTH IS? IN OTHER WORDS, DOES YOUR PLANET REVOLVE AROUND ITS TWO SUNS AND THUS CREATE DARK AND LIGHT AND SEASONS OF THE YEAR? (In an earlier communication, the Arcturians had told us that they had two suns around their planet.)

No. On Arcturus we do not have the divisions of minutes and hours that make up the evolutionary path of a culture. Instead, what we have are the increments of evolution that are absorbing our planet into the Great Central Sun. This is an entirely different process.

We do have a planet that rotates on an axis, similar to yours, but because we have two suns, (which, by the way, do not give off the same color of light that your sun does), we do not have the night and day syndrome that you do. We can tell only the degree to which we are evolving in the universe. We care not for the finite moments of measurement that the minutes in your calendar give you. Instead, we rejoice at the measurement of the soul which has obtained a higher vibrational frequency, for we know that enlightenment will bring peace of mind and harmony.

Our measurements come from those of balance. In reality, so do yours. You are constantly looking for the balance in your lives too, but have developed a false system to measure it, based upon time. We find the balance by the accurate measurement of the radiance. That is all we know. The minute by minute analysis of your civilization does not exist in ours.

The seasons on Arcturus are those which we choose to manifest. We do not have to wait for natural changes to occur, and then become victims of these situations. We witness many who perish in your intense spells of heat and cold, as though they were not in charge of their reality. We learned long ago that we are in charge of our realities, and we can manifest anything we wish to occur.

Furthermore, two Beings can manifest two opposite kinds of seasons in the exact moment of time and space. That is probably very difficult for you to understand, but nevertheless, that is a reality on Arcturus.

PLEASE DESCRIBE THE COMPOSITION OF THE ATMOSPHERE ON ARCTURUS.

Our atmosphere is one which has a reddish-violet light that surrounds the planet. This coloring serves as a natural, protective coating for the sensitivity of our eyes, and especially the inner eyes. We could give you the names of the various gases that surround our planet, but they would mean nothing to you. So, therefore, let us describe their function and how they support us.

One of the gases that is the most prevalent is of a nature that would be described as a poison to you on Earth. It is a gas that has a corrosive quality to it. This gas is necessary for our development, for it has the tendency to cleanse the negativity from around the planet. In short, it does not allow the negative quality of energy to function in the same way it is allowed to float and function around the Earth. So, to us, this quality is not dangerous, but one which we desire the most.

A second gas in the atmosphere is one which is watery in nature. But, keep in mind that we do not have any water on Arcturus. This gas is similar to a fluid, and it indeed is of a liquid nature. It has the quality of supporting our ingestion processes and it also does much for the transformational systems we have for changing energy into that which supports our life systems.

The third gas that we have surrounding the planet is one which is likened to a dust. This gas is for shielding out the rays from the two suns that support life on Arcturus. This gas is essential because it has the qualities that will prevent damaging forms of microorganisms to multiply. We do not want any foreign forms of organisms to invade our planet, and this third gas represents the shield that prevents this from happening.

The last gas that surrounds our planet supports what you would call our breathing system. Though all of these gases help support our life forms, we also need a primary gas to sustain our lives. Just as you have oxygen, we have this fourth gas for that purpose.

All combined, they produce a hazy environment surrounding the planet. The density, however, is our protection. We are what we are because of the interrelationship of this atmosphere and our planet, just as your air relates to the beloved Earth. We have created that which is necessary to support our existence. You have done the same.

In another communication, a Being who was proclaimed to be named Ascheana, gave us this information. This same source for information was recorded in other transmissions, as well.

YOU MENTIONED THE WORD "PLANET" IN REFERENCE TO ARCTURUS, BUT OUR UNDERSTANDING HERE ON EARTH IS THAT ARCTURUS IS A STAR. WOULD YOU PLEASE EXPLAIN WHY YOU CALL ARCTURUS A PLANET?

We call the star Arcturus a planet because, in the universal language code, the word planet is a symbol. The word planet means, in the symbolic sense, home. It refers to a place of one's consciousness and a state of vibration that is literally transferred into reality for those Beings who reside in that space and time. It is the highest of places in consciousness for each individual Being to journey to move to the place of safety and security. It is the situation that supports the learning that one must master on the path to the Great Central Sun.

In many ways our definition of planet is likened to the definition that you give to Earth. Is it not? Is this not your home, as well? And, is Earth not a planet? Just because Arcturus has the frequency that naturally resides in another, higher dimension, that does not mean it cannot be a star and a home, as well. We use this word freely to designate our home. We share this feeling and the word with you now, to expand your definitions of both planet and star.

CHAPTER III:
THE REVELATIONS OF THE ELDERS

OUR CURIOSITY about several mystifying universal concepts prompted the questions in this chapter. While there are several philosophical questions and transmissions sprinkled throughout the book, the majority of our efforts in this area are presented here. Included in this chapter are questions that address the different dimensions of time and space that the Arcturians refer to so frequently, our spirit guides, the path of our souls, and much more.

It is certain that many of our readers will find the responses transmitted here to be threatening. They are not what we are used to hearing, and many shake our present belief systems; at least they did ours. The information that we received is provocative, to say the least.

There was one constant, reassuring theme, however, and that was the Arcturians' belief in God and in the concept of oneness, which they defined as God. This concept seems to us to be the distilled essence of every religion on Earth as well, once all dogmas and rituals are put aside. It appears that we have this in common with our unseen friends.

Many questions flowed through our minds as we pondered which ones to ask. One that burned deeply within all of us concerned the origin of humans on Earth. We all, at some point in our lives, seem to wonder about this.

Accordingly, this question was asked one evening and the Arcturians informed us that we should not ask. We were then surprised at what happened. Computer problems developed, and the transmissions to Norma became fractured. Everything cleared, however, when we decided to drop this question for the evening and go ahead with others.

Not to be daunted, we persisted the following week with the same question. As you will read, we were chastised slightly and told to reword our inquiry.

HOW DID HUMAN BEINGS EVOLVE ON EARTH?

Juluionno Speaks of the Origin of Humans.

The origin of the species is a long and difficult story to tell. We choose the word "story," for it may remind you of that when you hear its entirety.

The soul of the human was cast at the same time as the souls in the other galaxies of the universe. The creation all came at the same instant of the moment of the wonderment. That is a true statement.

What we will now explain is what will seem like the "story," for we will have to explain some things with analogies.

While receiving this transmission, we were interrupted. We then proceeded to end the transmission, but returned to the same question the following week.

LAST WEEK YOU BEGAN TO TELL US OF THE ORIGINS OF HUMANS ON THE PLANET EARTH. WOULD YOU CONTINUE WITH THIS EXPLANATION?

No.

WHY NOT, PLEASE?

Because you have not asked the appropriate question.

The question is not of the origin of humans on the Earth, but of the origins of what you call extraterrestrial life on Earth.

We have already revealed to you that we were here first [see Chapter 9, The Mission], *and it is on this linear foundation that we actually set up the establishment of the human species on the planet Earth.*

This may sound a bit confusing, so I will now ask if you wish for me to continue, or if you wish to hear of the origins of the Arcturians on the planet. The word "origins" implies the beginning.

WE WISH TO HEAR OF THE ORIGINS OF THE ARCTURIANS ON EARTH AND HOW THEY CONTRIBUTED TO THE ORIGIN OF HUMANS ON THIS PLANET. WOULD YOU PLEASE DESCRIBE BOTH?

In the beginning of time, with the casting of the souls, Arcturians were of the highest of consciousness, and could manifest many things with the right conditioning and vibration. In this state of being, the Elders came to planet Earth to set up a colony. In this state, they did so with the utmost of care and affection.

The colony on this planet prospered for many centuries of Earth time, and in this prospering the citizens of the planet grew to love and nourish many aspects of creativity.

We were settled here until a more warlike life form came and destroyed much of the civilization. Many of us who remained on the planet were rescued and taken back to our home on Arcturus.

Those who were not rescued were left in the void, or in a neutral state of Beingness of the soul, and were given the privilege of reincarnating in other forms.

In the transition of our souls and species returning to Arcturus, we experienced a moment of consciousness that can never be repeated.

This moment of consciousness held in it a deep cry of love for the planet Earth and what had happened to the energy that was manifested there. We had begun an incredible civilization. It would take eons of time to repeat the efforts.

The most disappointing moment was when the Elders decided that it was no longer feasible for any of us to return to Earth. We were saddened, but this decree was such that none of us could disobey.

Instead, what we did was to work with a nearby galaxy to set up a Tribunal Council and make arrangements for the first inhabitants of other species to journey to Earth, and set up the conditions of their civilizations. This was acceptable to many of us, for we were delighted to observe our sisters and brothers of the stars rebuild the energy we brought to the planet so long ago.

In the interim period, the warlike tribes had gone. They had destroyed what they came to destroy, and left no forms for rebuilding the civilizations. Earth was once again ours to rebuild.

We were not, however, allowed to return ourselves. So what we did was to send the first origin of the human species from another system. Beings from other systems

65

then made the journey. Over time, there was much in-breeding and also extraterrestrial breeding, to make the human form into what it is today. This is the origin of the human species.

Since all the life forms come from God, the origin is truly from that Source. It is only the modifications of the original forms that you are witnessing today.

Does this suffice for a beginning to the explanation? And does this satisfy your initial curiosity, or do you wish to ask more questions?

FROM WHICH STAR SYSTEM DID THE TRIBUNAL COUNCIL FIRST SELECT "THE ORIGIN OF THE HUMAN SPECIES" TO REPOPULATE EARTH?

The star system is not from the galaxy that you are familiar with today. The star system is from one which is so many light years away that it is not even on your astronomers' maps. It has a name, but it would mean nothing to you. The name is Andromorphus Rexalia, as written in our records. It means one form. It means the reuniting to the one, which is the direction in which the human species is turning today.

DID THESE ORIGINAL HUMAN SPECIES INTERBREED WITH ANIMALS TO PRODUCE US?

There have always been life forms who would tamper with nature; but that was not and is not the status quo. Yes, this did occur, but not for many centuries after the original settlers came to the planet—which was after we were forced to return to Arcturus.

In the beginning, things were of the highest. In the interim period of millions of years ago, many souls became tainted.

There is an energy form around planet Earth that is difficult to analyze. In this energy is a vibration that makes it difficult for many souls to stay pure and remain at the highest vibration.

These lower vibration forms eventually affected the minds of the other inhabitants, and it was in this condition that many of them turned to lesser ways for fulfilling their expectations of what the journey of life should be.

When this happened, the life forms took part in mating with other forms of lower life. This caused many problems, but eventually many of them were "weeded out."

Many of the great civilizations addressed this problem and tried to cleanse the planet once again. One of those civilizations that made an attempt to do this was Greece. That was at the time when many great gods walked the face of the planet.

WERE THOSE GREAT GODS SPACE BROTHERS AND SISTERS?

Yes, and no. They were a mixture of the two, who also had gained the rights of the highest. The space brothers and sisters did come and bring enlightenment, and they did teach many who were of the human origin. They also interbred with many of the human species, and left their qualities of godhood with those who were not of other worlds.

IS THE MIXING OF BEINGS FROM OTHER STAR SYSTEMS WITH THE INHABITANTS OF EARTH THE REASON SOME OF US FEEL AN AFFINITY FOR DIFFERENT STAR SYSTEMS AS OUR ROOTS? IS THIS FEELING A TYPE OF AWAKENING?

Yes, and no. Let me begin with the explanation that, at one time, there was a pure race on the planet Earth. It was only in the evolutionary period throughout time, that the mixture of races of star inhabitants and the Earth life forms began.

At one time there was truly a pure mixture of gods. It was then that the breeding of gods resulted from the pure Beings from star systems that inhabited the Earth. They were from one central source.

In time the mixtures began to weaken. Later the problem of this weakening produced many solutions (designed by those who still had powers). As a result the Beings who inhabited the Earth remembered the secrets that connected them to their roots—their home star systems.

Those who remembered, and consequently contacted their home planets, were strengthened. The results were always uplifting to the spirits of the lost. Over time, though, this reinforcement fluctuated in intensity.

The reinforcements were always sent. But over a period of time, no matter what reinforcements were sent to mix with the population, it seemed nearly impossible to achieve the same level of superiority in the human consciousness and existence. This has continued to be a challenge for us and for many souls on Earth who have the remembrance.

IN AN EARLIER TRANSMISSION YOU MENTIONED THAT GROUPS OF SOULS CAME BACK IN EMBODIMENT IN TUNE WITH OUR COMMUNICATION. WOULD YOU PLEASE EXPLAIN WHAT YOU MEANT BY THIS?

This is a very important concept for souls to grasp. This means that individuals who have reached a certain frequency and understanding of similar paths and ideas will choose to come back in embodiment together. Their lessons will be similar to learn, and they will be the ones who help each other gain a higher consciousness, together and singly.

In this pattern, many of the souls like yourselves have the interembodiment experiences of working with us, and with Beings from other star systems.

Therefore, what happens is that when one of these souls "wakes up" and suggests to the others that tuning into our communicative frequency is a viable course, then others usually do not doubt it. It is that simple.

As a result, groups will come to us more frequently than single contacts, for the pathway to higher consciousness can seldom be achieved in a vacuum.

YOU OFTEN HAVE USED THE WORDS 'WAVELENGTH' AND 'FREQUENCY' IN YOUR TRANSMISSIONS. PLEASE EXPLAIN THE DIFFERENCE BETWEEN WAVELENGTH AND FREQUENCY AND HOW THEY RELATE TO THE THREE OF US.

Juluionno Speaks of Wavelength and Frequency.

This is a rather difficult concept to explain, if one is not of a scientific nature. Let me try to do so with analogies.

A wavelength is like a variety of one of your Earth candy bars. It has special qualities that give it a distinction all of its own. When one eats the candy, the absorber of this energy knows that what is consumed is of a particular nature and quality. The wavelength, then, consists of the

69

distinctive attributes of the object or energy that is being identified.

On the other hand, a frequency is the elongated motion of the energy of that object. It is like the colors the candy bar may emit. For example, a chocolate bar may radiate the color brown in one instance, but it would radiate the frequency of the color white in another.

On the one hand, the candy seems different. In reality, it is not. It is like two varieties of the same energy, which is the chocolate.

This relates to you three when you are hearing a particular wavelength, and you are being tuned up inside your physical bodies with the wavelengths that are being transmitted to you from the spaceships. This can manifest itself as tones or ringing in the ears, and it can affect the toning within your consciousness.

When you are raising the frequencies of your consciousness, you are approaching a higher vibratory rate and approaching the speed of light. In this condition your changing frequency can turn from a dense color such as brown to that of white, similar to chocolate turning from brown to white.

Although we did not quite understand this explanation, we decided to go on with another question. We discussed the options and selected a question that had intriqued us for many weeks. It concerned the topic of Liquid Light.

PLEASE EXPLAIN THE CONCEPT OF LIQUID LIGHT. WHAT IS IT MADE OF AND HOW IS IT USED?

Juluionno Speaks of the Liquid Light:

To begin with, everything is made up of electromagnetic energy. With this understanding, allow us to say that we have many different "forms" of energy.

There are rays of energy, such as light rays, gamma rays, ultraviolet rays, etc. When we look from our perspective, we see that the Earth is a sea of an electromagnetic field of energy. All forms combine together to form a pool of energy. This pool is termed Light, because all that is in the universe is God. GOD IS LIGHT.

The sea of energy is called liquid because it moves like a fluid and cannot be contained. In this sea of energy is the oneness of All. The electrons and smaller particles of existence are truly the creator of the force that sustains all life.

It is this force that is the physical energy structure of the All that supports life. This force is used by all of us in this dimension and other star systems for our propulsion.

We understand that the natural flow of electromagnetic forces of the universe is the only truly intelligent way to operate. Once a civilization begins to understand this, that civilization becomes a co-creator of the physical world that surrounds them. We hope our sisters and brothers on the planet Earth will soon come to the same conclusions and discoveries we came to long ago.

ARE OUR SCIENTISTS ON THE VERGE OF DISCOVERING LIQUID LIGHT? OR, IF THEY HAVE ALREADY DISCOVERED IT, DO THEY CALL IT BY A DIFFERENT NAME?

71

Your scientists have discovered Liquid Light, but do not call it by the same name. They still think of it as separate waves and frequencies of the bands of energies. When they begin to conceptualize it in the holistic format in which it is intended to be used, then they will have a breakthrough in consciousness and technology.

They will have to reunite Eastern philosophies with advances in the technological world, and in this unification they will find answers to many of their nagging questions.

WHAT IS THE "CENTRAL FORCE" YOU REFER TO THAT YOU CALL YOUR MINDS? IS THIS CENTRAL FORCE FOR YOUR SPECIES ONLY, OR IS THIS SOMETHING THAT IS FOR US TOO?

Juluionno Speaks of the Central Force:

First of all, remember we are all one massive force of energy in this holism. This is very important to comprehend.

With this understanding, let me say that the central force we refer to is the projection of our thoughts through the sea of Liquid Light to your subconscious.

We do not have the same neural transmitters in our bodies that you do on Earth.

We can tell you that your "brains" will evolve. They will assume more of the nature of energy in the unseen form as ours do. It is this resemblance that will be difficult for you to understand.

The central force is many neural transmissions through energy fields. These are available to everyone. When one learns to tap this source of power, one begins to understand how psychic communication and telepathic communication work.

It is in the telepathic powers of the mind that one will discover the secrets of the central force, and how it is being registered and utilized on Earth today.

IS THIS ANOTHER TERM FOR THE UNIVERSAL MIND?

Very good. You are beginning to understand this, but only with the words you have read in books. It is the "scientific" interpretation you hunger for, and that which will help you to utilize this system.

It is difficult to learn and to "become" when one does not understand what one is becoming. For now, the best way I can describe how one becomes one with this central force is to quiet the mind through meditation. This will allow the energy to work slowly through you.

This central force has an intelligence you cannot begin to comprehend. This intelligence, if you trust it, will work wonders in your life and become your teacher.

IN COMMUNICATING WITH YOU AND YOUR STARSHIP RIGHT NOW, ARE WE TAPPING INTO THIS CENTRAL FORCE?

You are doing more than tapping into it. You are becoming masters of how to use this force to shake the old structures around you. Can you see how this verifies what I said just a moment ago? You are becoming the creator of reality with the central force, and you are able to communicate with other dimensional Beings.

This is a use of this force that we take for granted on this dimension and on our home star system. You, on Earth, are just becoming acquainted with this form of "technology." We observe, however, that most are still in the denial stages. This disappoints us, but we cannot interfere. We are only programmed to assist.

THERE ARE MANY CONCEPTS OF GOD AND DIVINITY. WOULD YOU PLEASE EXPLAIN WHAT YOUR CONCEPT OF GOD IS?

Juluionno Speaks of God:

There is only one God. There is only one eternal life. Both of these are connected and are one.

You are right that there are many concepts of God, but not all of them explain the power that belongs to the oneness of God. God is the force that is present throughout all the universes.

God is the Light of this world and all worlds. "It" is the intelligence of the universes, and is centered in the Great Central Sun. In this position it is the center of All that is.

There is an electron force that holds everything together on the physical plane. There is the love power that holds all together on the emotional level. There is no such thing as mind power of one kind that holds everything together on the mental level, for God is manifested in many different forms of mental energies.

So what you have are all of the tools you need to manifest God in any form on the Earth plane. What you also have is the fortitude and the courage to do so, if you so desire.

74

The word "desire" is the key here, for that truly is what propels the concept of God.

Most Earthlings do not have the desire to hold on to this force, and to use it constructively out of the love it takes to generate things. Most Earthlings give in to lower vibrations of the physical world, and refuse to practice their powers of the spiritual. They live in the manifest of the physical, instead of the spiritual. In this state, they never truly come to realize God.

While God is this—the physical—too, they are one step removed from the source when they choose to remain on that level. It is the source that each soul seeks.

Until each soul finds this source, a level of discontent arises. When the source is found, then all peace and tranquility go back into the consciousness, and a new level of manifestation results in the power of this wonderful source.

To explain it in more simple terms: love, Light, and the electron force are all God. WITHIN HIS BEINGNESS, THESE ARE ALL ONE. Within human consciousness these are three separate things, until the soul masters relearning each of them. When that happens, then all three become one within that Being, as well.

WHAT IS THE GREAT CENTRAL SUN OF WHICH YOU SPEAK?

The Great Central Sun of which we speak is the highest vibratory substance known in this universe and all universes. It is God, Himself and Herself.

We tell you that it is the white and the black. It is the presence and the absence of the All. It is the "gravity" of all that is, which holds the precession of the equinoxes in the order of the highest. It is the ruler of the Ascended Masters. It is the ruler of the forces that propel all dimensional Beings. It is nothing and it is everything.

Do you get the point of what we are trying to express?

NO, NOT ENTIRELY. WOULD YOU ELABORATE FURTHER?

We regret that we were not able to convey the message more accurately. Let us try again.

The oneness concept is fairly new to Earthlings. But to those who occupy the positions of the fourth and fifth dimensions of time and space, it is no challenge. That is because we experience more from the emotional level, without having our emotions running out of control. In this state, we can experience the energy, live it, and become one with it.

When a consciousness in embodiment experiences itself as separate, it has difficulty relating to the oneness, for it does not feel the connection on an experiential level. In this state of being, the duality of light and darkness, high and low, are a part of the consciousness.

In the experiential mode of the oneness, a soul feels that all degrees of differences are not opposites or in competition with one another. In this case, the soul experiences darkness as one aspect of the Light.

Does this explanation help you in understanding what it is that we are trying to convey? If it does, we would be happy to continue; and if not, we will try another version. What is your pleasure?

ARE YOU SAYING THAT THE GREAT CENTRAL SUN IS AN EXPRESSION OF THE ONENESS OF GOD AND OF EVERYTHING?

Yes, and no. What we said is that the Great Central Sun is the expression of the focal point of all that there is. It is the force that propels, stores, houses, emits, and elicits all other forms of energy within itself. It is like the generator of the universe, which is consciousness itself.

PLEASE GIVE US THE THIRD VERSION. WE ARE TRYING VERY HARD TO COMPREHEND THIS INFOR-MATION, BUT ARE STILL HAVING DIFFICULTY IN GRASPING THE SIGNIFICANCE. PERHAPS ANOTHER EXPLANATION WILL HELP.

God is the Alpha and the Omega. God is the beginning and the end. God is eternal. God is the spatial likeness of the darkness that comes to life only in the Light. God is the growth and the retardation of the progress.

God is It. That is all. That is the truth.

There is no separation in this concept of the oneness. It is only the conflict of the physical manifest plane that distracts souls from understanding this.

If one looks within, one finds the Great Central Sun there, and access to all universal knowledge is gained from this journey. When this connection is made, one finds that the limitations of the physical existence are truly that— limitations. In this awareness, another dimension of understanding of the power and glory of God becomes apparent, created by the existence of the Earth plane.

One cannot exit the Earth without the full knowledge, understanding, and love of the curriculum the God force on Earth manifests. When this curriculum is learned, a soul is ready to transcend to another dimension, and learn higher agendas. When one accepts this basic understanding, one finds no conflict anywhere, for in this acceptance of oneness, a soul sees perfection in all that there is.

God is everywhere, everything, and the All. God is love and goodness. Any conflict one perceives on the lower vibrational frequencies is a perception of the human condition. In these perceptions, humans do not learn of the goodness, but they will use their perceptions to understand their concept of evil.

Through the completion of the so-called evil acts, one learns how to raise his or her own soul's vibration. If, on the Earth plane, this duality did not exist, there would be little substance to the curriculum we spoke of earlier.

When a soul transcends this curriculum and can see the goodness of God in all, and the work of God, then that soul is ready for higher dimensions, for the Earth plane is no longer a challenge.

So this is why we say that God is the Light and the dark. Nothing and everything exists within God.

IS GOD PURE ENERGY, CREATIVE IN ITS NATURE?

[No response was transmitted through Norma.]

WHY ARE THERE NO MESSAGES COMING THROUGH?

Because we are putting you through a higher mental course right now. If you will take a minute and look over your questions again, you will note that we will have to answer "yes" to all of them. Remember God, is everything.

We felt a bit humbled at this point and decided to go on with another topic.

WOULD YOU PLEASE ELABORATE ON THE FOURTH AND FIFTH DIMENSIONS OF TIME AND SPACE AND TELL US IF WE CAN ACCESS THESE DIMENSIONS IN OUR PRESENT HUMAN FORMS?

Juluionno Speaks of the Fourth and Fifth Dimensions:

This is a complicated question, and the second part is even a bit more complex. Nevertheless, we shall try to give you the explanations you desire, through the use of analogies.

The reason we must do this is because we do not have "understandable" terms to use. The language used on the fourth and fifth dimensions of time and space does not parallel yours on the third dimension. With this brief explanation and apology, let us begin.

The fourth dimension is not the same as the fifth dimension. The reason that it is not is because it does not have the same vibrational frequency as the higher dimensions. Again, we go back to energy.

In the fourth dimension we see the differences between the parallel universes manifesting themselves. The lessons and contrasts between them are beautiful. In the fourth dimension, creatures of many universes exist simultaneously and the Beings of many worlds find one harmonious state on the path to a higher level of existence.

In the fifth dimension of the higher planes, there is a vibrational quality that is like what you would term "heaven." In this fifth dimension, the Beings and inhabitants all live on the highest octave of manifestation.

Anything that a soul desires is his or hers. I use the feminine and masculine terms here loosely, for on that dimension all the Beings are androgynous.

There is another difference between these two dimensions: that is, the color of the light radiates in two dimensions. While these dimensions actually exist simultaneously, they are in bands of two different frequencies of light. One is higher than the other. The higher frequency is also the path for those who are no longer seeking. In the higher frequency the Beings all choose to live in the totality of their oneness.

In the lower frequency, the Beings are still in the seeker mode, and therefore, have the opportunity to look beyond themselves for some of the answers. They are still in the exploration stages. In the higher realms, the Beings are self-contained.

Does this give you enough of an answer to the first part of your question?

YES, CAN YOU DESCRIBE THE COLOR FREQUENCIES OF THESE TWO DIFFERENT BANDS OF LIGHT?

We will try, but it will be most difficult.

We will begin with the analogy of the rose. In the smell of the rose, there is hardly a fragrance that can compare with its beauty. But how would you describe this fragrance?

The way we would describe it is that it is closer to the word and feeling of love than any other flower on the Earth plane. The reason that this is so is because the fragrance elicits a stimulus/response attitude in the individual that triggers a gentle power from the fragrance.

In this response to the smell, the individual has to make a decision about the attitude that is being expressed. By comparison, in expression and choice, one does not have to seek the Light unless one wishes to do so. Something must trigger the response.

Now, you might think these last statements do not make any sense. What we are referring to is the choice each must make of reacting on higher levels, which is equivalent to that of seeking the Light on a higher dimensional plane. Believe it or not, this is also equivalent to the state of consciousness that is usually elicited from the fragrance of a flower, such as the rose.

In this common response mode, the energy one absorbs in the process of making this choice is that which can be internalized and transformed in the process. For, we remind you, all energy is transformed and is transforming.

If we take this explanation back to the color and frequency of the higher dimensions, let us say that the color observed on an energy level is so glorious that it automatically transforms behavior, and leaves one in a state of Beingness that is like utopia. That is what experiencing the higher frequencies and colors is like.

Does this give you the idea, without describing a color, of what these two different bands of light are like? We know it is difficult when you cannot imagine that in your mind's eye.

YES. THANK YOU. WE REALIZE HOW MUCH WE HAVE YET TO LEARN. WOULD YOU PLEASE AN-SWER THE NEXT PART OF THE QUESTION, WHICH IS: DO WE HAVE ACCESS TO THE FOURTH AND FIFTH DIMENSIONS IN OUR HUMAN FORM?

You do have access to these other dimensions, and you do access them on a regular basis in your etheric forms. In this state of Beingness, you have the possibility of the oneness being stripped from you on the fourth dimension, and reunited on the fifth dimension. This probably does not make sense to you, so allow us to explain further.

The reason we said that you have access to the oneness being stripped from you on the fourth dimension is because this dimension is one which has diverse activity going on within it. Some of the souls get confused, and actually think they are on Earth, the planet of duality, or they believe they are in another existence.

You have been told that the Earth school is the third grade curriculum, and that you must learn this curriculum before you exit that dimension. That is correct.

The fourth dimension is revealed to you now as being a part of the fourth grade curriculum. Once on this realm of reality, one has to learn to differentiate this curriculum from the third level curriculum, and in this act of discernment lessons become much easier.

Many of the souls on Earth right now are actually learning the fourth level curriculum so they may enter the fifth dimension. It requires an opening of the heart center. They are seeking their birthright after so many centuries of separation from the Creator. Therefore, they are adjusting and accessing the fourth and the third dimensional frequencies at the same time.

Much of the access one has to the fourth dimension comes in the dream state. When one makes it through this vibrational frequency, the soul can also interact on the fifth, which is the Ascended Master realm.

Then there are many higher realms, as well. This is only the beginning.

IS THIS FOURTH DIMENSION THE REALM IN WHICH ALL OF OUR PAST, PRESENT, AND FUTURE INCARNATIONS EXIST SIMULTANEOUSLY?

Allow us to divide the answer into two parts. First, it is important to note that it is a fact that the past, present, and future are all one. It is also important to note that all dimensions exist as one, as well. With this firmly anchored, let us proceed to answer your question.

What we would like to say first is that you have several bodies existing all in one, within each of your units, so to speak. In this understanding comes the knowledge that each of those bodies has access to different dimensions of time and space and awareness. This is part of the duality of consciousness and the many conditions you can experience simultaneously.

What is known about this is that you actually are existing in all the past, present, and future time periods in the moment. As you know the concept of time, you can, with awareness, actually slow time down or speed it up.

In the fourth dimension of time and space, there is simply one more dimension of awareness open to a soul for integration. In the third dimension you must first learn the lessons of that space before grasping the lessons of the next. This is accomplished before you have conscious access to the higher levels. In the fourth dimension, it is no different.

We can tell you there is a clearer realization of the past, present, and future all being one when you are in the fourth dimension. In your dream state you access this awareness all the time. That is why your dreams often do not make any sense. But if you go inward to where reality is, you have the tools you need to gain understanding of what those images and words actually mean.

Juluionno Continues the Discussion of the Fourth and Fifth Dimensions:

Juluionno apparently wanted to add more information to his previous transmission, so this time he initiated the questions himself.

We suggest you ask this question: "What is the nature of the fourth and fifth dimensions?" You asked a similar question earlier, and we would like to elaborate on this further. Is this permissible?

YES, PLEASE CONTINUE.

The nature of the fourth and fifth dimensions is the process of learning. One can learn the path of evolution of a soul by the journey of moving through the various dimensions of the universes.

The fourth dimension has been coming to the Earth since the time of Jesus. He came to the planet to introduce the quality of the fourth dimension. That quality is the journey inward and the expression of love. He taught all souls to love each other as they love themselves. In preparation for this new journey that is to come for many on your planet, He also taught that they must forgive. These are the two major qualities the fourth dimension imparts to the inhabitants of Earth. When one masters these, they alter the vibrational frequency that prepares them for the fifth dimension, which is that of the manifestation through thought.

The electron force of the Great Central Sun, which is God, is that force which is equivalent to "The Father Within Me." This very famous quote is another from our dearest Brother in the Light, Jesus. He came to teach that all people must learn love and forgiveness (the fourth dimension) before they can master the fifth dimension, which is the ability to manifest things using the force of love.

With this new introduction, I am ready to answer any more questions you may have on this topic.

HOW LONG WILL IT TAKE FOR EVERYONE ON EARTH TO ACCESS THE FOURTH DIMENSION FULLY?

Life is eternal. Does that answer your question?

YES.

ARE THE DISEMBODIED SOULS AND SPIRIT GUIDES A PART OF THE FOURTH DIMENSION?

The disembodied souls to whom you refer are not a part of the fourth dimension. They are considered to be a part of the Earth plane, and the astral plane that is connected to the Earth.

ARE DISEMBODIED SOULS AND SPIRIT GUIDES THE SAME THING?

They can be, but sometimes are not. A disembodied soul, within the progression of the soul, can obtain a higher frequency and become a guide to a living person on the Earth plane. Many disembodied souls around the Earth plane are still attached to the gravitational pull of the third dimension. They have difficulty rising above this frequency. They are often trapped between the dimensions, and find it difficult to understand where their path lies.

Spirit guides are those who have demonstrated greater wisdom and a higher frequency. They are assigned to souls who are working to attain their own freedom in the Light. They are in the position of guiding. The astral plane souls, who are mischievous or confused, often will interfere with an individual's path to the Light. They seldom try to help. Instead, they try to relive their own desires through the soul on the Earth plane.

WE THOUGHT SPIRIT GUIDES WERE ON A HIGHER FREQUENCY. ARE THEY ONLY ON THE FOURTH DIMENSION?

Spirit guides have access to many dimensions. The higher the frequency of a soul, the more dimensions it can access with ease. It is only souls who vibrate at a very low level who have difficulty accessing dimensions that are on a higher frequency. Does this answer your question?

ON WHAT DIMENSION DO THE ASCENDED MASTERS RESIDE?

The Ascended Masters reside mainly on the seventh level and higher. They, however, can access all, just as we described a moment ago. They can move with the grace and swiftness of thought, and pour out their love to all of God's creation. They are every living creature's best friends, but so few understand this on the Earth plane. No matter at which level souls reside, the Ascended Masters do welcome them to their hearts.

AT APPROXIMATELY WHAT TIME WILL THE EARTH BE GROUNDED IN THE FIFTH DIMENSION?

The time period you wish for me to convey is not my projection, but a projection only the inhabitants of Earth can make. The reason for this is that this transitional period of cleansing has to be completed before the Earth will be stabilized in the new energies of love and understanding for all. Out of this higher frequency of love and Light will come manifestation by thought, which will be powered by the minds of the humans who are the masters on Earth. In this state of being, all things will come to pass. It will be perfect.

If I could make a projection, I would say that it will come within the next fifty Earth years. If I am wrong, it is only because I cannot predict the emotional patterns of free will that constitute the human consciousness. I would like to say tomorrow. If I did, I fear I would be quoted as another prophet who did not see the vision accurately. I can only say we see collectively that it is written, and will come to be.

WHAT LIES BEYOND THE FIFTH DIMENSION?

The sixth dimension.

YES? PLEASE CONTINUE.

In the sixth dimension the powers of manifestation are increased to a point of brilliance. In the fifth dimension, the curriculum is such that the electron force is just beginning to be used. In this use of it, the Being who manifests is also a Being who is competent, loving, wise, honorable, and patient. In the sixth dimension, we add other qualities. The rays or emissions that emanate from a Being who graces the sixth dimension and higher are so intense that they can disintegrate the highest of frequencies that are known to the planet Earth. Entire universes understand the electron flow coming from these Beings, for they are the creators of those universes. They use color and sound frequencies in a manner that would be totally foreign to your minds. It even would be difficult for us to pass this information down to you in the form of analogies. We could try, if you desire. Please remember, even we do not have the total picture of the existence, for that is our destiny. We will always be just one step ahead of our Earth brothers and sisters in leading the way on the path of evolution.

I can tell you what we have been told, and nothing more. Also, much of what I have revealed comes from our Magnificent Chamber for Manifestation, that is described in the chapter on the Starship. [We had already brought this information through at an earlier time.] *That is where I received this information. The Ascended Masters reveal this information to us at times, as well.*

CHAPTER IV:
THE LANGUAGE

OUR HUMAN concept of communication involves the use of words, signs, and symbols, as defined below by *Webster's New Collegiate Dictionary.*

Language: The words, their pronunciation, and the methods of combining them used and understood by a considerable community. (1): audible, articulate, meaningful sound as produced by the action of the vocal organs (2): a systematic means of communicating ideas or feelings by the use of conventionalized signs, sound, gestures or marks having understood meanings.

As more and more incidents of communication between humans and extraterrestrial Beings come to light, it is apparent that communication between the various species is often telepathic. When we asked the Arcturians to explain their system of language, we were told that their language is indeed telepathic. Their system provides for more accurate transmissions of messages, they said, both in content and in quality of emotion, than our system of words and symbols.

The information that follows is in response to our inquiries regarding their language systems and general patterns of communication. It constitutes a detailed explanation of the concepts and mechanics of telepathic communication.

89

Juluionno, our most frequent communicator, turned this subject over to the Ship's Elder, Herdonitic, who greeted us by asking us a question.

We greet you in the name of Our Most Radiant One. I am Herdonitic, Elder of the Starship Athena, who will address your questions of language.

Before we begin our dialogue, I would like to ask you one question regarding your language. Would you mind?

NO, PLEASE ASK WHATEVER YOU WOULD LIKE.

Thank you. My question is brief. I should like to ask you, "How do you speak?"

WHAT DO YOU MEAN, "HOW DO WE SPEAK?" DO YOU MEAN PHYSICALLY, MENTALLY, OR WHAT?

I should like to ask again, "How do you speak?" Please offer whatever answer you wish regarding the interpretation of this question.

WHEN THOUGHTS COME TO OUR HEADS, WE FILTER THEM THROUGH OUR MINDS, AND THEN MOVE OUR TONGUES AND MOUTH TO FORM WORDS THAT INTERPRET SOME OF THOSE THOUGHTS. EVENTUALLY, SOME OF THE THOUGHTS THAT BECOME WORDS HAVE A SOUND ATTACHED TO THEM. DOES THIS ANSWER YOUR QUESTION?

Yes, a part of it does. What you said in the beginning of the first sentence more clearly describes our language system on Arcturus than it does your language system on Earth. At least for this moment of human evolution, that statement is true. The latter part describes the way in *which you interpret **your** language abilities on your planet. Thank you for attempting an answer to my question. What I would like to do now is to build upon that answer, and use that as the foundation for the comparison I will provide between how humans on Earth use language and how we on Arcturus communicate.*

Please note that at times I will use the collective "we" to describe the group's explanation for a particular question. It will be done in this manner, for it is written in our laws that we indeed must submit to the commonality of the group. In this way of life, we know only the oneness, and one single Being does not try to take credit for the accomplishments of the many.

It has taken many eons to refine our culture and system. It remains one of the highest civilizations in the universe, in the opinion of many who are deemed capable to judge. One of the reasons we remain in the highest of esteem is because we honor the oneness of the laws that fit every Being. In so honoring, we do not compete. We instead build upon the mutual contributions of the many. In this way we support the masses who inhabit Arcturus.

Therefore, during this dialogue, you may often see a reference to "we." When you do, know that I am referring to our civilization and its laws. When I refer to the least significant "I," I refer to only one Being's opinion regarding the interpretation of a question or topic.

You might wonder why it is even necessary that I have to interpret using the insignificant "I," coming from a culture as advanced as Arcturus. There is a logical explanation for this. The reason is that we are communicating from a fifth dimensional existence to a third dimensional existence. The interpretations of many of our explanations are not as easy as one might think. It is in this transition that I often must explain a concept that has no common analogy in the civilization of Arcturus. When this occurs, the group's laws and common meanings cannot support the information that I will be sending; for, up until now, there has been no need for this kind of dialogue or communication. Therefore, some of what I reveal to you will be my own interpretation that seems to best fit the needs of the communication channels for your psyche. It will also be on a frequency where others can receive it, as well.

This is only one of the reasons why I, Herdonitic, an Elder of Arcturus, have been called upon to answer the questions about the language. A second reason is that I have had the privilege of visiting your planet before, and have even incarnated as a human on one occasion. While it was many Earth centuries ago, the programming of language was very good in my Akashic records. I am able to translate many things that my colleagues on Arcturus have not yet been able to decipher. They honor me in their trust of this dialogue. I now wish to try my best to explain our systems of language in a manner which you might understand.

Herdonitic paused for a moment to let the information just transmitted sink in. Many concepts described by the Arcturians are difficult for us to really internalize, from the basis of our own human experience. We cannot, for example, truly understand the concept of oneness when our human values extol the virtues of individuality. Apparently unity of a species enhances accurate communication. This seemed reasonable, especially in view of our awareness that communication on Earth is so difficult to achieve with any degree of accuracy. We were glad Herdonitic, with his previous incarnation as a human, had been chosen to address this subject. His awareness of our thought processes might make it easier to understand, we hoped. After our brief discussion, he resumed:

Let me begin by defining the terms.

The word "language" implies a coded symbolic system that is used to carry concepts and feelings from one life form to another. This is not the precise definition you use on Earth, for your systems include vocal transmissions as well. This, however, is an acceptable definition from the Confederation of Planets, for the purposes of our work here.

*The word "speaking" implies the ability to move a part of the outer body physically, and to produce a sound that is transmitted to another life form. This allows for the transmission of language and/or decoding to take place. Sometimes the transmission is accurate, and sometimes it is not. The **sound frequencies** that are exchanged make the difference in whether or not the information is transmitted accurately.*

Speaking also implies that the emotion of the message is transmitted from one to another. Again, this is an exchange produced by the transmission of sound frequencies.

The third word that we would like to define is the word "communication." This word means the sending of a message across a distance. It has no other hidden meaning to it. The definition does not place a value system on the message, it only states that one is sent.

The key to understanding the kind of language system we use on Arcturus has nothing to do with the above three definitions. They are only in this communication because they are definitions that are used as the standard for describing concepts. They are also universal definitions, to a degree. At least they are in the way which we analyze Earth behavior and humans' acceptance of them.

What I would like to do now is offer a definition of our form of language. This would allow for comparisons of the two communication systems to begin.

*First, on Arcturus, the word "**language**" implies the energy that is formed within one's consciousness that directs the visualization process. This allows a Being to communicate not only the encoded messages, but also the feelings that were intended when the message was sent.*

*The second word that is important to define in understanding the Arcturian language system is "**message**." This word means carrying energy to the appropriate section of the consciousness. Message implies the beginning and end points of a communication. Message also implies that the communication has been delivered. If a message is not received by the "target" to which it is sent, it does not contain the impact of the communication for which it was designed. This is a critical element for civilizations that adhere to the oneness concept, as we shall point out later.*

*The third word that is vital to understanding our language system is the word "**volume**." Volume means the amount of energy that is directed in the visual and emotional modes to another Being. Volume implies the fullest possible use of the system of language. Volume is what is steadily increased throughout our own language training programs on Arcturus, as we are taught to communicate.*

*The last word that is critical to understand is "**communication.**" Communication means the ability to see the same visual and emotional pictures between two or several life sources, and to present a common solution to the inquiry being made, when inquiry is the mode of exchange.*

*Communicating is the **critical element** in our training and development. Unlike humans on Earth, who use their own interpretations of symbols and meanings when communicating with others, we on Arcturus do not allow individual interpretation to confuse others. In your systems of development and training, we observe one soul often trying to bring others to a common point of understanding. In actuality, that common point is only the picture stored within that soul's mind and brain. Through lengthy communication sessions, that individual is often successful in making all the others believe that the visualization within his or her mind is the same as what they also see.*

We believe the term is called "winning," but we do not see a win situation developing at all. What we observe is the destruction of the visualizations contained within the others' consciousnesses. This dissipation of energy prevents the will from flowing through to higher levels of the collective consciousness of the universe. Much is lost in this mode of operation. As you see, your definition of "winning" does not agree with ours.

We hope you see that the word "communication" means two very different things to the Beings of our two planets. Just as it may be difficult for you to understand and accept our way of defining that word, please allow us to struggle to understand the benefits of your application, as well.

Again, Herdonitic paused for us to absorb the material he had given us. Apparently he felt that with the definitions firmly in place it would be easier for us to understand the information to follow. In a few minutes he again began to send his message through Norma.

Now that we have defined our terms, let me provide you with a different aspect of our language system. That aspect is the one of symbols.

On Earth we see numerous symbols being used that formulate many concepts from different geographic parts of the planet. We also see many souls learn more than one set of these complex symbols, for the purpose of helping them learn to communicate with others. We find this very admirable. But we also find this system to be a very lengthy training program, and one which only fosters the misleading concept of "winning."

What we witness in this process on Earth is that language interpreted between individuals (who traditionally use different symbols to communicate) often is used to gain acceptance of each other's viewpoint. Or the language is used for comparisons again, which serves to reinforce the individual systems of separateness.

Within this system and usage of languages, we see very little room for the use of common visualization exchanges between souls. There is also less assurance that the emotional quality of the energy being sent will be received in the manner in which it was intended.

If an accurate communication is sent on both accounts, it appears to be a bonus. This can be seen as an exception, and not the rule. Also, when an accurate communication does not result, we observe that there is little room for concern, unless there is a problem. In the identification of a problem, what we see is that the individual interprets his or her position as one of losing ground in this competitive game you play with your symbols.

On Arcturus, we only allow symbols from the universal mind to permeate our consciousness. We learn from these symbols information from the source, the Light force.

There is a big difference in this approach to language, for we learned many centuries ago that we do not wish to be misunderstood. When one is misunderstood, the entire group suffers. For in the oneness of civilization, there is no room for regression. If one has a different interpretation or opinion, then the coding and visualization of that one is honored and synchronized with the others, to form an even higher form and level of vibration.

The Light force is what guides our visualizations. We do not entertain concepts of "good" and "evil" on Arcturus. We only know the Highest, and use this frequency to benefit the consciousness not only of our own inhabitants, but also of those anywhere in the universe whom we are asked to serve.

The Light force is a direct ray from the Great Central Sun that allows us to know and understand much of what is taken for granted by civilizations from the fourth and fifth dimensions of time and space. Soon the planet Earth also will be coming of age, and will adopt a whole new approach to understanding this concept. That is because the beloved Terra will soon be vibrating at a much higher rate herself, as the planet is being rebirthed into the New Age.

The language barriers that exist today on the planet soon will have to change, for the language systems that have been developed on the Earth have sustained duality and not the holistic patterns that await. Therefore, the language systems are archaic, and that will soon be evident, as society moves into the higher forms of visualization patterns of communication.

That is yet another reason why we have been asked to come to Earth, to help our sisters and brothers achieve this leap into the unknown that is awaiting them. We can see, from where we are situated, the past and future. You cannot, for you have limited your sight by your duality of nature.

Through this limitation, you have closed down many of your systems out of fear and disbelief. In this state of mind you have closed down the visualization powers that are lying dormant in your brain structures. The visualization patterns are the key to your survival in the New Age. They are the foundation for the accurate communications you all desire.

You are beginning to tire of the long road which has required you to justify your existence and patterns; for in this mode you have to compete. Competition consumes much of your energy and tires you. It is competition that is aging you and making you hold on to your fears.

May we suggest that you take this opportunity to work towards a new system of learning and advancement based upon the tools of visualization, emotional transmission of accurate messages, and telepathic communication?

IF YOU ARE ASKING US, WE WOULD LIKE TO LEARN MORE ABOUT THIS; BUT IF YOU ARE ASKING FOR THE WHOLE HUMAN RACE, THAT CHOICE IS NOT OURS ALONE TO MAKE. PERHAPS YOU COULD

EXPLAIN HOW THIS IS ACCOMPLISHED AND HOW
WE COULD BETTER MAKE A DECISION. WOULD
YOU PLEASE EXPLAIN THIS "NEW" SYSTEM OF
LEARNING AND ADVANCEMENT?

Yes, I would be delighted.

*The first instruction is forming visualization patterns.
What this means is that a Being on Arcturus has the
capacity to synchronize its consciousness to those frequencies that sustain the encoding of symbols. Another
word for symbols on Earth might be picture forms. They
can be linear, two-dimensional, or of a holographic
nature.*

*Whatever the image, it is encoded with an emotional nature.
The emotional nature is evoked from past lives and recollections of the happy and fearful experiences a soul has
collected.*

*A Being on Arcturus always has the image of these rec-
ollections imprinted on its brain structure. I am using
the word brain only as an analogy here, for in our reality,
we do not have brain structures that are common to your
species. Instead, we have a very complex system of fibers
and what you would call neurons that control the frequency
patterns of our essence. But for simplicity's sake, allow
me to use this term.*

*Since we have access to universal language codes, symbols,
vibrations, and frequencies, we can draw from all the
collective records which support our present mission. We
can move symbols to any dimensional frequency we wish,
for it is the nature of our command of the symbols to do
so. In this state of retrieving frequencies, we can form
them into any picture or visualization we wish. By doing*

so, we are then able to move our messages from one transmitter to another.

One of the reasons we are so highly telepathic is that we have the ability to access any of the symbols in another's consciousness, as well. We can use this ability to retrieve information or visualizations, for we know we are all one. In this understanding come the skills to access information from the collective consciousness. In this accessing of the information, an individual Being understands that all have the same privileges, and therefore, does not abuse the system.

You are probably wondering how we filter and organize the information and visualization frequencies we are capable of receiving. We can tell you that this was a difficult task when we first began to open our energy centers on our evolutionary path. What it did at first was to cause many problems by confusing the visualization patterns as the emotional nature of our existence was not yet fully developed.

It was this lack of emotional development that caused a retardation in our evolutionary progress for eons. It was not until our Elders realized that the lack of progress of our entire civilization was caused by this inadequacy that we began to study the problem and find ways in which to perfect it.

We began to study the universal coding for peace and harmony. This code vibrates on a high frequency and is one which rests within the capacity of each created Being. This seemed to be a very desirable state, and we decided collectively to find an operational mode that supported this quality and way of life.

We began to study other star systems, and other planets. One of the most advanced at that "time" was that of Alpha Centauri. We learned much from our space brothers and sisters in that star system and, even though we needed their information and knowledge, we did not have the courage to adapt totally to their way of life for many centuries.

Nevertheless, the learning proved to be very helpful, and in this information exchange we gave them some of our scientific propulsion secrets. We did this because even though they live in another dimension of time and space, they were not as advanced in this area as we were. This exchange proved more beneficial than we had imagined, for what resulted was that the information we acquired also augmented our language systems. While this may sound a bit strange, let me explain. It was in the exchange of information that we were able to develop coding that helped facilitate communication between our star systems.

This meant that we were able to have access to more than a technique for aiding our civilization to reach a higher frequency. It also helped us solve the problem of visualization interference. We now had access to universal coding for a higher frequency of the Great Central Sun. The Beings from Alpha Centauri understood this, as they have a civilization that has long been consumed by the Great Central Sun. It was in this process of being consumed that they merged with many of the Ascended Masters of the ethers, to develop a plan for continuation of life, far removed from and above the incarnation of inhabitants of Earth.

Although Norma is not aware of the contents of the transmissions as they are sent through her, and therefore, not tired or overwhelmed by the information, Herdonitic apparently felt it would be better if the group understood each section before proceeding. For this reason he let her rest while Betty and Cynthia read and discussed the previous message. He then continued:

The issue, then, was the disturbances in filtering out visual pictures of the collective consciousness.

We discovered that the frequency at which a Being vibrates is directly related to the command it has over its thoughts, actions, words, and emotions. When a Being is vibrating at a lower frequency, it permits many other, lower forms of energies to mix and mingle with its pool of energy and its cycles. When this happens, the thoughts have a tendency to get confused which causes the Being to experience frustration. In this state of Beingness, one who is operating at this frequency can get very discouraged and depressed which only has a tendency to keep the vibratory level at a constant, lower level.

When one increases one's frequency to that of the speed of Light, then the mastery of the process begins. This means that the Being now has access to more information in the universal consciousness; but that Being also has the command to dictate what will or will not come through the filter.

The process actually becomes more complex as it becomes more simplified. When a Being does not understand this principle, that Being may go through cycles of high and low frequencies that direct its consciousness. This is because the frequencies are controlling it. When one discovers that he has command of thought within frequency levels, then there are steps he can follow to assure that these vibrations will be maintained.

The reason a higher frequency protects a Being from receiving other, lower vibrations is that the Light consumed within the essence of that soul is impenetrable. When the Light within is deliberately changed by the Being who has assumed that consciousness pattern, then a transformation and stillness overtakes the body. In this transformation process, the Being becomes centered. When centered, the energy patterns are more logical, holistic, and unrandomized.

When we are centered, we are accessing the universal code, and when we tap into this frequency, we understand another's frequency patterns too. That is, again, because we are one. In the oneness of this existence, we are able to transmit and receive messages; and, more importantly, we can become the sender and receiver of messages in perfect understanding.

In most of our communications, we learn how to shield ourselves. We do this with White Light. This frequency protects and nourishes us. We then can only call upon our Higher Selves for the direction we need to advance as a group.

When our shields are up, we are masters of what we wish to receive and to transmit. This also includes what you would call a group dialogue. We have the power to "hear" all that is being "discussed" telepathically. In this mode, we are conditioned to adjust our own vibrations, so that we are all in tune with the centeredness of the group energy. That means that not all of us "think" at the same time. A part of the process of mastery in this form of life is learning to clear the mind. A soul who cannot achieve this, even on the planet Earth, is not a master. A clear mind is essential in our mode of telepathic communication, for we do need to learn how to receive as well as to project.

As we observe your cultures on the planet Earth, we are amazed that souls have not learned the quality of listening. Listening is another form of clearing the mind and allowing it to receive information. We believe a part of the reason is because you still have ownership of your egos; and in this state of being, you are constantly in a competitive mode.

Competition will produce only behavior that is aggressive rather than passive. Sending messages is the aggressive mode and receiving messages is the passive. If a soul has not learned to receive, then it only stands to reason that there will be greater difficulty in understanding and learning this form of communication.

In order to be passive and receive, a soul must learn how to increase its vibratory rate. As we said earlier, we know the lower frequencies are much more unstable and disruptive. When a soul is vibrating at the level of hate, envy, or greed, which is the feeling of not being satisfied, then it stands to reason that its consciousness would be bounced around from one temptation to another. A soul's needs have to be met, and there must be a sense of peace and satisfaction within, before the frequency begins to rise. When this frequency begins to rise, it begins to work miracles within. One only needs to bathe in the Liquid Light to feel the cleansing, purification, and peace that it provides.

Allow this discourse to conclude the first part of our explanation on the topic of language. In a second communication, we would be most honored to delve into a more complex issue, which is that of the electrical impulses that facilitate the transmission of thought patterns from one Being to another or between groups.

The following week Herdonitic continued his transmission on the subject of language—or more precisely, communication. Although this message was supposed to deal specifically with the mechanics of electrical transmission of messages, it led inevitably into the philosophical matrix in which communication takes place.

> ## Electrical Transmission Of Messages

To begin a dialogue on this subject, we must anchor, again, the concept that all is energy. If one does not understand this concept, one may have difficulty understanding the explanations we will try to communicate to you about our ability to send messages telepathically.

All thoughts are electrical impulses surrounded by an electromagnetic field of energy. This field of energy has the ability to move at speeds the human mind cannot even begin to comprehend. In this movement, images are transferred that are directly related to visualizations, emotions, and the coding systems of the universal language.

It is a Being's choice whether or not to send electromagnetic impulses to another place. The choice is determined by the amount of emotion and will power that Being is able to gather. In this choice and the consciousness of the mind, a Being determines the degree of mastery over telepathic communications that he, she, or it will obtain in one lifetime.

The force that propels and projects thoughts is based upon a tensor equation. This tensor equation is made up of 2 parts electromagnetic energy and 1 part emotion. It is the brain and mind of the individual, coupled with choice and conviction, that determines the ability to send messages.

Being a sender is experiencing one form of communication; being a receiver is experiencing another form. In both, the determining factors of the communication's success are the choice, the free will, and the emotional commitment. Remember, we defined our word communication earlier as transferring energy from one place to another and having the ability to send and receive the same visualization between two parties.

It is important to remind you that it was my experience on the Earth plane to witness that all humans think and behave in a linear fashion. Therefore, I am choosing to use words "from one place to another" only for the purposes of satisfying your mode of thinking and facilitating a clearer interpretation of the explanation we are providing. In reality, these limitations are not appropriate, for there are no linear points in the universe of oneness. Oneness supports only the concept of the holistic mind; which when translated, means the mind is all points inclusive. Each point contains the oneness of the universe. How could a thought even be conceived of as moving only from one point to another, as if it were truly self-contained?

This explanation is inserted here only for clarification. We hope that you will request a more detailed explanation of this subject, for the explanation is one of the foundational shifts the Earth will be experiencing in coming years. Having an explanation from us, even though it may be a limited one, undoubtedly will relieve many individuals who are currently struggling with the limitations of their own research. One of the reasons your research moves so slowly on Earth is because the "learned" on the planet are trying to apply limited restrictions and variables to a multidimensional world. This approach is always indicative of the finite awareness of the universe rather than the infinite. Let us now return to the concept of thought forms.

At this point he once again paused. We assumed it was for the purpose of keeping us "with him" as he continued his teaching. We reread the message as it appeared on Norma's computer, absorbed it as best we could in the few moments he allowed, and tried to internalize the following information as it came through her hands on the keyboard to the monitor screen.

*The force that propels and projects thought forms is the electromagnetic energy of the universe. It is the yin and the yang, as defined by Far Eastern civilizations on your planet. It is the Prana, or life support system of the universe, as well. This force is the positive and the negative, or the light and dark sides of one's consciousness. It is the substance and the void. It is the **ALL**.*

In this force, the tensor equation is used to determine the degree of manifestation of the thoughts, for the tensor equation is a shared power between the force and the free will of the Being. It is designed to be the foundation of co-creation, and the paths that are designed to achieve mastery of this power are as diverse as the thoughts themselves.

Thoughts are part of the universal consciousness, and the energy that moves them through one's consciousness is the intensity of conviction of needing to be one with this power. All thoughts that can ever be created "are." All inventions that will ever be designed "already" exist. All freedoms that will ever be invented "are" present. In the totality and oneness of the ALL, everything is already in the past, present, and future.

Therefore, it does not make much sense for one individual to claim a thought or invention, and try to hoard the discovery for his or her exclusive use. The concept in itself, of controlling and claiming one thought, is absurd. In the limitations of the ego, a soul does not understand this. Therefore, the lower vibrations of fear, which are governed by feelings of not having enough, take over one's consciousness and limit reality.

Individuals limit themselves, for they are unable to see the vastness and abundance of the ALL that is available to them. They cannot see the opening of manifestation and power, if they claim thoughts or inventions to be theirs alone.

On Arcturus, we learned and experienced this concept of the oneness eons ago. Since then, we have adopted the mode of behavior that we understand, adhering to practices which bring through information in the collective form.

Since each of our Beings is a part of the whole, we often have group telepathic sessions whereby we put out a question to the universal consciousness. In this process, we all participate in bringing in a piece of the information that will contribute to the holistic concept or understanding. In this collective visualization we take the image and resonate it within each Being's mind. This develops the collective through focusing the energy. One can see clearly how important group work and meditating is in this process.

We understand that each of us has access to the universal holistic concept, but each of us may also have limitations in retrieving the entire visualization clearly. It is for this purpose that we collectively use those who resonate on specific sound and light frequencies to bring forth information on different questions.

Let us explain in another way. For example, when we wish to bring forth a visualization on the subject of a scientific discovery, we measure the frequency of those Beings who are in the light vibration of the color blue. This intensity will then be double checked with the combinations of selected "sound frequencies" that Beings may have, since so many scientific discoveries are based upon the combination of light and sound waves. This process serves as a screening device for Beings who will be selected to communicate telepathically with the universal consciousness, with themselves, and finally with the advanced communication technology we use to retrieve and decipher information.

*When the groups are selected, they are in the mode of operating. What this means is that the mode in which they choose to bring forth the information will be designed according to the mode that is set for the investigation. If the inquiry is the mode of investigation, such as the activity of sampling and analyzing selected specimens, then the sound frequency closest to the **physical mode of existence** is used to determine which Beings will be a part of that group. If theorizing is the mode of investigation, then only those Beings who register a frequency of sound closest to that of, what shall we say, **Tchaikovsky's Concertos,** are selected to participate in that process.*

There is an important reason for this. All manifestations of creative energies result from combinations of Light energy frequencies and sound vibrations. By combining them, one is able to channel the power to create from the universal consciousness and access its codes.

Our education utilizes the processes in this explanation. We humbly hope this application helps to further your understanding of our life and civilization on Arcturus.

Allow us to note again a very important point about our doctrines and beliefs on Arcturus. In the situation described above, if a Being is not selected to be a part of a certain telepathic group discovery session, there is no shame or dishonor. It is because that Being has the talents for another, equally important characteristic, which adds to the quality of life on Arcturus in another area of our civilization.

If we had not learned to be the masters of our emotions and to be centered Beings eons ago, we might not be able to function so well during this period. But we have indeed achieved this level of understanding, and are able to work collectively for everything we achieve. This is only one reason we look so much alike, in the minds of all those who have witnessed our appearance on the Earth plane. We have no need to use our egos to be better than one another. That is nonfunctional in our civilization and existence. It is contradictory to our beliefs, and to experiences of progress.

Our progress is definitely dependent upon our abilities to access the universal codes collectively, and to adhere to the nonemotional commitment of the advancement of our civilization. If you had to describe our civilization on Arcturus, you would have to use the word "peaceful." We are not happy or sad, for those two words are also nonfunctional in our civilization. Instead, we are considered to be peaceful. In this peaceful state of mind, we are in harmony and walk a path of great contentment and accomplishment. One of the reasons we are able to do so is because of our mastery of universal symbols and telepathic communication.

These telepathic communication abilities are now being made available to many humans on Earth. Many souls on Earth are moving into the sound and light frequency of the color indigo. Visualization is being used to access incredible depths of power and talent, even in those individuals who do not realize they have these powers.

We delight as we observe this process, and we take great pride in all of you in this accomplishment, for it brings back memories of our own civilization of so long ago. We honor your path and are here to help make it easier and swifter for you in your third dimensional consciousness. We have the recollection in this present moment of time and space of the long struggle we endured to find peace and an advanced level of achievement. Watching the transformation on planet Earth brings this visualization back to us. In many ways you are living an historical moment of Arcturus in the present moment of Earth. If you wish, you could describe this transition period as one in which you have pulled the Arcturian drama from the universal consciousness mind as the script that is unfolding for Earth at this time. We see the main actors and actresses in this drama from the place where we reside. We also see the villains and the victims. Behind the drama is the brilliance of the Great Central Sun that assures the dawning of a new day for all of you.

The unfolding of your drama is definitely coming to the end. A play is now being directed. Soon the universal consciousness will bring the inhabitants, or characters, of this play another script, which will usher in the symbols, emotions, tools, and behaviors of a higher level of consciousness. That is assured. That is always how the Great Central Sun's energies work, for that source of power is truly dedicated to the highest forms of evolution one can imagine.

So, allow me to leave you with this great visualization for your future. **YOUR FUTURE ON THE BELOVED TERRA IS ONE OF GREATNESS.**

We thanked Herdonitic for the information he had brought through and felt good about the positive way he had predicted the future of our Earth; but he was not yet through for the evening. He continued with a summary of his messages about language/communication.

Before I depart, let me complete a summary of this chapter for your document, which includes the description and application of what I have explained, and how it relates to your receiving our messages telepathically.

In the beginning, I defined the word "message" to be that which has a beginning and an ending point. I also explained that the "visualization patterns" and "encoding" from the universal consciousness were of utmost importance for sending clear messages in our civilization. We also described the concept of "volume" as being most important for sending and receiving messages, for that concept determines the degree of commitment and emotion carried by a message.

In this present communication, you have received my dialogue well, even though this explanation is somewhat foreign to your own consciousness. Our concept of the importance of the message has been explained and fulfilled. In this holistic pattern of consciousness, you have become one with us in bringing forth the information of encoded messages, and have been the facilitator in the decoding of those messages for the masses.

Often, you have been able to decode our visualization patterns because we have communicated through an exchange of energy patterns using the tensor equation. You have made a commitment to work with us and expressed a desire to bring forth this information. Therefore, Part One of the formula was strengthened, which automatically allowed the force to use positive and negative energies of the electromagnetic currents to place selected visualization patterns of words in your brain. The Part One automatically facilitated the development of the other two parts of the tensor equation.

The concept of volume was fulfilled because of your emotional desire to bring forth the purest communication that you are able to receive. Also, by being passive and open, you were able to receive our messages, therefore gaining skills to decode them for the masses.

This is not a special skill reserved for you alone. All humans, with proper training and commitment, can do this as well. This is the same process we had to learn from our sisters and brothers from Alpha Centauri, when we first began communicating with them and exchanging ideas. So, although this may seem "alien" to you, let us assure you it also appeared the same to us long ago. We are now sharing with you the same information and skill training that we received from them in that historical moment of the now.

We are honored and pleased that you have made a commitment to communicate with us. We only hope our intentions from the heart center are received by the people of Earth in the same manner in which we send them. We come here with great admiration and love for our sisters and brothers on Earth, and we hope we will be able to help you address many situations that lie ahead with greater ease and harmony than what we experienced in our own transformation.

113

We see the coming of a new day and a glorious future awaiting all of you, and we are honored that we have been asked by the Ascended Masters to come to Earth at this most important time to be a part of this new birth for humanity.

CHAPTER V:
THE EDUCATIONAL PROGRAM

EDUCATION, AS defined by the Arcturians, is quite different from what we know on Earth. At least, that appears to be the case for the definition of education in the United States. To most here, the term means having to go to school for approximately 12 years to become "educated." To others, it also means completing additional years in our postsecondary institutions and universities for the purpose of gaining skills for careers and/or self-development. The curriculum emphasizes facts, figures, historical knowledge, scientific investigation, and learning processes. Progress is measured by the amount of information assimilated, retained, and used. Often, the measurement of knowledge is taken at the expense of depriving the students of an understanding of values, leaving them in a position of having to focus their attention on facts and data rather than on the spiritual and moral consequences of their behaviors.

The Arcturians report having a completely different approach to education from ours. They describe their systems of learning as ones based upon the acquisition of higher states of consciousness and vibratory frequencies. They educate to achieve patterns of mental development that are compatible with the fifth dimensional frequency of the universe. They state that they are totally telepathic Beings who can manifest objects with their minds. They also claim to have the ability to tap into a universal consciousness, and state that in the future, humans also

115

will have this ability as we progress into their fifth dimensional frequency. They measure only the Light frequency of each Being as the true measure of that soul's success, and do not seem to concern themselves with the tallying of facts and data within each Being's records.

While a comparison of our two systems suggests that the two approaches are indeed different, there are also a few commonalities. First, it appears that both of our species are concerned with our future development, regardless of what we define that to be. Second, we both seem to have a hierarchical structure in our worlds that directs the knowledge and learning taking place within our systems. We have teachers and professors, they have their Elders. Third, we both take the activity of learning to heart and treat it with the sincerity and sophistication it deserves. The ultimate goal in both cases seems to be evolution. In spite of the fact that we are reportedly different in appearance and mind structure, we both appear to want to evolve. It seems that we just value different paths in creating our futures.

When we studied the messages transmitted, one of the things that impressed us most was the Arcturians' ability to compare their system with ours. They seemed to have the ability to "target" many of the weaknesses of our system, and they did it with a grace and finesse that we were unaccustomed to seeing. Were they only critiquing or comparing our systems or were they actually criticizing them? The presentation of their analyses leads us to question whether or not the Arcturians are truly unemotional Beings with the ability to compare, or whether they are masters of psychology and the use of words. At times there appeared to be some hostility present in their comparisons, but then maybe that is only our own shortcoming and bias as the readers of this information.

We on Earth are often accused of having closed minds. Sometimes we deserve this criticism, and sometimes we do not. The problem seems to be that if new information does not fit our parameters of "taught thought," then we often tend to dismiss this information as untrue. The same is true of criticism. Perhaps the questions we pose in the paragraph above are unfair, and based only upon a defensive response on our part.

The concepts presented by our unseen friends in this section are indeed different. That, few can deny. We hope that our readers will be open to receive them as a comparison of our two worlds. The Arcturians have included some new ideas for our consideration. There are a few suggestions that are even appealing. Maybe we can learn from them.

Following is the transcript of the transmission that was received when this section was brought through. Norma had already made the connection in the usual fashion and had been told that a new Being with the name of Ascheana would be the one who would answer her questions concerning the educational systems of Arcturus.

GOOD EVENING, ASCHEANA. I AM HAPPY TO MAKE YOUR ACQUAINTANCE FROM THIS TELEPATHIC COMMUNICATION. I HAVE SEVERAL QUESTIONS FOR YOU THIS EVENING. THE FIRST IS, WHAT KIND OF EDUCATIONAL SYSTEM DO YOU HAVE ON ARCTURUS?

Our educational system is much different from what you are accustomed to on Earth. One of the major differences lies in the fact that we do not have any grade levels on our planet. Instead, we have what are called, in your language, increments. What this means is that the frequency at which an entity vibrates is being monitored continually, and when the frequency reaches a certain level, then the "learning" is deemed to be increased to the next increment.

On our planet we are competing with no one but ourselves. We have no standard curriculum. We offer all knowledge from the collective consciousness of our planet and the universe. Our species learns to open their "centers of learning" from their "birth." Each Being has equal access to information and knowledge.

Each one can and does accelerate at the rate which each finds comfortable for his or her enjoyment and happiness. The collective spirit of the planet prohibits anyone from competition; we are allowed only to support.

Frequency levels are the measure of enlightenment. All of us understand that enlightenment is the measure of true growth of intelligence. What we learn in one increment is automatically used for the good of the planet. Therefore, there is only "progress," and the good that is shared among our inhabitants.

This means that we are a planet of one. Duality is reserved for the Earth. We know only the one, and, therefore, we have no stress. The only stress we observe is that which your species puts themselves through when they constantly fight the forces.

On our planet we learn in our instruction from our "birth" that we need not fight the force. We learn to flow with it and in so doing, we learn to increase our life span and knowledge.

Many souls on your planet are just beginning to catch on to this wisdom, because of the exchange program we are conducting between some of the souls on Earth and Arcturus. This exchange program is serving both of us well, for it is in this exchange of ideas that your inhabitants are learning of the power of the Liquid Light and the Great Central Sun, and we are learning more of friction. It is this concept of friction that I will explain at a later time, if that is permissible with you. Right now, it would be helpful if I could stay focused on the curriculum of the educational system.

We agree on our planet to use the powers of the mind to create and not to destroy. This not only includes our physical manifestations, but also the life we support. We are not able to destroy on Arcturus, for that is not in our understanding of natural forces. We have not yet learned how to reverse our learning processes, but I can tell you we are getting quite an education as we observe our sisters and brothers on your planet.

The life force that is available to all is truly the most dynamic and stimulating curriculum to be learned. On Arcturus we observe this instruction with much discipline and love. We learn how to channel love to all of our counterparts. It is difficult to learn anything other than creation when one is channeling love.

On your planet of duality, these concepts are difficult to understand, as lower vibrations of energy and frequencies are so prevalent. It takes a very strong remembrance of the Light and love to break through the lower frequencies and to enable souls to remember to channel only higher ones.

The souls on Earth who are learning to channel love right now, however, are indeed finding that this way of life is much happier and more productive as compared to the life of stress and fears from lower vibrational frequencies. They also are finding that the forces that support them on the planet are adding to their life spans. For this discovery alone it is well worth learning the new curriculum. Do you not agree?

Our mission on planet Earth at this time in history is to bring concepts of this new education to the planet. We, the Arcturians, are designers of the curriculum, so to speak. We are the "experts" in the structure of learning, and we are the leaders in communicating much of the new information to Earth.

We have conducted some experiments on your planet for comparisons that we are making. In all cases, our results are just as surprising to us as they are to the animals and minerals we study. We use the information to make comparisons of the two worlds. Our plan is to share more of this information with experts on Earth as soon as we are welcome to come forward.

The "curricula" we are presently assigned to write is mainly one of enlightening the mind. Each star fleet that has sent its representative groups to Earth is in charge of a different aspect of the birthing process of the planet. Ours is the curriculum of the mind.

Ascheana then proceeded to outline the "new curriculum" that the Arcturians are planning to write for us on Earth.

Our main assignment is the programming of messages and information into the minds of those Earthlings who have given us permission to communicate with them. We are in the process of sending a new curriculum which will soon allow for a higher level of information to come forward. This information will include:

1. ingredients for the process of enlightening the mind;
2. making of the product;
3. secrets of digestion of information on an energy level; and
4. the evaluation process that structures the individual's progress.

Does this not sound like a biology unit in one of your Earth science classes?

With your permission, allow me to explain this mission, while at the same time interpreting the curriculum process of Arcturus. In many ways they are one and the same. This process is also a description, in part, of the evolutionary step that souls on Earth will be experiencing in the next decade; therefore, I deem this information to be of much importance to humans.

Ingredients for the Process of Enlightening the Mind

The first part of our course of study has to do with those aspects of energy that affect the functioning of the minds of humans. These aspects of energy are within the forces of the winds of change. Once they are learned, they are the keys to all future levels of enlightenment. Call them your building blocks, so to speak. In your science/physics courses they might be referred to as the laws of nature.

The first law we wish to give to you is that of reversed friction. Reversed friction means the removal of all blockages that stand in the way of energy flowing smoothly and easily through a life form. Reversed friction is the first step Earthlings must learn before they can move to higher levels of consciousness.

On Arcturus, we do not have to deal with this law, because we do not learn negative forms and frequencies of vibration. When one does not learn friction, one does not have to learn to reverse it.

On the Earth it appears that the one step in your curriculum, so prevalent in all of your subjects and grades, is that of learning much of the negative and lower forms of energy. When these are learned, it is hard to progress to higher levels of thought and manifestation. So, one must learn to eliminate this subject and conditioning by mastering the process of the reverse law of friction.

There are several ways to accomplish this reversal. The first is to work on "open mindedness." This is very difficult for many of your people to do, because the negative conditioning is so strong and deep. We advise some simple exercises to practice that will help you to overcome this conditioning and to change the law on your planet. Follow the instructions below to learn a process for acquiring an open mind:

Take your head between your hands and look forward for a period of one Earth minute. Then close your eyes and visualize the vastness of the space and sky running between your hands. If you perceive clouds or dark forms of energy in this visualization, then let these cloud forms pass from your left side out through your right side.

While doing so, breathe deeply, and pretend you are breathing in the vastness of a perfect, cloudless day. Feel how good the energy of this light of day feels.

Take this sense of expansion and the "lightness" it gives you and hold it in an area within your forehead, between your eyes. Focus on this for at least five minutes, but only experience the feeling and the lightness. That is the key.

Then, when you feel like doing so, open your eyes and feel refreshed. Try to hold this feeling in your consciousness throughout the day.

122

Let us now give you a related tool to use to help you open your minds.

Hold on to this feeling of lightness and expansion and note the vibrational frequencies throughout your body. Monitor it carefully when you do this exercise. Then take this newly acquired knowledge of sensing your physical feeling of expansion and note throughout the day when you begin to lose this feeling. What happens to your body when you begin to lose the feeling? Where are you? With whom are you speaking? How is your body reacting? Calculate what the differences are at these moments.

Log the mind's reactions at those moments, as compared to the way the mind felt when you were expanding the energy and light through it. This duality exercise will give you important data. It is the first step in learning the process of open mindedness and how to begin to reverse the friction of the conditioning that surrounds you.

The second ingredient of the process is that of an understanding and appreciation of God. God is the Force to which we are always referring. It is in the understanding and appreciation of God and this life force that we begin our curriculum for advancement in the powers of enlightenment.

What Earthlings do not understand is that all knowledge and life comes from this force—the God Force. When this is denied within one's consciousness, one does not have the opportunity to grow and become one with the force. We on Arcturus know of this force from the moment we are conceived, for there is a ritual of energy transformation that occurs and the knowledge is implanted in our consciousness. From that moment on the concept is taken for granted. In understanding this basic law we are prepared for the curriculum of the God consciousness that is to be developed later.

The third ingredient in the process of enlightening the mind is learning how to channel unconditional love. It is in this aspect of knowing the "oneness" where we are tested. If a Being does not pass this increment of the educational process, then it does not reach the vibrational level of other situations for learning.

The amount of love that a soul channels can be measured by a frequency counter. This device is used only in the highest of structures for learning on our planet. It is in this measurement of love channeling frequency that we undergo the learning of another form of curriculum. It would be called "incidental learning" on your planet, a term that you understand so well.

While we are being measured for tolerance and levels of emotion of the highest quality, the results of these measurements are posted for others to see. If the frequency is not equivalent to the increment level designed for our progress plan, others are assigned to help the one to reach the highest possible increment. The others know that to raise one is to raise all. So, instead of working at the remedial level of diagnosing problems and highlighting the low frequency, the Elders concentrate on the picture of perfection and help the individual Being to raise its consciousness to that level. The Beings of our planet know that when consciousness is raised, and vibrational frequency is higher, rewards for the all are much greater.

So, in celebrating achievement of the higher increment, honor goes not only to the one who is raised, but also to the group's combined effort. They have increased their own enlightenment just by focusing the powers of the collective to assist another.

There is no room for disgrace or dishonor on our planet. We are all one. Increased enlightenment brings increased powers in the realms of creation and manifestation. On Earth you would call it increased intelligence. It is the same, but many on your planet do not know this yet.

Since the force, which is God, is the maker and creator of the all, then it stands to reason that intelligence would be a part of this holistic wonder. If enlightenment is increased, so is power. Intelligence is only one aspect of this force that is enhanced.

Our curriculum guarantees that fundamentals of the laws are provided in the basic ingredients of the plan. Once these fundamental ingredients are transplanted and integrated into our consciousness, we are able to build the products with our powers. This would be similar to the curriculum and fundamental concepts you teach to your students.

Does this gives you a basic idea of what the educational system is like on our planet?

YES, BUT WE ARE EAGER TO LEARN MORE. PLEASE CONTINUE.

We will be sending this basic information to many of your Earth inhabitants in the next few years. Mastery of the fundamentals is necessary before the information and powers can be increased. If you feel you have a working knowledge of our basic system, I will continue with the description of the fundamentals of learning we teach our inhabitants.

Making of the Product

"Making of the product" simply implies that we work to enhance our qualities and those of our planet with the tools of our consciousness. We learn from a very young age that we are one and that we support the single highest cause and goal of our civilization. In doing this we are allowed total freedom with the powers of our minds; for in attaining a certain vibrational frequency we automatically earn the power of manifestation.

With this power comes a considerable amount of responsibility. We learn to acknowledge the roles of each of our colleagues around us, to sense their needs, to read them telepathically, and to assign a quality of assistance or dependency to them.

We do not need to use a language, for we transmit our messages through telepathic communication, just as we are doing with you. We also do not need the highest forms of symbolism or language signs, for we do not need to record our messages. All of our information is stored, if we so choose to store it, in complex machines that are part consciousness and part equipment with cells. Those pieces of equipment or devices are only used for projects that are considered too cumbersome for our own minds to handle. Therefore, those pieces of equipment are primarily used for storage of information for future generations of our inhabitants.

In the evolutionary process, we do understand how important it is for all of us to learn from one another, from the collective consciousness, and from the past and future in the present moment of time. Therefore, we store some of our information for the future and from the past, in the present moment of time. That explanation may be a bit confusing, so let us explain further.

The future is the past and present moment, all in the same instant. That is easy for us to understand, for we do not live in the third dimension where the past and future are viewed as linear. In a holistic concept of evolution of life and consciousness, the three aspects are all in the present moment of time.

It is easier for Arcturians to be noncompetitive and more relaxed about their existence than it is for Earthlings, for we understand this concept of time. We are not like you, rushing with an imaginary clock and measuring our accomplishments against this timepiece, which is perceived to be the judge. Instead, we only measure our own frequency and the vibrational qualities of love and Light—and anyone who has ever felt these two qualities automatically knows that this is indeed a desirable state in which to be.

Out of this state come the products that are manifested and created for societies. These are not measured against time. Instead they are measured by how much the manifestation adds to the vibrational quality of those who will use it. If it lowers the frequency, then it is located in another area with other inhabitants. Or, in worst cases, the structure is vaporized and the electron structure is redesigned for another form and function.

The products are judged solely by the levels for which they are intended to satisfy. That is the only criteria. Never is fault found with a system. Instead, it is like your negotiation process, where the structures of manifestation are telepathically examined and then the determination is made for its placement.

127

There are no grades for the work that is produced. The only grades that we have are those of the Elders, who grade themselves on the numbers of our species they can help each moment of their lives. They pride themselves on the numbers, but never reveal the actual count to others, for if they did, a system of comparison, similar to the one found on Earth, would be born. While we study the Earth system, learn from this system, and honor it, we do not recommend it for those on Arcturus.

Products are also developed by those on other star systems and planets, and brought to our planet. When this occurs, we honor the contributions as though they were our own works of art. In these cases, we are allowed to study them and to learn from the creative processes we have not yet achieved. In this transfer of creations we can tell you that we are truly in a state of excitement, for the works of art brought here are very stimulating.

We are especially interested in the manifestation process of those items we have not yet learned to create. And even Earth has some of those structures and creations. Although we may consider ourselves more enlightened than our sisters and brothers from your planet, we do not consider ourselves to know and understand everything.

One of the things that we have learned from you is the process of dynamics. This process is the one which creates the structures of water and the many different energy formations that are manifested from these structures.

We do not have liquids on our planet as you have on yours. Therefore, we do not have the chance to learn from the dynamics of this force. While we know the God Force is in everything, we do not have all the same ingredients on our planet that you do. The reverse is also true—you do not have all of the ingredients we have, either.

We wonder at your inventions with this creative power. We also learn from what you are doing with it, as we watch your heating and lighting institutions function from this activity and energy.

We do not have any form of energy other than the Liquid Light, and we do not have any other form of liquid other than the minerals that run smoothly, like celestial granite. We are amazed and applaud your ingenuity and the progress you are making with substances available on Earth.

While we could go on forever regarding the making of products from our educational processes, let me continue on with the next phase of our explanation. This information will include the "application of products," which reveals secrets of the digestion of information on an energy level.

Secrets of Digestion of Information on an Energy Level

Digestion simply means absorption. On Earth, when a human eats something, the food is turned into energy and is absorbed by the physical body. In our definition this analogy is also true, but it applies in a little different way.

What we mean by digestion is the slow breakup of energy and its transformation into a higher source. In learning and concentration on Arcturus, we see results of this process in the products that we are able to manifest and transcend. The energy is absorbed into our consciousness, and in this process we are transformed into higher levels of awareness. It is in these higher states that we are able to perceive other dimensions of reality, and process information on a much more complex level than most Earthlings are able to do.

What we refer to is the process of digestion. It is different from the product, and this is the "physiological" part of our learning. It would be equivalent to your eating certain foods, in order to perform at a different level. An example is that you believe carrots make your eyes perform better.

On Arcturus, we digest energy and frequencies as though they were foods. In this belief system and practicing of these principles, we are able to do many things that you on Earth are not able to do. You have a vibration of a much more dense nature than we do, and it is in this physical condition that you are not able to digest the energy as quickly as we are able to.

A lower frequency has the ability to reduce the rate of transformation. It would be equivalent to a motor of your automobile, which is having a difficult time in turning over on a cold winter day. In this condition it vibrates on a slower level, and the faster action takes a longer time to resume.

Your bodies are like this example. You need to fine tune them, and if you do, the reaction is the digestion of energy at a much more rapid rate. After a while, this has the tendency to make you rotate your cylinders, so to speak, to the tune of the vibration of Light.

There are three primary bodies that need to be synchronized into one. Those include your physical, mental, and emotional bodies. As we have said earlier, our emotional bodies are in control, and we do this by disciplining our minds to follow the higher frequencies of the oneness.

The physical bodies need to be tuned occasionally and we find this is the weakest of all three areas.

In humans this is sometimes the most abused body also. We see that your ingestion process includes many items that do not quicken the vibration, but instead actually retard it. Such items are those of your animal life forms, sugars, and white flours.

These are not harmful to the body, as such. They are only harmful to the vibrational increase. When you do not know that you need fuel for the increased frequency, then the foods you consume do not bother you. When you are on an accelerated path, the foods that you consume can either make or break your energy patterns. In fact, there are presently many Beings on your planet that can tolerate only the consumption of the highest forms of energy.

We do not have the food problem that you do, for we ingest very little. We do not ingest food, for we have outgrown the emotional quality of desiring it. That will occur to many Earthlings over the next century, as well. While there are many who would not believe this statement to be true, we can assure you it is so.

In summary to this section, let us say that the ingestion of energy is another very important part of our curriculum. We learn this at a very early age, and we advance to mastery soon afterward. There is no other part of the curriculum that is as important as this one. For if we "fail" to learn this in the beginning, all the other lessons must be continually repeated. Nothing results in our development if we do not have the power absorbed within our systems and consciousness.

Evaluation Process That Structures an Individual's Progress

The evaluation process is the final step in what we refer to as our educational process. This is different from the measurement of an attained frequency of vibration, which we refer to so often. It differs because, in this step, we assess only the application and usage of this information and frequency.

While one of our species is studying and learning "how" to increase the vibration, it is not necessarily judged on how it might apply the exercises, and what it might be able to produce. This stage of development is left for the time when one of our species maintains a certain vibratory level over what you would call a period of Earth time. When this is measured and maintained, then at that moment the outcomes of the application are evaluated.

Again, we do not have the situation where we measure one against the other. We do not have criteria for measuring, placement and appreciation of the products, just as we described in the product development section. What we have here is the total reexamination of the purpose for using these powers of manifestation and the documentation of one's judgement for their usage.

When one is asked to document a judgement of the usage of manifestation powers, one is asked to qualify for the highest of ranks on Arcturus. In this situation the subject is placed in a room with the Elders. They are in a position to read into our Akashic records and document the areas of growth and achievement we have had over eons of time. We stand "accused" of past situations and are given the data related to those situations in which we did not handle the circumstances in an "appropriate" mode.

The standards of "appropriateness" are pre-set by the Elders, and a group of Cosmic Beings. They determine from the Karmic Board level, who is deemed suitable to progress to a higher state of Being.

In the examination, we are asked to resolve the unresolved situations from our past lives that are read in our Akashic records. We are presented, or re-presented, with those situations, and asked to provide the solution to the "case studies."

Since we have been measured to be vibrating in a higher dimension and frequency, our range of responses are only acceptable within an acceptable range of solutions. Our answers are measured against the range of behaviors that are acceptable for that frequency.

You see, we are really only measured against ourselves. Our "tests" are those which we have not passed in earlier situations. We only compete against ourselves. The range of measurement is solely that which is based upon the frequency level of behaviors. So, we earn the opportunity to keep only one focus in our consciousness—that is, of taking the best of our accumulated responses to past situations and making them even better.

There is no pride or shame in "passing" or "failing" this measurement. There is only progress. We do not go backwards in our frequency and vibration. We only stay at the same level or we go forward. We do have the opportunity to rest at any time and we take this option very seriously.

No soul on Arcturus wishes to remain at one level for an extended length of time. There is no such thing as emotional attachment to any one level, or to achievement. The only emotion that is attached to it is one of mentally mastering the keys and secrets for constant evolution.

Now you have the educational "curricula" of Arcturus.

We are proud of this system, in that it maintains the oneness we claim to be. We find this much more desirable than the duality of Earth and the emotional crippling we observe taking place because of your educational systems.

Please do not think we criticize, for we do not. We just observe that your system provides an opportunity for only a limited number of your Beings to be successful. Because of the processes to which they are subjected, we observe that the masses of people do not feel elated and successful. They feel the hurt and pain of those who do not move to the highest frequency of consciousness.

Those who do not make it out of the lower vibrational frequencies often make more mistakes of the lower nature, as well. They are lost and do not know how to find their way and they do not know for what they are looking.

What they seek is the Light within their physical bodies. The Light is the source of all power in the universe. The density of the physical structures that encase this Light body is such, however, that it makes it very difficult for the individuals to remember what it is that they are seeking.

For us it is not that difficult, for we were born out of a higher frequency and contain our consciousness within bodies that can transcend the third dimension. We seem to have a head start in accepting and understanding this. But on your planet, you have a difficult time releasing the friction of the learning of the physical world and, therefore, have an even more difficult time in accepting the new information and awareness that awaits you.

In the New Age that is impacting your planet each of you will find that the information provided to you in this correspondence will indeed carry the secrets to what it is you desire to know. You will also find that as the vibrational frequency of the beloved Earth increases in the years to come, your own bodies will begin to change as they absorb the new energy of the planet. When this occurs you will first see these changes affect your consciousness. You will then discover weaknesses in the emotional and physical bodies.

Only when the three bodies are in the harmony of the one will you be able to begin the transformation into your Light bodies and make the quantum leap into the new dimension that awaits. That dimension is the one in which we operate and it is within your range of consciousness and Beingness.

That is why I am taking the opportunity to reveal this information at this time. In the correspondence I have been honored not only to explain our system of educational progress, but also to reveal some of the new information that will be coming to planet Earth.

Please note that this broad explanation is hardly enough to provide the basis of what you will need to know in order to apply and proceed with this information; but we can assure you that all of those details will be provided.

CHAPTER VI:
THE LAND THEY LEFT BEHIND

In ONE transmission, the Arcturians kept referring to "the land they left behind." When asked what it meant, they replied that it referred to Arcturus and they wanted us to add this information to the book.

We therefore asked a specific question regarding this land, and received the following information from our unseen friends.

TO WHAT DO YOU REFER WHEN YOU SPEAK OF "THE LAND YOU LEFT BEHIND?"

What we mean when we use this phrase is that, like yourselves, we too have a home from which we came. Our home is considered to be a land mass similar to yours. The land that we left behind is sacred to us. We would do nothing to hurt the creation of God that has placed this important mark in the heavens for the purpose which it holds.

The significance of a planet or star is its purpose for existence. In the creation of the universes there was and is a masterful plan that takes into consideration the meaning of life for all forms of creation. All is energy and manifestation of the Divine.

Arcturus is a sacred dwelling of the highest forms of life this universe is capable of producing in the fifth dimensional frequency. We are proud to claim that we and the energy of Arcturus are of this vibration. That is why it shines so brightly in the heavens during the evening hours of your time patterns.

The vibrations of Arcturus affect the entire universe. They are designed to penetrate the consciousness of all Beings who are nearing entry into the dimensional frequency in which it resides. Compatibility is of the utmost importance for this action and reaction to occur. Therefore, we are assigned to assist any and all of our brothers and sisters in the universes who are on a similar path.

Arcturus is the teacher. It is the conceptualizer of the planets. The teachings from Arcturus will free humans and other Beings in the Light from their own entrapments. The pulsating power that emanates from Arcturus is similar to the sphere of musicians of the ethers. The frequencies are split between two sources of radiation. One comes from the energies of Arcturus itself, and the second comes from our instruments aboard our ships, which were created for the purpose of the mission.

These sources of power are honored and respected by our species, and have significant meaning for our Beingness. We cannot survive without either of these connections. Just as Earthlings will not be able to survive in the future without the vibrational qualities and linkages to fifth dimensional frequencies, we also need our life support systems back to our homeland.

These two sources of power feed our energy needs while we are away. We need to return periodically to our home base, and this is a respected ritual among our species. We need this for the nourishment of our souls. What we receive from this connection cannot be achieved or received by any other format.

You are beginning to understand on Earth that your soul is the only eternal life there is in your three-dimensional existence. We also understand this in the fifth dimension. The difference between these two understandings is, however, the fact that we take life and actually flow with it in the natural positive states of existence. We observe that you fight the natural, positive flow of energy and actually cut your physical lives off at a much earlier rate than we believe is necessary.

Arcturus has a natural abundance of positive energy which we call our universal fuel supply. This source of energy is filtered through our consciousness and our Beings by the process of osmosis. We need this life line; otherwise we too would die a premature physical death. Therefore, what we have done is to cherish and honor the source of our nourishment, which comes from the Great Central Sun to Arcturus. In this honoring, we have created and maintained a true paradise on our world. It is desirable and it is envied by many sentient Beings.

We observe that you do not honor or respect the planet that has given you life. We observe that you have little care or vision for its welfare beyond your own present existence. We wonder why this is, our sisters and brothers of Earth.

The love that we have for our supply of energy is indescribable. We honor this feeling even more as we are on our long journey away from home. We cannot understand why you take so much of the power and source for granted. It does not make sense on our level of understanding. It is a saddening experience to see.

WE, THE ARCTURIANS

An analysis of the two worlds shows that Arcturus was once like Earth before it journeyed into the fifth dimensional frequency. We remember in our historical recordings what those days were like, as the progression of the equinoxes took its steps into the giant void for our future. We cannot remember reaching a point of limited vision where we did not take responsibility for our mother and father of energy that supported our life systems.

This may sound like a lecture to some who are in the mode of absorbing this dialogue. We apologize if it does, for we do not mean it to be. We only ask again, "why?" The answer to this question haunts us on our journey, for we must provide our Elders with full reports upon our return to Arcturus, and they will expect answers to the questions we have posed. We cannot understand, and therefore, we do not begin to interpret the answer to this question.

Why is the beloved Terra in its present state of negativity? Why does it cough at the intensity of the pollution that surrounds it? Why do the boils flow from its grid points, in the form of volcanoes? Where do the constant lacerations come from in the midst of your earthquakes? Finally, why do the bowels of the Earth hurt so much from the eruptions and the explosions that are permitted to continue on the planet?

The intensity of the energy forms that reside within and on the Earth is so strong that the equilibrium of the positive and negative energies is unbalanced. We fear that this situation may cause the Earth to shift on its axis in the future, if these disturbances are not curbed and blessed. We also know that these disturbances cannot continue in the days ahead, but we say no more at this time.

We yearn for the tranquility and beauty of the horizons of Arcturus, cloaked with reddish-violet frequencies. We hear the sounds of sirens in the distance as we are constantly reminded of the bliss and the peace we left behind. You could have this, too, if you choose.

Arcturus is a sister star in the heavens for the beloved Terra. We are the caretakers of the fifth dimensional frequency inhabitants, and Earthlings are the caretakers of the physical, third dimensional realities. We can manifest the third dimensional realities in our space and time. You can observe the beauty and feel the inner love and tranquility of our world just by manifesting it within your meditations. We are the inner world of reality, and you are the outer world of reality. We are the soul's existence of the Light, you are the Light manifestation of the soul. It is perfect in its relationship. For you are the yin and we are the yang of the God Force of the universe.

Observe for a brief moment the bright star in the Bootes constellation some evening, as you ponder the thoughts we have just transmitted to you. Believe in your heart and the inner reality, and take this thought to the level of the manifest plane. Use your strength of mind and emotion to manifest that reality on your Earth plane and know, dear sisters and brothers, that we do exist simultaneously in all aspects of time and space.

While we began this transmission with the thought regarding "the land we left behind," we advise you that in many ways that is incorrect. We are within the reality of Arcturus while visiting your planet and you are in the midst of our home as well. It is all in the matter of perception.

Go inward and you will find our home. Journey outward and you see the Earth. Learn the brilliance, the strength, and the magnificence of understanding both worlds, and you will then have the totality of the oneness of God at your feet.

That, we hope, will be your realization in the days to come, but do not take too long. The world that you know will change in the twinkling of an eye. It is the wisest of souls who will take this message to heart, and understand it for the true wisdom that it contains.

CHAPTER VII:
THE STARSHIP

IN ONE communication to Betty, Cynthia, and Norma, the Arcturians identified thirty-five major divisions of their Starship. They requested that Norma refer to this section at a later time, because the explanations needed to describe each of these divisions would take too long to transmit during that particular evening's session.

In any session, Norma could hold the energy for no longer than two hours. At the end of that time period, she was always very weak and often began to shake. This was the sign that it was time to quit, for in this state there was a danger that she might do harm to herself or that the transmissions would not be as accurate. Therefore, each of the sessions had to be carefully monitored so as not to exceed that time limit.

During that particular session, and at the end of the two-hour limit, a question about the divisions of their spacecraft was asked. The Arcturians sent through, in a matter of minutes, a list of thirty-five major divisions of the Starship Athena. The session ended with this listing only, as Norma was too tired to continue the communication that evening. The divisions listed were as follows:

1. The Commander's Bridge
2. The Reuniting Parcel, which serves as the point of reentry to our Ship
3. The Remembrance Headquarters, which gives us the data on the manifestation level

4. The area that you would call the kitchen, but we call the Energy Transformer Storage And Retrieval Area
5. The Sleeping Quarters
6. The Ship's Motivational Chamber, that propels the movement
7. The Reunion Quarters, for those who are in the reproduction mode
8. The Duty Free Port
9. The Magnificent Chamber for Manifestation
10. The Learning Facility
11. The Movement Chamber for Locomotion
12. The Chamber for the Captives
13. The Storage and Retrieval Area, for the parts of the ship
14. The Communication Chamber
15. The Navigation Rehearsal Area
16. The Motivational Storage Motion Area
17. The Motion Carrier
18. The Shuttle Craft Area
19. The Jet Propulsion Chamber
20. The Information and Communication Information Area
21. The Motion-Remotion Lodging Apparatus Carrier Chamber
22. The Integrative and Supportive Area, for the development of new plans and access to new information
23. The Old and New Vaporizing Chambers
24. The Intelligence and Debriefing Chamber
25. The Intelligence and Vaporization Chamber, for the production of the multiple forms of gifts that we bring
26. The Captain's and Commander's Quarters
27. The Crew's Quarters
28. The Light Rejuvenation Chamber
29. The Mechanism Chamber, for manifesting our bodies in different places
30. The Ship's Engineering Apparatus Area

31. The Engineering Crystallization Area
32. The Influx Setting
33. The Increment Learning Facility for the Elders
34. The newest area, which is the Debriefing Room, for the Light children from the planet Earth, and
35. The Chamber for the Holistic Concept of Universal Law

The Arcturians also requested, when Norma later returned to the subject of their spacecraft, that the questions and dialogue be phrased in a "process format." They defined "process format" as a mode of communication that would require one to learn more about the functions of the Ship, rather than the visual descriptions of the various divisions and compartments. This approach, they said, would facilitate a better understanding of their function and existence in this galaxy; for they were dependent upon their Ship for their life support systems. The Ship was designed to support their mission here on Earth; therefore the spacecraft and their own essence were interdependent upon one another. What we found is that by honoring their request, the Arcturians were able to provide information far beyond the descriptions of their Starship. Somehow, it always seemed to relate.

This chapter is reserved for that communication. It took several days to receive this information, because the content is long and somewhat complicated. The most difficult part of receiving the information was adjusting to the Arcturians' new terminology. All the sections have been pieced together to make the chapter appear to be one long report, but in reality, it came through in four shorter sections of time, each section about two hours in length.

Before sending Norma descriptive information about the Starship, however, the Arcturians played a little name game with her.

In August of 1988, Norma was alone, receiving information from the Arcturians on the language section. At the end of one of the sessions, a symbol suddenly appeared on the computer monitor that looked like this: "ÿ". This symbol appeared at the bottom of the screen without Norma's hands having touched the keyboard. The cursor was in the upper left hand corner of the monitor. The symbol remained on the screen for approximately 10 seconds. Norma studied it, and then tried to reproduce it by pressing various keys on the computer keyboard. At that time, the symbol disappeared, and she was unable to make it reappear.

The symbol was unlike any Norma had ever seen on the computer keyboard or in any software program she had ever used. But, not being a computer expert, she thought that maybe somehow it was possible for combinations of symbols to be projected on the screen, by using certain commands or directives.

Norma's husband, Rudy, was home and she ran out to tell him what she had seen. She asked him to determine whether this symbol could have come from the computer or the software package (Professional Write 2.1 version) that she was using.

Rudy is a computer expert. His career has included 22 years of working only on computers, both mainframe and microcomputers. He was stationed in Houston, Texas, at the Johnson Spacecraft Center during the Apollo Missions, where he received several commendations for his contributions to the success of these missions. Later, he was transferred to Sandia National Laboratories in Albuquerque, New Mexico as the project manager for an important contract that his company had received. Still later, he held a position in Pasadena, California, at the Jet Propulsion Labs, working on a project for the Viking Mars Mission. For his work there he again was presented with a wall plaque of his significant contributions in solving some of the major problems that the project encountered in 1976. In short, Rudy "IS" a computer.

His present title is Senior Technical Systems Specialist for Unisys, which was formerly Sperry Corporation, and originally called UNIVAC.

Rudy studied the situation that Norma described and concluded that there was no way in which the computer could have generated that symbol on the screen by itself. Unfortunately, he was not in the room to witness it, and therefore, only had the drawing that Norma produced to use for his criterion.

Rudy is a pragmatist, and his first reaction was that the symbol just could not have appeared on the screen. All his training and credentials have taught him that there is always a solution to any problem with a computer, and that this solution is always logical and tangible. He has an impeccable track record for solving mainframe problems, and has made computers his life. He thrives on computer problems, as they are the challenges that keep his mind moving on to higher dimensions and levels of reasoning. In his work, there has never been a problem with a solution that has escaped him, and these solutions have always been within the realm of tangible reality.

For this problem, he had no immediate solution. While he tended not to believe what had been described to him, he also did not doubt it. Since the fall of 1987, when a Being named "Monka" had begun to come through Norma's channeling, he had been the primary witness to several unexplainable things that would happen to the microcomputer while Norma was at the keyboard. For these situations, he also had no logical explanations.

Over the course of several months, Rudy had gotten rather frustrated with the problems that occurred when Norma was at the computer. They were not of a kind he had encountered before. Fortunately, there were always many witnesses present during these occasions. Office workers, a few members of the University of New Mexico faculty and administration, and friends all had had first-hand experiences when the microcomputer would just take off and "do its own thing." This just seemed to be one more on the list of things that were above his level of explanation or reasoning.

The problem plagued Rudy for months. One day he was able to discover the exact symbol in ASCII characters and he did reproduce it by hitting, simultaneously, the following combination of keys: ALT, 152. There was the symbol! But this still did not solve the problem of how or why it had appeared automatically at the bottom of the screen. The only plausible answer was that some electrical impulse must have sent the command to the computer.

A few days after her initial experience with the symbol, when Betty and Cynthia returned for their regular Tuesday night session, Norma told them what had happened and again drew the symbol for them to see. The three of them decided to ask the Arcturians what the symbol meant. They entered the following two questions into the computer, and received these answers.

LAST WEEK YOU PROJECTED ON THE COMPUTER SCREEN A SYMBOL THAT CANNOT BE REPRODUCED BY THIS KEYBOARD. [At that time it had not been determined that this symbol could be reproduced on the screen.] THE SYMBOL IS "ÿ". WHAT DOES THIS MEAN, AND WHY DID YOU PROJECT IT ON THE SCREEN?

We projected this symbol on your screen to give you the name of the Starship that we are on. This means the Athena. It is the symbol of the highest and wisest. It is also a Greek goddess. Can you now begin to see the relationships that are forming in your consciousness?

The response was discussed by Cynthia, Betty, and Norma, and they did not understand what the question at the end meant. Instead of asking for clarification at that time, they decided to continue retrieving information about the projected symbol.

CAN YOU GIVE US MORE INFORMATION ON THIS SYMBOL?

Yes, we can. It also means the wisest, who never go astray. We ride this symbol to determine our destiny and return to the planet Earth. We also give this symbol as a secret code, to those whom we honor and trust, and who will ride the safest journey with us. We welcome all of you to our ship at any time, and look forward to the moment when we can be reunited.

WHAT IS THE NAME OF YOUR STARSHIP?

We address her in the feminine, just as you do on Earth. She resides in the pride and glory of your most magnificent eagle on the Earth plane.

Her name is Athena, just as the goddess of your planet. She is truly one of the finest Starships in the universe. Few Ships can match her magnificence. She is indeed of the stars, and is not designed to do battle. She is equipped for protective measures, but is designed to be the transporter of the Most High to their systems of home and radiance.

DO YOU HAVE A SYMBOL THAT IDENTIFIES YOUR SHIP OR YOUR CULTURE?

We vibrate to the colors of red and purple. These are like the colors that you sometimes choose in your cultures. We have a symbol, but we would have to write another program, as we did for the face identification, in order for you to see the visual aspect of what we are referring.

Approximately two months elapsed before Norma could return to the subject of the spacecraft. At that time, additional information was solicited about the Ship and the question was worded to try to accommodate the Arcturians' request to ask the questions in a "process format."

WOULD YOU PLEASE EXPLAIN YOUR STARSHIP IN GREATER DETAIL AND DESCRIBE THE FUNCTION AND FORM OF EACH GENERAL DIVISION? WE ARE ESPECIALLY INTERESTED IN THOSE AREAS THAT SUPPORT YOUR LIFE SYSTEMS, RATHER THAN THE COMPONENTS OF THE SHIP THAT ARE USED FOR STORAGE.

Thank you for honoring our request. I, Herdonitic, will provide you with the descriptions of the vessel. I am pleased to be the one selected, but I will not take all the credit for this explanation. For I am the language expert, and not the ship's technician. Therefore, I will need the assistance of many on this Starship to accommodate your request.

THE COMMANDER'S BRIDGE

First, let us describe the Commander's Bridge. It is oval in shape and it is in this position for a particular reason. The Commander's Bridge is where all major decisions are made. Therefore, it is fitting that it should follow a curved shape and not one with many angles and points.

The point of power is within one's consciousness, and it is the wisest Beings who understand that all energy flows in a circular form. When one surrounds oneself with this form of energy, the function of this measurement is increased many times over.

The Commander's Bridge has access to every division and component of the Starship through its vast computer systems. I use the term "computer systems" loosely, for in reality, we have long outgrown the use of computers. If I initially gave you the name of our information system it would not be of any use, for you could not imagine what the system would be like.

Our computer system is called the "Hyper-Propulsion System" for its interconnections with the main components of the Ship's operating systems. It is operated by the power source of crystals that do not come from your planet. These crystals come from another planet that is many light years away from yours, in a constellation that has not yet been discovered by Earth scientists. The crystals have a means of attracting and conducting the light energy from the Great Central Sun, and they operate the Ship by the means of the locomotion and motion factor. The crystals are also of a vibrational frequency that attract the positive and negative energy forces, which allow the propulsion of the matter/anti-matter gravitational pulls to flow through the various aspects of time and space.

The Commander's Bridge is in the bottom area of the Ship. The Bridge is situated there because, in the design of our vessel, that places it in a central location, allowing it to draw from all the energy sources on the Ship. Areas surrounding the Bridge are mainly those of living quarters, storage, etc.

All main energy sources are equally distanced from the Bridge in a circular fashion. This allows the support systems to interconnect with one another and to support the central control headquarters, which is the Commander's Bridge. This creates a circular flow of energy and provides for more efficiency in the operation of the Ship. This design is especially helpful for tracking problems such as in the flowing of currents that support our life systems. Every system is interdependent, and if a problem occurs, we are able to move very quickly, in a circular fashion, to determine where blockages may occur. This design becomes an important safeguard for our survival.

The Bridge has viewing screens all around it, but has no windows. There is no need for windows, as we transcend time and space. We see with our telepathic abilities and with the instruments and technologies that are within our vessel. We also have equipment that allows us to view beyond the walls of the Ship without having to use a camera to gather images.

The Bridge supports only the crew who have the rank to be in that area. The Bridge is the smallest of areas, and contains the most efficient systems to support all of the Ship's needs. Whether one is worthy of these positions is determined by the vibrational frequency of that individual Being. The colors that support the vibrational frequency are similar to your colors of blue, blue violet, and red. These must be balanced in our essence, and when they are, they are integrated into the design of the Ship's structure. This integration is only evident on the Ship's Bridge.

Within the energy force field of this area are certain symbols and vanishing points of energy that detect any frequency that is not in alignment with the structure of the Bridge. When this occurs, the individual Being who is intruding becomes very ill, and can even lose consciousness. The contrast of the energy sources and forces causes this to occur. This provides protection for this area of the Ship for there is no area more important than this one.

This will conclude our introductory section about our Commander's Bridge. We would now like to describe the Reuniting Parcel.

REUNITING PARCEL

In this chamber all of the plans are made for the mission of the Ship's crew. We call it a Reuniting Parcel because our mission is to come to Earth to bring enlightenment to our space sisters and brothers. In order to accomplish this we must continually leave our Ship and manifest on the Earth plane.

This chamber contains subdivisions used for various stages of planning and retrieval of our inhabitants. In the headquarters we have access to the information and plans that contain details of the mission. To be in this location automatically places us in the midst of our mission. It reunites us with our goal and the oneness for which we have journeyed to Earth.

Another area is reserved for drawing details. This area supports all decisions that are made, for we continually change our plans and projected activities to accommodate the constantly changing conditions on your planet. We find that this room is the most flexible. In your terms you would call it frustrating, but we do not know that emotion. We only know adaptability. Therefore, we use the word "flexible."

Another section is for debriefing our crew who journey outside of the Starship. When they return, they are brought to this location, and must report what they have learned and observed. We have all the records of these journeys stored in this area, and find solutions to our problems by channeling this information into our hyper-propulsion system.

A last area that is proportioned for our use is the directory command. Since we have several activities enacted simultaneously, we must have a recordkeeping system to store the information and data. In this directory are the names of our crew who are on assignment, as well as names of Earthlings with whom we are in communication.

Many individuals from Earth are not even aware they are communicating with one of us, or that there is an interaction taking place. Even so, the individual's name is recorded and a log is kept of these interactions. We use these primarily for a system of tracking.

THE REMEMBRANCE HEADQUARTERS

The Remembrance Headquarters is the area of the Ship that reunites us with our home star system of Arcturus. We have a need to return to our roots, just as humans do on Earth. These quarters have been designed to connect us with our home base whenever we feel the need. This is the only area of the Ship visited on a spontaneous basis, when a Being feels that it is necessary. All other areas of the Ship have a definite function which requires a schedule of visitation. This one is special and is there for the support that one may need to regain strength.

It looks like a replication of the planet Arcturus, and is situated far from the other major functional areas of the Ship. In this reclusive position, it has the capacity to actually take the etheric body of the Ship's crew member back to home base. This helps strengthen and rejuvenate the vibrational frequency of the Being who feels this is necessary.

We find that the longer we stay in the Earth area, the more frequently our members use this. Earth has a vibrational frequency that is very harsh. It has a tendency to penetrate our consciousness in strange ways that even we do not fully understand. We recognize this, and support the use of this special chamber. Therefore, the Being who chooses to use it must go through a cleansing of negative energy before entering the room.

ENERGY TRANSFORMER STORAGE AND RETRIEVAL AREA

This area of our Ship is designed to penetrate all of the hydro-propulsion systems. This is different from the system described earlier, the hyper-propulsion system, that replaced our computers. The Energy Transformer Storage and Retrieval Area is designed to eliminate much of the collected waste and energy that is manifested from the operations of the Ship. The base for such power is water, for that is what the Ship's design will tolerate, in the atmosphere of Earth.

Our Starship was specifically designed for this mission to the planet Earth and this part of the universe. The design for the Energy Transformer Area was researched long before the Starship design was completed and is one of the best systems existing.

Earth has many unique features in its environment and energy sources, and one of these is that it is a water-based planet. Not all planets can claim this. Not every planet can find so much flexibility in design, based upon the abundance of the minerals and elements it contains. We had to learn this before we launched our mission, and had to design systems to support our needs in this part of the galaxy. We can both store energy and collect it from outside the Ship. This department is an Energy Transformer Area that has the capability to convert different forms of energy.

We have the capability to convert all the Ship's waste to the energy source of light, and to use this form of energy to bring in water from outside the Ship to produce pure food supplies. This is one of the reasons why we can stay away from our planetary system for so long, and not return for supplies. The compartment supplies our needs for what you would call food substance, and what we call energy to sustain our lives.

We repeat, water is the basis for this energy conversion operation, because this is unique to your planet. If we had been assigned to a mission in the Pleiades, we would have had to design a Ship with other abilities to transform energy.

It is important to remember that not all life forms can live in the same environment together without additional life support systems. While we do not eat, as you humans do, we have the need to transform energy continually within our systems. In this area we get our ingested amount of energy to support our life on this Ship. This area is connected to the individual living quarters we use for sleeping. We are able to obtain the required dosage of energy just by visiting our assigned quarters. This description now brings us to the next area of explanation: the Sleeping Quarters.

THE SLEEPING QUARTERS

In this area we activate the dream state. We find we do not need this as often as humans do, but we do have a need to make contact with our celestial Brothers and Sisters of the Tribunal Council. We have regimented our schedules so that once every seven days, (in Earth terms), we are allowed to return to our Sleeping Quarters and access this very important mode of existence.

In this state, we are reconnected to our Higher Existence, where we receive the spiritual knowledge and guidance to continue on our path to the Light. We find this is essential for many reasons:

1. *First, this reunion provides us with the balance necessary to continue on with our mission. It is very easy in the Earth's atmosphere to get "off balance." Reconnection prevents disharmony or disruption of balance. This activity is given the highest of priorities and anyone who expresses a need to participate in this process is automatically granted leave to do so. The Elders are all in agreement that this request holds the highest of respect, and there are few reasons why it should ever be denied.*

2. *A second reason why we are so involved in this activity is because pursuit of the highest goals is ingrained in the Arcturian culture. We have made a commitment to raising all the vibrations on Arcturus, as we understand the importance of the progression back to the Great Central Sun.*

3. *We honor this activity highly as it expresses the essence of our Godhood. We may be of a different shape than*

what you imagine your God to be, but we are none-theless, a part of the God creation. This reconnec-tion in the dream state is used for the purpose of furthering our powers, through increasing our sound and Light vibrations. We have controlled quarters for transmitting these selected, higher frequencies to and through our consciousness while we sleep. In the state of dream and sleep, we actually access higher realms of the universe, and participate in the fre-quencies that support the highest councils in this universe.

Only those Beings who are considered to be fourth and fifth dimensional Beings have access to these channels. In your etheric bodies you have access to these states, but often do not recollect these events when reuniting with the consciousness of your physical bodies. This is one of the things that will change for those souls who will graduate from the Earth curriculum in this lifetime, and those who will take the first step towards the evolutionary path of the Light, upon exiting the Earth plane.

Let us now continue with another critical chamber.

THE SHIP'S MOTIVATIONAL CHAMBER

This section of the Ship is reserved for grooming the leadership that is constantly necessary to head up the various aspects of our mission. There is hardly anything more important than leadership in any dimension of existence. We find this leads many of our species to higher realms of understanding and integrating, as they prog-ress on their journeys. This area of the Ship is reserved for training. It is here we support the Beings who undergo programs that help them detach from the energy forces of the new environments they encounter.

Our journey takes us through many dimensions and areas of the universe. The final destination is that which the Ship is primarily prepared and designed to accommodate. In this case it was Earth. In the transitional periods, there is a great need for many of our crew to access new and higher modes of existence, just to help them overcome problems, and it is the Motivational Chamber that helps them do this.

In your educational systems, you probably would refer to this chamber as a school or training center. We do not call it this, for we do not measure the content that is learned. Instead, we measure the energy effects that learning has on a subject, and consequently, the effects which that Being has on others as a result of its own increased frequency.

When a Being uses the Motivational Chamber, the result is always positive. Not all of the crew members have access to this area, however. That is not saying that they are deprived of motivational training and assistance. This is most difficult to describe, for it appears that we discriminate in our systems. In our reality, we do not. Our civilization assures that over the course of a soul's existence on Arcturus, it will have access to all of the systems and pleasures that it wishes. This may take several embodiments, but it is assured.

Allow us to close this area of description now, in order that we may continue with another.

THE REUNION QUARTERS

Unlike the planet Earth, which does not control its population, we learned on Arcturus long ago that, in order to survive in the highest realms, we must be willing to do so.

The first step in the process of controlling our species was to learn two things:

1. *We discovered that we must control our emotions with our thought patterns, and there is a designated part in our central learning structure that is designed to help us understand how to accomplish this control.*

2. *To reproduce is an honor, and one of the highest professions on Arcturus.*

Before we integrated these concepts into our consciousness, we had great difficulty in raising our young to assume the same vibrational qualities and frequencies that were deemed to be of the Light. This was so because there were no systems for monitoring or aiding the Beings who were mass producing the offspring. In short, we had many of the same problems that you have encountered to date on your planet.

This situation caused much alarm for our Elders, and we met with the Tribunal Council of Arcturus to decide what would remedy the situation. The Council determined that the gift of life was a gift from God. It was the statement of procreation and the making of the image in God's likeness. The Council designated that this situation should be treated with respect and the highest of honors.

159

We, therefore, developed a ritual for the chosen ones who were to perform this very important function in our society. We began with a selection process which is comprised of two steps.

1. *The first step is the selection of the many who are deemed to be perfect "candidates" for this function.*

2. *The second step includes their preparation by ingestion of energy. It is important that this take place before this function is actually completed.*

Not all candidates will be called upon to fulfill this role in our civilization. The reason is because some of them may become weakened in the process. The energy ingestion patterns that must be developed within our species, before reproduction can commence, comprise a process that is very difficult to complete. Not all of the candidates can accomplish this part of the curriculum, for the tolerance levels required sometimes cannot be developed within a Being.

To develop tolerance levels means that we are actually building the frequency of Beings to the vibrational speed of Light. This is developing them to be in a positional frequency nearer to that of the Ascended Masters than it is to ours. Some of the Beings who are led through this process find that their bodies cannot take this shift, even though we administer the treatment in small dosages and steps.

Those who cannot complete the training program are often led to another chamber that helps them with the decelerating process until they are ready to come back to the mainstream. The end result is that they are better for the treatment; for how can any deny the privilege of being a chosen one?

Increasing their vibratory qualities to assume a position closer to God is indeed a privilege.

For those who make it we conduct a ceremony. When the time is appropriate, each Being goes into the Reunion Quarters Chamber. The reproduction process begins. The two Beings are not in physical contact with each other at all. One Being represents the masculine energy source of the universe, and the other represents the feminine energy source. Through a mind link process, the two energies are stabilized to be in perfect balance. Through the procreation process of the Light, the electron Force flows through two Beings, and actually creates another Being that is a replica of the Light. It is manifested out of love, honor, deep respect, and the thoughts of the chamber.

The chamber that supports this process is especially designed so that it has a unique programming contained within the walls and interior. The process is perfection. If anything happened to this chamber, our species would be in great danger of deterioration. We cannot produce this same frequency on Arcturus, because the energy patterns are such that there is some contamination that can interfere with perfection. Therefore, our ships are the only places where we can accomplish this important function.

The celebration commences when the new Being is created. The new life form is then carried to a special unit that encases it in the proper vibrational frequency until it is ready to be brought down to Arcturus for integration into family units. The special Beings who care for these new life forms are all waiting and prepared for the deliveries that occur on a regular basis. The regularity of the schedule is never violated.

We complete the reproduction cycle only once in every seven years, according to your Earth time. When this cycle is completed, we seed other planets with some of our finest. We do this because we have been commanded by the Councils of the universe, who are interested in the evolution of the God process. We have earned the right to be one of the selected species to perform this function and, therefore, fulfill our roles and responsibilities with great dedication to the Ascended Realms of the Universes.

This final explanation brings us to the description of the next part of our Ship and the function which it holds.

THE DUTY FREE PORT

On Earth this term represents the activity of exchanging materialistic goods between countries without having to pay specific taxes. Our "Duty Free Port" represents the area that supports a constant exchange of goods between our world and other worlds to which we journey. Instead of participating in the exchange of goods that are manifested only on the materialistic plane of the third dimensional reality of Earth, we exchange the gifts of God.

This means we transport many souls from our world to yours. Those souls are destined for embodiment on the Earth, now and in the future. In this area of the Ship we carry our precious cargo and proceed with the process that dispenses them on the Earth plane into embodiment when the time is right. There is no charge or special tax for these gifts. Their only duty is to learn to fulfill the will of God.

While we make light of this at this time in our communication to you, we understand the intensity of

162

feeling that this knowledge may invoke in humans when they read this. We are only trying to ease the shock of this information, and mean no disrespect. What humans have not understood is that this process has been going on since the beginning of time.

We call this compartment of our Ship the Duty Free area for we charge nothing to deliver our gifts. God does not charge for the Light, and we bring to the Earth some of the finest Light bearers that the planet has seen. There are no taxes on these gifts, either, and we offer them with the utmost of pride and joy.

Many of the Light bearers on Earth today are beginning to wake up. They are connecting to the thought processes that provide them with direct communication to us aboard the motherships. Their remembrances are beginning to reawaken in their hearts as the longing for home is getting stronger. The commitments made between embodiments, to serve the commands of the Tribunal Council of the Universes, are now beginning to surface in their minds and hearts.

We honor and welcome them back with this communication, which will be one of the first to emerge on the planet providing a direct contact with us. In reading this information, much will be triggered in their souls. We are pleased to say that those re-emerging memories will be just one more step in the process to help them reclaim the data unlocking the mysteries of their missions on Earth.

163

THE MAGNIFICENT CHAMBER
FOR MANIFESTATION

In this chamber we have the most advanced mechanism for manifestation that humans can ever begin to imagine. We, on the fourth and fifth dimensions, are closer to the vibrational frequency of the electron Force of the Light. We have, within our created environment, a support device that represents the ultimate process in our existence.

In this chamber we are guided by the Elders to create the highest forms of which we are capable. A direct correlation exists between a soul's growth and that which a Being is able to create, or manifest, in any embodiment. It is our code that once a Being has performed on a higher level, it is nearly impossible for that same Being to perform at a lower one. The experiences in this chamber are guided by the Elders.

We make an assumption that all of our Beings wish to journey to the Highest, and we are in the position of sharing this magnificent chamber with any Being aboard our Ship. This chamber is designed to complement and support rearrangement of the molecular structure of the Being's central nervous system, for inducing the pleasure of performing at the level of the fifth dimensional frequency and higher.

The experience cannot easily be explained in words. It is more than telepathy and visualization. It is more than walking in the etheric form and transporting oneself through various dimensions of time and space. It is more than joy and happiness. It is the feeling of actually "being" the Force and the Light. It is the experience of the All.

The planet Earth will someday evolve to this existence, but it must first experience the fourth and fifth dimensional qualities. That is why it is undergoing this incredible transformational process at this moment.

We, the Arcturians, come from and exist in the fourth and fifth dimensions. We are in the process of evolving to higher ones ourselves.

The plan is perfect. We are here to help our Earth brothers and sisters make their transformation to the fifth dimension with as little pain as possible. Helping you successfully through this period automatically helps us in our own evolutionary process. All souls are being consumed by the Great Central Sun. In the alignment of the universes and star systems, all Beings help each other with this progression and evolutionary process.

We also receive assistance from those who are much higher evolved. The only difference is that we do not fear those who assist us, as we perceive you fear us.

THE LEARNING FACILITY

The Learning Facility is for the enhancement of knowledge. Since we understand the curriculum of Arcturus and our civilization we use this room for the accumulation of knowledge concerning other worlds.

The Learning Facility supports the growth and development of all on the Ship. It has a complete data bank and information retrieval area that includes important material on every aspect of Earth. Equally important is the topic of astronomy. This includes reference material about our charted course and even the destinations of sister Starships working in other areas of the universe.

Our method for learning is a simple one. We ingest information through our telepathic abilities and central nervous systems. We have the ability to work knowledge through our systems as humans ingest and digest foods. We are capable of absorbing concepts and information at a rate approximately 100 times faster than the average human. We do this through a stretch-elongated technique of mind expansion.

This technique is used in conjunction with some specifically designed instruments that have the capability of absorbing data and implanting it within our "brain" structures. We can assimilate information in a one-directional mode, like this method, or we may tap into the universal consciousness of the Great Central Sun.

In using this latter mode of operation we find greater truths and mysteries are revealed. When we wish for specific, mundane pieces of information, such as spatial distance through the universal equation of thought projection, we will use the stretch-elongated technique.

Although this area is different from our systems of education on Arcturus, many of the processes of measurement and motivation are the same. Allow us to continue on with the next division.

THE MOVEMENT CHAMBER FOR LOCOMOTION

The Movement Chamber for Locomotion is designed to facilitate movement when we are in the Earth's atmosphere. This chamber protects us from those outside forces that have a tendency to hold us to a three dimensional existence. It provides us with the energy sources and means by which we can increase our vibratory rates and move outside of that existence.

We need to utilize this chamber whenever we are preparing to "surface" within the third dimension. We use this chamber to assist us to rise above the energy forces that lock us into a pattern that keeps us dependent upon the positive energy currents of Earth.

The Arcturians learned long ago that in order to maintain a higher existence, one must always maintain a balance. This includes the balance of everything in existence. Mastering the positive and negative energies of the electron Force is most critical in this process.

In the Earth's atmosphere, the thought processes of its inhabitants have produced an energy field that is out of balance. Therefore, most of the humans on the planet find it difficult to maintain any kind of balance in their lives. They are swept into the currents of the mainstream of the "yang" energy—currents which are the positive, masculine energy. They have no idea who or what is available to aid them to re-adjust their lives or to bring them the happiness and peace they are seeking.

We experience these currents around the Earth, and have a chamber that assists us to maintain a vibrational frequency that is above the one most strongly represented on your planet. We honor those on Earth who automatically do the same with no assistance from such chambers.

The chamber we use has perfect balance of energy sources built into its design. It supports our physical, emotional, and spiritual needs. This allows us to be fortified by the currents of equality of intellect and drive. The chamber is used by those who leave the Ship frequently and manifest near the Earth's surface.

All Beings who enter our Ship are required to use this Chamber. This is the first area to which strangers or guests are introduced. We do not use our limbs and projectiles for our main source of movement when aboard our Ship. We, instead, move by floating and using our minds to project us on the force of the Liquid Light. Those Beings whom we take on this Ship are often required to use this same format for moving. A visit to this chamber, when they are in the dream state, is deemed to be a very effective way to accomplish this.

When a Being is balanced, he has the power to raise or lower his vibrational frequencies to any level that he desires. He has the strength of commitment, also, to accomplish many feats that are deemed to be extraordinary. Walking on water would be one of the activities that would demonstrate this kind of power.

Your records show one Great Man was able to accomplish this in the midst of your energy forces on Earth. He came to teach you this and we are here once again to transmit more technical knowledge to help you all achieve this feat too. We all do "work" for this same great soul, Jesus, who also is known to many in the highest realms as Sananda.

Since we are on the subject of working together to raise all of humankind's vibrational frequencies to adjust to the New Age, let us now direct our efforts to describing the next area of our Ship, which also supports this activity.

THE CHAMBER FOR THE CAPTIVES

To describe this area of our Ship, we must take you on a journey. The journey consists of traveling back to a time when the souls on Earth were not as enlightened as those presently gracing the surface of beloved Terra.

This consists of the time period between Atlantis and now. It is recorded in the footsteps of the ethers, and is in the historical annals of your civilizations. It is the here and now, and it is the past. It is also the future.

During all of those moments in your third dimensional existence, there have been souls who have walked the planet and given the masses enlightenment and the teachings of the Great Masters. Throughout all of history, since Atlantis, there have always lived the "Way Showers" who have come down to the planet and incarnated in bodies that kept the vigil light burning for humanity. They have toiled and worked to lead the masses out of the darkness.

These great souls have chosen to come to Earth and to open energy vortexes which could be accessed for future events. Every continent on the planet has been blessed by these Masters, and every Master has had numerous followers who were dedicated to the teachings and the way of true Enlightenment.

As these numerous souls have continued their own journeys toward the Light, many of them have chosen to come to Earth again at this time of transition, to repeat the same curriculum of the ancients. They are here so that Mother Earth will be helped with the birthing process into the new day and age.

These souls are embodied in a sea of negativity that chokes them and makes it very difficult sometimes for them to see through this illusion. This is especially true of those souls who are in isolation on the planet. The isolation makes it very difficult to remember who and what they are.

In this struggle for their identity we have assisted them on their journeys of awakening. We take them aboard our Ships to help in the removal of energy blockages. In the oneness of it all, we are truly working for the same purpose. We are to help each other remove the illusions of fear and doubt.

In your books many souls have reported to have visited us, many whom you would describe as religious. They are the ones who have irreversible programming in their souls to move forward on their missions in this lifetime to help bring enlightenment to the planet. They truly are in service to God and to the Light.

Many have access to us in the dream states of the fourth dimension. Many of them appreciate help in recalling all of the secrets they once knew and fought for, to aid the Masters in the way of Truth and Light. They all have given us permission to work with them, even though, on the conscious level of the third dimension, many do not remember they have done so. This is acceptable. We must continue on with our work for the people of Earth.

Time is running out, and Earth is at a moment in its history that will determine its fate. That future direction, and the amount of pain that will be endured, is truly in the hands of the humans who walk the surface of the planet.

We are committed to help with this reawakening. We are committed to help our brothers and sisters to walk in the higher dimensions that are their destiny. We are committed to fulfill the plan of God and the Scriptures.

These souls can consider their journeys aboard our ships to be one of aid and assistance. We hope that those who journey with us and remember know that the selection process automatically classifies them among the finest souls who ever walked the planet. We wish they would integrate these two ideas in their third dimensional consciousness, work at removing the illusions of the fear that surrounds their journeys, and focus only on the incredibly wonderful service they are doing for humanity.

The chamber designed to assist these souls in the reawakening process is the Chamber for The Captives. We call it this not because these souls are captive aboard our Ship. These souls are captive only to their own fears and doubts that comprise the negativity that surrounds the Earth in the third dimension. We bring them to this chamber to remove these illusions and eventually to set them free. This is the truth of our mission and higher purpose.

THE STORAGE AND RETRIEVAL AREA

We offer no long description for this area of our Ship. It is not exciting. It is only functional. This area is for storage, and for a Ship the size of ours, we do need large areas for storage of replacement parts.

Many items cannot be reproduced through the powers of our minds and the dimensional frequencies we access.

We are limited, just as you have such limitations on the Earth plane. But we are also in the space where most of what we need may be accessed through the process of time travel. Therefore, we are able to gain many things in a matter of moments, by your standards, just by accessing and using some of the tools that we have mastered in our own evolutionary process.

THE COMMUNICATION CHAMBER

We will begin the description of this area of the Ship by defining the word "communication." What this means is "the passing of messages telepathically between two or more Beings, and the process of receiving this information accurately." With this understanding firmly in place, we will now begin to describe the purpose of this chamber.

The Communication Chamber supports continual growth and development of our telepathic powers. It is equipped with a mechanism that absorbs our mental thoughts and records their significance and power. What is exchanged is a "readout" of what we sent. In this readout, we are able to determine our own power and potential for the sending abilities we have. We are given information, or feedback, if you will, that helps us make decisions as to how we might improve our telepathic abilities.

This chamber is actually a learning facility for accuracy and skill development. The mechanism in this area will let us know of any difficulties we are having in focusing, for example.

An unfocused Being will experience the problem of sending unclear messages. This is described in the chapter on Language, and a problem such as this is not acceptable to a species as advanced as ours. This does not mean that we take things for granted and do not continue to practice the lessons that are ours in this curriculum of existence. Instead, we take our roles and lessons seriously, and we discipline ourselves to use chambers such as this to ensure that our skills do not deteriorate.

The room is the transmitter and receiver of totally accurate information. It receives the electrical impulses from our thoughts, transcribes them for us in minute detail, gives us a telepathic readout of the areas needing improvement based on the data it obtained from our communication, and then prescribes exercises for us to follow. Whatever your mental image of this chamber may be does not matter. Its function is truly for us, to serve us and our continual development.

Every Being is required to use it at least once each Earth month. It is like a medical check that is recommended in your society once each year.

Another purpose for this area is the socialization process that takes place here. Since use of this chamber is a requirement this is like a reunion hall for the many who use it. We do not have many opportunities to socialize on our mission, nor do we feel a need to do so in our culture. This chamber provides us with just about all of this activity we feel we need.

THE NAVIGATION REHEARSAL AREA

This is a very special area of our Ship. It is here that we practice a combination of maneuvers like your military moves on Earth. We plan, write out our activities in detail, and actually rehearse the maneuvers that we must complete for the continuation of our mission on Earth.

The room we use is a very large room with a large area for strategic drawings in the etheric form. Often we take visitors from other Starships aboard our Ship, and when they arrive we use this room to jointly plan the next stages of our activities. These rehearsals involve many steps of telepathic communications before any diagrams are actually completed.

The plans are promoted and enacted to perfection for each of the smaller parts of the mission. When we actually fulfill the plans, say on the Earth plane, the maneuvers are compared with the data stored in our central storage areas. In comparing the findings we are able to constantly improve and make decisions to complete our assignments with even more accuracy.

In this rehearsal area we have what you would call sensing computers that react to energy movements. These collect data from such movements as thoughts, physical forms, and even emotions. They are especially sensitive to emotional energy emissions, as those are the most unstable of all. Although we pride ourselves on being the masters of our emotions, we still recognize this part of our nature to be the weakest.

These sensing computers do a remarkable job of dictating all of the innermost movements of our maneuvers. They can access movement in all dimensions simultaneously. They can offer instantaneous reports of the images and perceptions received.

Since efficiency is something our species truly honors and respects, we take these rehearsals very seriously. We use the data to make every move of our strategy as effective as possible to accomplish our goals.

The Starship on which we ride is one of the few that has this special chamber. It is unique to our needs, and, therefore, we are honored to have many visitors aboard our Ship who take advantage of this technology. We share our inventions with those whom we honor aboard the Athena, and we learn of the power this device has in simplifying our mission.

The purpose for this area is only to support our journeys out of the Ship. It serves us and our other visitors well. It is a valuable part of this Starship.

THE MOTIVATIONAL STORAGE MOTION AREA

Seldom has an area of our Ship been more misunderstood than this one. We begin with this statement, for we would like to use this as the basis for the explanation that we are about to share with you.

The Motivational Storage Motion Area is a compartment of our Ship that supports the learning facility. It is designed to take information about the planet Earth and our mission and to place these data in a holistic framework of the many dimensions of time and space. This area will take many of the completed plans from the Navigation Rehearsal Area that result from the information gained from the Learning Facility, and rearrange these plans into parallel constructs that support operations on the third, fourth, and fifth dimensions. This is necessary, for we continually fluctuate between these dimensions, and we need assistance to help us bridge the gaps between the "distortions" that appear to occur when thoughts, words, actions, and emotions are transferred from one dimensional frequency to another.

This chamber is given the word "motivational" in its title because it performs a function that truly does keep us motivated to continue on our mission. What we have been asked to do is not easy, by your Earth standards, although perhaps not that difficult by ours. Without the assistance of this kind of device, it would be very difficult for us to continue to function simultaneously on these different dimensional frequencies and still keep the holistic goal of the oneness in our focus. With this technology, we proceed with much ease and assurance.

This area of the Ship is the refinement of the process of our primary mission and does keep us motivated, as we rely on its interpretation, trust its assistance, and are dependent upon the mechanism for much of our motivational support that enhances our journey.

The word "storage" is in the title because this area integrates and stores the data from two other areas of the Ship: the Learning Facility, and the Navigation Rehearsal Area. Both of these chambers are necessary and must be operational before this area can perform its function.

The word "motion" is used in this title because the integration process takes the valuable information from those other areas and puts it all in motion with our personal energies, to provide us with the holistic patterns for performance outside the Ship. This is just one reason why the practice sessions must obtain such a level of perfection. The refinement process of collecting and manipulating the data and activities must be such that there is no room for error by the time they are sent to this area of the Ship.

We are dependent upon this chamber to a large extent only for assisting us on that part of our mission when or where we manifest ourselves outside of our Starship support area. When we are within the Ship's contained space, we do not need to use this area at all.

In the beginning we said that this area was misunderstood. It is misunderstood by the Earth inhabitants who have worked with us in the past. There are certain government and scientific workers on Earth who have had access to some of our information and "secrets" for advanced technology. They are continually amazed when they learn of what we do with the use of our energy systems. This area is one they have not been able to comprehend as yet. One of the reasons an understanding of the function of this part of our Ship has been so difficult for them is because when they were exposed to this technology they did not have the holistic support systems programed in their computers. Their own brain structures were not able to comprehend this multidimensional level of holistic learning without the assistance of your computers that enhance understanding. Therefore, this part of learning has been largely ignored by those who have been exposed to us in your recent past.

We tell you today that this is the area that holds the secrets to our own success in our journeys to Earth. So in many ways, one might label this section of our Starship as one of the most critical parts and support systems for the Beings who work among you.

THE MOTION CARRIER

The Motion Carrier is situated in an area adjacent to the one just described. This chamber supports the changed essence of our Beings before they move away from the Ship and continue their journeys on the Earth plane. The Motivational Storage Motion Area performs the function of integrating necessary information and data into a holistic design. The Motion Carrier Area programs the holistic data into the essence of the Beings who journey outside of the Ship.

The Beings who are assigned to leave the Ship are led into this chamber. All the members of the team are present, for they must receive the same "treatment." The Beings are placed in a circular pattern and are momentarily separated; that is, their souls are separated momentarily from their physical structures through a primordial scream process. The sound vibrations used are on a level higher than those within their own normal range of "hearing", so this does not hurt them.

In this separated form, the chamber's energy frequencies work with the soul and reprogram it to ensure that each Being receives all the information necessary to accomplish the next part of the mission. When the programming is complete, the souls and physical structures are reunited and the team is ready to journey to its destiny.

This entire process takes only a fraction of a moment according to your Earth time. There is no pain. There is no physical deterioration. It is simply a process that supports the work they are destined to fulfill. It allows us to move. We could not be "put into motion" if we did not undergo this treatment.

There are many benefits to this. One is that the team that actually leaves the Ship does not have to be the team that has practiced all of the learning and rehearsals. The practicing is done by those who have greater vision and patterns of perfection within their essence. This greater

178

team absorbs the refinement and perfection patterns, and the workers are the ones who benefit from that procedure by being imprinted with these patterns in the Motion Carrier Chamber.

Storage of the information and holistic patterns for performance are not permanently implanted in the Being's consciousness. Because this is a function of team work, when those Beings return from their missions they do not use that pattern of programming anymore, so they are individually positioned around the Ship once more. The programming breaks down so that the Beings are no longer affected.

This form of learning and performance is very efficient. Need we say more?

THE SHUTTLE CRAFT AREA

This may be the only area of our Ship with which you can identify, because of the recent film productions that are sweeping your planet. We, too, can leave our Ship via smaller craft. Contrary to your popular beliefs, many of our smaller craft are global in shape. They are also much smaller in dimensions than you would imagine. We call them sensing devices. They are sent out to roam and collect data in closer proximity to Earth than our Starship is able to cruise.

The purpose of these smaller vehicles, which we call "vicama," is to access energy points in the Earth for the purpose of reactivating them. There are many such openings into the Earth about which humans are only recently learning. These openings into the Earth's energy fields have, for the most part, been lying dormant for centuries.

We are here to reenergize these for all of the inhabitants on the planet and for all of our other celestial sisters and brothers.

We use the vicama to tenderize the electromagnetic lines of energy that are flowing from these pressure points, and to refocus the currents if it is necessary to do so. Sometimes the energy currents are in misalignment because of scientific endeavors that you are completing on the planet. An example would be your nuclear power stations. Some of them emit such strong energy currents that they mix with the natural alignment energy forces of the planet. When this happens, the electromagnetic forces around the planet are placed in jeopardy of being put out of balance, as they become unstable. We then journey over one of your stations in our vicama, and reprogram the computers or the sources of power for that plant that produces the misaligned currents. Sometimes this action is just slightly noticed, and other times the changes are quite dramatic. This has a tendency to alarm some of the inhabitants of Earth.

We do this out of our sense of duty and love for the planet and its inhabitants. We do this because it keeps the Earth in alignment with the electromagnetic currents that have kept it stabilized for so many centuries.

There are many other purposes for these vicama craft. They are used as the primary means of communication between the Starship and the destinations to which they are sent. In addition they are our primary life support systems for a portion of the journeys that we take. The vicama also are equipped with instruments and "computers" that can trace energy sources and data. These data are utilized for further study of systems on Earth.

We also have transported some of the humans from Earth on these craft.

These craft are global in shape. By global we mean that, as you see these disks in the heavens, you see a round vehicle that appears to look like a globe. However, the distance from top to bottom is actually not as great as the width of the craft. These craft are shaped using the principles of aerodynamics which have recently been employed on the planet Earth.

Would we present an arrogant image to you if we stated here that it was the Arcturians who gave the planet Earth its present information on aerodynamics? In truth, it was we who brought this information down, but your applications of these principles are still far removed from the extent to which we use them in our civilization.

We have transmitted much information to many souls on the planet since the beginning of time. While they, in embodiment, often take the credit for these discoveries, in reality the source of the creative ideas was transmitted from a higher collective consciousness.

Much of the information received by Earth inhabitants results from the work that is accomplished in the vicama and by the advanced technology that they contain. If it were not for these advanced systems for processing data in our computers, we would not be able to convert our civilization's information to the third dimensional frequency. Therefore, the primary purpose for these craft is for the collecting and transmitting of data and information.

THE JET PROPULSION CHAMBER

This chamber resides within the Shuttle Craft area and is used as the main source of power for launching our shuttle craft. It is also a stabilizing unit for the return of our Beings aboard the Ship. You might call this area a decompression chamber.

The function of this area is not only for the inhabitants aboard our craft, but also for the craft. We use metals that are unlike any you are aware of on Earth. We have to realign these metals, or at least check to determine whether or not they need realignment, when the craft returns. Sometimes currents of energy collected on the mission can destabilize the particles in the craft. We use this Propulsion Chamber to detect if any misalignments have occurred.

Therefore, this chamber has two primary functions. It is the launch pad, and the decompression chamber as well. It takes the combination of these two functions to initiate and terminate our missions of smaller significance. This is accomplished in a brief period of time, but with the greatest of efficiency.

THE INFORMATION AND COMMUNI-CATION INFORMATION AREA

This is one of the most important areas of our Commander's chambers. We, the Arcturians, have a great need for ongoing communications that enable us to ingest incredible amounts of information and data at any given moment.

On our own we have limited abilities to accomplish this. Without an area equipped to serve the Ship in this capacity, our abilities would be very limited indeed.

This area of our Ship allows only Beings of selected rank to enter: those who are entitled to know all the information stored in the retrieval banks. In order to access this area, a special code with which to activate the kind and amount of information is needed.

For many, this area does not even have interest, for the other Learning Facility area serves the need for the continual mental and emotional stimulation of new knowledge. For a few, however, this area is essential.

The special code is based upon the vibratory frequency and color that the Being emits. This is registered in the entry chamber. If the two match, the Being is entitled to pass through the doors to review information stored in memory. If the frequency is not recognized, the door simply does not allow passage. In the event that more than one Being moves into the entrance chamber, each must pass the coded "inspection." In the event that a guest is being admitted, the Being who is entitled to approve the admittance must use a "voice" command that also activates the chamber door.

The information contained within this chamber consists of the propulsion matter/anti-matter formulas necessary for advancement of our hyperspace travel. We guard this information, for not all Beings who ride in the celestial skies are what you would call friendly. We must guard some of this information for evolutionary purposes, as it stands to reason that, if our civilization were to fall, it would produce a "domino effect" reaction throughout several planetary systems.

All of our work on Arcturus and beyond is completed with dutiful respect to the oneness concept of the All. We are dedicated to bringing peace, harmony, and love to all of those with whom we come in contact. But, unfortunately, not all share our same viewpoint. Many on your own planet would tend to dispute this motive or intention. Do you not agree? We, therefore, must be very careful with whom we do business for we truly are about Our Father's business and we do not wish to carry the unhealthy karma of giving such powerful information to those who are not aligned with the highest of intentions and frequencies.

For this reason we call this area the Information and Communication Information Area. It contains the most powerful information of the universe, and it is our responsibility to share it only through communications with the appropriate individuals. We are told with whom we are to share this information by the highest in command.

Even though all individuals have access to these data through the collective consciousness and their own higher resources, few are advanced enough to know how to access this information. We, therefore, are presently in charge of dispensing the communications that allow humans and other entities slowly to assimilate this learning.

THE MOTION-REMOTION LODGING APPARATUS CARRIER CHAMBER

The name is long, but this simply means the area of the Ship that carries the cargo from one planetary system to another. Much of what was on our Starship when we arrived in the Earth's atmosphere already has been deposited on Earth. We use many locations on Earth to work that are not decipherable by your human eye, to operate our bases and to complete our assignments. In order to maintain these sites, we constantly must import much cargo. It is needed to sustain the functions of our different Earth bases. We also have a site on the moon, in fact three of them, but we do not bring much cargo to that location any more. It is more imperative that we station ourselves on or nearer the Earth's surface because of an increase in the instability of the gravitational pull around the planet.

Many of our Earth stations are situated inside mountains and within the crust of the Earth itself. There are a few on Earth who know this to be true, but most will find this a shock and try to dismiss it as a fairy tale. The reality is that we are on the same dimensional frequency as the fairies and other little people who have been described for centuries by your poets and writers. There have been only a select few who have been privy to a view of this existence in the course of history. So, if you hear someone dismiss this as a fairy tale existence, use the positive feedback techniques that you know so well on the Earth plane, and tell them, "You're right!"

The reason we label this area the Motion-Remotion Lodging Apparatus Carrier Chamber is because this precious cargo, in order to exist in the middle of matter such as the mountains, has to be pure energy in a highly refined state. It can move and assume its same form to support our needs and the functions of the mission. Perhaps this does not make sense to you, but to us this title does convey the sole purpose for this part of our Ship.

The walls of the Ship are designed to hold the frequencies intact of each piece of precious cargo that we carry to its destination. There is a special ionization unit in this chamber that is used to stabilize the movement of energy *of each item we carry. It detects any irregular movements or patterns in this cargo, and those patterns are corrected and held in confinement before they have a chance to disintegrate or change form.*

If we had to name one area of our Ship that is the most vulnerable in the event of an attack, this one would probably be high on the list. We tell you this with much ease and confidence, though, for we are not a civilization that is prone to attack or to destruction. In fact, we report with pride that many in the universes stay away from our ships only because we have earned the reputation of being a high-minded civilization that is very technologically advanced. This reputation has lent centuries of peace to our civilization, and we are pleased to say that it is not fear that keeps lower vibratory souls from attacking us, but wisdom.

THE INTEGRATIVE AND SUPPORTIVE AREA

You would call this a "mess hall," "lounge area," or a similar name. It serves a similar function as your areas for rest and relaxation. It has the purpose of socializing and telepathic exchanges of non-classified information. The only difference between your lounge and ours is that our frequency sensors can detect if classified information should ever be exchanged telepathically, whereas your areas would not.

To date we have not had an incident where this became a problem. It is not a problem with our species. Only when our invited guests are taken aboard do we need to monitor the information that is being exchanged in this area. With our guests, our awareness is a bit more sensitive and alert.

But we have gotten off track, to a certain degree. Let us repeat. This is mainly a socialization area. As you might expect, though, this area is seldom used by our species.

> ## THE OLD AND NEW VAPORIZING CHAMBERS

There is a difference between these two chambers, but basically they do the same thing. They are also one unit. This may seem confusing so let us first define what these are.

The vaporizing chambers are those areas that instantly vaporize Beings and objects which are extinct. In this action the item that "was" is definitely turned into another form of energy. We use this chamber for extracting waste from nonfunctional materials, and for providing everything the opportunity to return to the state from whence it came.

We have two chambers within each unit, because we honor the old and the new. Each area has a distinct function and place, and the energies are definitely aligned in different patterns, depending upon which category they fall into. Something that is new might be an object that was manifested with a flaw. Since it is new, it has not had the opportunity to collect and mingle with other forms of energy. This is the kind of object that would be placed in the New Vaporizing Chamber.

Something that might be placed in the Old Vaporizing Chamber is an item that is a part of a system. In a system, all units function as one, and the combined ener-gies of those units are united into one energy field. This situation demands that we place the object into the old chamber. It performs many different forms of operations on this to separate the energy systems as it is being trans-formed back to its pure state. In some ways this is like the different forms of rays your scientists have discovered on Earth. While they are all energy, each has its own recognizable quality. Therefore, the same distinction is made when we do our work, distinguishing between the forms of energies that are designated for vaporization.

We on Arcturus are precise and we do not leave anything to chance. If you notice, Earth is also moving into that state, as well. We wish to point out there is a parallel here, for this is just one more affirmation that we are here to assist. We inform you again that it is we who have been guiding you for many Earth centuries.

It is important to note that we do not use this Vaporization Chamber as a kind of death chamber. That would be barbaric, and we have no use for that kind of practice. The only time this chamber is used for a Being is when that Being's life has expired, and the remains are left for us to care for. In this case, we provide the remains with a form of disintegration, but, in reality, it is a process of returning its essence to the purest form of energy. We thus do our colleague a favor and honor.

The Vaporizing Chambers have the capacity to reunite energy sources, as well. In other words, when vaporiza-tion is complete, a program of the exact structure that was changed is recorded and stored in the Ship's records. We can use this program and create that same object once again, at a later time. You see, the process is reversible.

This is truly a pure system for cleansing and restoring all that we are and have. We use this system because it keeps our civilization in the highest of energy sources. It is a quick, efficient, pure, and accelerated process which integrates the Light with the properties of our existence.

THE INTELLIGENCE AND DEBRIEFING CHAMBER

Your definition of this kind of room has a negative connotation in many minds. The function of this area for us is a very positive one. We view this area as the essence of our mission to Earth. We view this area as that which provides us with exciting cultural exchanges from one world to another.

This debriefing room is exactly that. It is for both our own officers and for those Beings of other races that are visiting our Ship. The purpose of this area is to exchange information, and we do emphasize the true meaning of exchange. For if the Beings with whom we are communicating are of another world, we conduct these sessions with the diplomacy of our civilization, and honor our sisters and brothers as well.

Much of the knowledge that is presently coming to Earth during these times is a result of the information that is exchanged in this area of our Ship. Often, souls are brought here in the dream state, and work with us for many Earth hours. When the discussions are over, they return to their physical bodies to awaken to a new day.

Many of the Earth souls who are being prepared to work with us in the higher realms and on Earth assignment use this area frequently. They are assuming the roles that were written with us between embodiments, and they are freely coming aboard and participating in our plans for raising the frequencies on Earth. Each of these souls has gone through an awakening process that is irreversible, once the programming for their missions on Earth has been revealed. This area of the Ship is one of the reasons why the programming is slowly surfacing within the consciousness of many of these star children at this time. We have spent many hours in this debriefing room, giving them instructions in their dream states. They have recollections, occasionally, of strange things that have occurred to them in the nights. What they are actually remembering is the interaction with us.

We use this area for other exchanges, as well. When our species returns from assignments, they sometimes will report to this area for an exchange of information that has to do with the master plan of knowledge being transmitted to Earth. When a part of their activities has had an impact on the overall mission, it is then that they are asked to come to this area for the stimulating exchange of information and telepathic dialogue.

If I were to select one area of our Starship that I am the most attached to, it would be this Intelligence and Debriefing Chamber. I see moment by moment the progress that is being made by our efforts with the children of Light on the beloved Earth. This special area for the reunions of our forms is why this progress can be witnessed on Earth today. As a group, we collectively bless and love this room of Light for the dedication that it has to help the souls on Earth to advance.

THE INTELLIGENCE AND VAPORIZING CHAMBER

We have an abundance of gifts that we bring to your star system and to the others we visit. We carry precious cargo of another kind in this area, however. In the Intelligence and Vaporizing Chamber, we can carry and manifest various forms of gifts that are products of our thought forms.

This chamber is used to increase our powers, our friendship, and our protocol offerings. It serves a dual purpose, as do all the chambers and areas of our Ship. We do not design anything that is strictly functional with a sole purpose in mind.

Although we are time travellers, we still must use this area to help us with our mission. We cannot manifest anywhere we wish at the precise moment of time we desire. That is left for those higher on the ascension ladders, and for the levels of the Ascended Masters.

We find we must make use of what we have and the technologies that we have developed. We cannot do this in isolation, and while we are on the Ship, we are in an isolated position. Therefore, we rely on this area for manifesting and vaporizing inadequate ideas, objects, and things, when we are in atmospheres similar to that of Earth. We can manifest that which is unique or common to your civilization, and our gifts can have a greater meaning.

So far, we have given many secrets of our technology to some in your military and to scientists of different countries.

In order to do this, some of the models had to be manifested and brought to Earth. We consider these to be forms of gifts we create in this chamber and share with our colleagues.

Other forms are gifts of adornment, and many of the star children are already wearing these gifts on their bodies. These have dual purposes, as you might expect. They not only serve as an object for beautification, but also as energy transmitters. Perhaps one might call them communication devices, if one really wished to get technical. These "gifts" are not detectable by the average person. It is only those individuals who are finely tuned to energy sources who would understand their importance and significance.

We, the Arcturians, do consider our species to be a very giving group. In the understanding of the Universal Laws that have been presented to us by The Brotherhood of the All, there is no law more essential than that of giving love. That is the primary motivation and cosmic glue, so to speak, that activates the electron force of creation, which is Light. The law is simple: "The more you give, the more you will receive." While this law was given to all on Earth 2000 years ago, there are still many on the planet who do not believe this is true. Interestingly enough, those souls who have not mastered this basic law are the same ones who are in a state of lower vibrations and misery. Need we say more? The point here is that we learned this law eons ago, and have practiced it as a group. We are in the process of assisting our beloved Commander, Sananda, to reinstate this teaching on your planet once again.

This chamber on our Ship exemplifies this law and provides us with many opportunities to practice its perfection. It is a delightful part of our Ship, supporting our *own spiritual and mental development to a degree that cannot be measured.*

THE CAPTAIN'S AND COMMANDER'S QUARTERS

By combining the two titles "Captain" and "Commander" it appears these two positions are the same, but they are not. They do not even share the same space in the privacy of their own lives. Let us explain why we have dictated this section in this manner.

The Captain of our Ship is the Being who commands all of the Ship's routines. This Being also commands all of the life forms on the vessel who perform the common mission. The Captain's position would be equivalent to that of the captain on one of your vessels. It is the highest position for orders that the crew would turn to for direction and guidance.

The Commanders are those Beings who guide the mission. They control the overall strategy that guides the maneuvers of the plan. For the Commanders, there are many Starships, Beings, maneuvers, and locations that must be directed for the missions to be successful.

These Beings are in the roles of serving the Galactic Command and the Brotherhood of the All. They are in charge of all aspects of the plan. These Beings reside above the fifth dimension and wield a power that is far beyond what our technology can provide. They hold their tenure through the Tribunal Council of the universe and work tirelessly to assure that the mission to assist the beloved Terra in her hour of need will proceed with confidence.

The quarters designed to house these two levels of Beings, are in a part of the Ship reserved for a vibratory frequency. The Captain's Quarters are sealed off in a special electromagnetic field that protects its frequencies. It contains energy from the Great Central Sun that provides an effervescent energy absolutely maintaining integrity of the purest form.

When the Commanders visit our Starship, they must have surroundings of the highest quality. They must be preserved, so to speak, in a frequency that supports their level of love and integrity. Therefore, the quarters reserved are in an area separate from, yet in general proximity to, the quarters designed for the Captain.

The Commanders' quarters must, at all times, be adorned with an area that manifests Liquid Light. This is the universal substance that comprises the Force of all that sustains life. While it is present everywhere, and all souls have access to this Force, it will only manifest for those who are the purest of channels, and who have earned the right to its use and wisdom.

The keys to accessing this at will are the three ageless wonders: faith, hope and charity. Within these three concepts lie the mysteries of the universe, but few Earthlings have awakened enough to find the true value of these words and their meanings.

Let it be known that our Commanders do not require sleep. These quarters, then, are only a courtesy which provides them with opportunities to gather, share moments of reunion with colleagues, and radiate the intensity of love and Light they are known to provide.

All the other Beings know when the Commanders are in the closest proximity and are present aboard our Starship.

Their radiance announces them without any communication. It is honoring and uplifting to be adorned by such magnificence, and we are pleased to be working with such power and magnitude.

THE CREW'S QUARTERS

In an area of the Ship that is not in the general proximity of the Captain's and Commander's Quarters, is the section of the vessel reserved for the Crew's Quarters. This area is designed with magnification of sound and color frequencies to stimulate intelligence and levels of evolution.

As we reported earlier, each of our assigned posts and levels of responsibilities is selected by our frequency levels. It is these frequency levels that we continually sustain and raise for our own and the collective evolution.

The Crew's Quarters is an area that supports the integrity of each of our frequency levels. Using a holistic concept of light and sound frequencies, any crew member may enter this area and be immediately supported by the frequency that is recorded to match that Being's level of development. The programming for chosen subject areas is encoded in this holistic design, and those who are the historians will immediately receive their intellectual nourishment as they are residing simultaneously next to the Being who is dining on the technical knowledge of the universe.

This area is not the same as the learning facility that we briefly described earlier. This is the holistic chamber for supporting the integrity of the evolutionary process of each crew member. This is designed mainly for the crew, but any Being, including those from Earth or other planets, may enter this area. It is not a chamber. It is an area patterned after an important hologram that represents the Universal Mind. It is the heart and depth of creation. It is the understanding philosophy of the All. It is truth. The perfection of the design of the system is that it reaches the precise area of a Being's mind in which there is a need.

Needless to say, many of our new members use this area frequently. It is designed so that one can pass through it in a brief moment of time, or a longer stay is also accepted. There are no rules or procedures for using this area. There is only the concept that "The Crew's Quarters exist for all."

THE LIGHT REJUVENATION CHAMBER

This part of the Ship produces the power that propels the Starship. This function is critical for our journey, for if we did not have the means and ways to do this, we could not sustain our own life forms or the activities of our mission.

The Light Rejuvenation Chamber is a small area that transforms energy from crystals we use for our main source of power to Liquid Light. In this transformational process the energy is stored and "recycled," so to speak, and used to support our efforts.

Liquid Light is drawn through the crystals from the universe and locked into the transformational process. It accepts and rejects no other form of energy or supply, but is self-contained in this continuous cycle.

196

There is no other purpose for this area. It is known to be our life support system. If we did not have this power source, we would not be able to complete our work.

THE MECHANISM CHAMBER

A very complex area, and one vital to our existence, is the Mechanism Chamber that allows us easy access to many places outside our normal area of operations. We have several modes for operation that we can use. One mode is the process we use when we wish to transform our physical nature into another dimensional frequency. When we have a need to do this, we do use this special chamber.

It has the capability of recording our exact molecular structure, containing the program through hyperspace, and then reforming it in another location. What this is similar to on Earth is the decoding of the DNA and RNA molecular structures and the creating of a duplicate life form based upon that information.

This chamber can hold the program of individual life forms indefinitely, so that even if there is a malfunction in the process of transporting us, we still can be brought back into our original form by the decoding process of the program. We much appreciate this advanced function of its design.

This chamber is vital for areas where we have to work, but where we have not physically set foot. We use this chamber as a testing ground to decode a life form's genetic structure, and then send a replica of that pattern to the surface of the planet we are visiting. We learn much about survival conditions of that space by the way the replica pattern operates. We are then able to make *adjustments to our needs before we send our own to complete the assigned work.*

This area is also used to detect manifested defects that are occurring within a Being's constitution. So, from that standpoint, you might call it a medical facility. This chamber can detect malfunctions and reprogram them instantly. It has no biases, unlike the human doctors on your planet. It can detect the source of the malfunction immediately, and prescribe solutions that are always "exactly what the Chamber ordered!"

It is because of this advanced engineering and scientific knowledge that we have no sickness on Arcturus or on our Starship. We have yet to encounter a galaxy or constellation that had a defect we could not identify and rectify within our own Beings by use of this chamber.

THE ENGINEERING APPARATUS AREA

On the Earth plane, humans deem this area of their ships to be the most important, for they can see no support systems beyond the technical. On the fifth dimensional frequency, we also deem this to be an important part of the vessel, but we think that it ranks second in importance to those areas that support the life-raising frequencies of the mission.

The Engineering Apparatus Area is the section that maneuvers the Ship between the third, fourth, and fifth dimensions of time and space, but mainly through the third and fifth dimensions. This section of the Ship is designed for the subtle, yet abrupt, transition of magnetic frequency changes necessary for the Ship to become visible and then non-visible to the human eye. While we can

observe you and the energy force fields that are in opera-
tion at all times, you have a limited knowledge and belief
system that you can only see things in the third dimen-
sional frequency. While this is not totally accurate and
true, you believe this, and therefore it becomes your real-
ity.

This area is equipped with a device that not only maneuvers
the Ship in and out of current affairs, but also has the
capacity to change the intonation of the moment. This
means it actually can change the tonal qualities of
communication exchange and allow, or not allow, further
communications to proceed, even though one does not see
the vessel any longer.

This section consists of that what the engineers of your
planet would love to investigate. It has the transitional
frequencies and mechanisms that a scientist would be
delighted to adapt to the present structures of the programs
that are in place on Earth today.

This section of the Ship also can be operated by humans,
if they should be invited to do so or wish to come aboard.
Other areas of the Starship, because of their energy inten-
sifications and vibrational shields, would not allow the
intrusion of an Earthling. We have in your past brought
souls aboard our vessels for the purpose of exchanging
theoretical and practical knowledge.

We also call this section the transitional mode, for it allows
air to flow through the chambers when we are manifest
in the third dimensional frequency. This is an important
function, for air is the vessel or the holder of the Liquid
Light that we use for our main source of energy and
propulsion. It contains the electronic substance that
facilitates transitional changes from the third to the fifth

dimensional frequencies. It can only be used to its maximum power with humans who have cleared their channels and who are in the primary mode of becoming one with this Force.

The same Force is also available around Arcturus and our star system. It is not contained in what you would call the air around your planet. Our Force is contained within the energy of the gases that puts the violet protective shield around our planet, and which is used to filter the highest and lowest rays.

It is important to note or clarify here that this Force is contained in everything. It is important to restate that this Force is everything. But the distinction we are making is that there are certain channels or ways in which humans or Beings from our system can use this Force more readily than others. We tell the individuals on Earth, that breath and air of the purest forms contain the primary way in which a soul can access this Liquid Light and fuel for evolution.

On Arcturus, we absorb this Force in a more concentrated form in our survival patterns. This is because we have a screening device in the violet rays that allows this energy to be absorbed into our Beingness.

The Earth, in the New Age, also will be experiencing a similar concentration of this energy. As we have said many times, the Earth is being consumed by the Great Central Sun. When this occurs (and it already is occurring at an incredibly rapid speed), then this will automatically move and position the beloved Terra into a place in the universe that provides a permanent, higher vibrational frequency to nurture it. In this higher positioning will come a new atmosphere and way for the inhabitants of the planet to use this energy source more readily in the fifth dimension, which will be its new culture. We can only tell you that this process is a delightful and beautiful one.

We honor this part of our Ship that provides for the enjoyment and ease of the transition between the dimensions for you and us. The Engineering Apparatus Area that sweeps in the air and electronic Force of your existence provides us with another source of Light and power for our own existence. We truly can identify with the saying on your planet, "It is like a breath of fresh air!" For every time we experience the motion and nourishment this section of the Ship provides us, we rejoice in the rejuvenated spirits that we obtain.

If more Earthlings would understand the power in the breath, they would make a conscious effort to change their breathing habits. If more Earthlings would change their breathing habits, there would be less sickness, more happiness, and more wealth and prosperity on the planet. For breath holds the key to mastering the electronic Force of the universe, and the power of manifestation in the fifth dimension. For those who conquer this understanding, the Earth will be theirs to inherit. For those who do not, the Earth will be theirs to leave.

A soul cannot be breathing deeply and relaxing in the Force and still channel fear and hate. This is not possible when the spirit and practice of the breath are managed as they are intended. One cannot conquer the lessons of the fifth dimensional frequency in a state of fear or stress, for that frequency supports the love and Light of creation. Therefore, if the souls who are channeling fears and lower vibrations wish for a way in which to free themselves from their bondage, the first step that they must accomplish is that of changing their breathing. If they try this, the Force, which is truly much more intelligent than they are anyway, will automatically begin the transformation process.

But souls must choose which one they will master. There are only two choices: there is love and Light, or there is fear. Choose, our dearest sisters and brothers of the universe. And make the choice before the portal of time into this new dimensional frequency closes and makes the choice for you. But if you analyze this further, the bottom line is that if this is allowed to happen, then, ultimately, IT HAS BEEN YOU WHO HAS MADE THE CHOICE!

With this explanation complete, allow us to proceed with the next area of our Ship, which is the Engineering Crystallization Area.

THE ENGINEERING CRYSTAL-LIZATION AREA

Little is really understood about crystals on Earth today. In previous civilizations, such as the one of Atlantis, many scholars and the spiritually elite understood the use and care of these important minerals. The term "minerals" is perhaps not accurate, for the silicon in the crystal is indeed a powerful communicator, which sends an electromagnetic impulse signal to and from its center to other transmitters and receivers. It is more equivalent to an energy source, but your Earth scientists have integrated the substance of the crystal "rock" with the other stones, comprised of minerals.

In the part of the Starship called the Engineering Crystallization Area, crystals are transformed and energized for purposes that relate only to our mission. In this area there is much hyperactivity on the levels of static and propulsion. The static is created during the transformational process; the propulsion is acquired through the momentum of the energy that is programmed into the crystalline structures.

Many of these crystalline structures are used to make contact with power points on Earth. We find that the need for energizing many spots on and within the Earth is an ongoing duty. We also find that Earth is constantly changing its influx of magnetic energy impulses, and this has a tendency to shift the polar points and connectors that we depend upon for communication. Therefore, we have to continue to program and create new crystalline structures, and they are used for the various communicative aspects of our mission.

There are many points on Earth that historically have been Light receiving areas. We use these power points to sense changing vibrational frequencies. We take the readings and use them to give us an indication as to just how much intensity we need to channel to the Earth at any given time to help it remain stabilized.

As many children of Light know, there has been an ongoing crusade of Light frequencies directed to Earth to assist it in its transition into the New Age. These higher frequencies have been directed to the planet with our help, and we are presently processing much information with these frequencies to help souls move their consciousnesses to a level that is considered higher.

The Earth receives this information through vortex areas of electromagnetic energies, and distributes the forces throughout the planet by the ley lines and grid line force fields. These have been described accurately by some as acupuncture points for the living Earth body. We also use this description, for this information helps us to address this concept.

The points of power are those that are in tune with the crystalline electromagnetic energy signals or impulses, and it is these force fields that carry the higher thought forms of the Light. We usher dosages into the planet at regular frequencies; then we give the humans on Earth the time it takes to adjust to the new, higher frequency. Within a planned, respectable length of time, another dosage is administered. This process continues throughout the years.

We do this because the human consciousness needs to adjust slowly to the higher vibrational frequencies that the New Age will demand. We do this because the human psyche needs time to make the adjustment on an emotional level. If this change were administered in one full dosage, it would cause such a shock that many would not recover from its effects. Therefore, we take the process slowly and with much deliberation.

There are many aspects to this process, and they all are implemented with the use of crystals. The crystals that are manufactured, so to speak, by us aboard our ships allow for signals and higher frequencies to be transmitted to the planet. We produce many different forms of these crystals, and we also register many different programs within them. This programming allows for the storage and retrieval of information, just as Earth scientists are now beginning to discover in their work in Silicon Valley.

Often, we have had to implant gigantic crystalline beds of crystals in select locations around the planet. When we have had to do this, these centers have been spots on the planet where much UFO activity has resulted. The reason is that these spots have become what some would call

*communication bases, and we need to frequent these loca-
tions to obtain information and data that are being received.*

*Our Ship has the capabilities to produce many different
kinds of crystalline structures, and we use this part of the
vessel frequently. In fact, if we ever had a malfunction in
this area, the completion of our mission would be in serious
jeopardy.*

*Our Commanders do not hesitate to abort missions that
are not productive. But in the case of our mission to this
sector of the galaxy, the work we are doing is too important, and we find we cannot afford to be lax in anything
that we accomplish. This area of the Starship is protected with great care. It is an area that carries much
significance for the physical survival of the inhabitants of
the planet.*

*If we could not produce and program the crystalline
structures as we do, the Earth would not be as far along
in its consciousness revolution as it is. That is Truth.*

THE INFLUX SETTING

*Before we go any further with these explanations, allow
us to examine a concept that you all understand on Earth.
The concept I speak of demands a regimented approach to
following and obeying orders, even though one's heart
does not agree. We believe that you call this approach to
running an organization, your military. Is this not so?*

*We find this approach to running a civilization to be one
of barbarism and control, but please note that in this*

expression of feeling we are not calling humans of Earth barbarians. What we are saying is that any system of command that does not allow for individuals to express their freedoms and free wills is a system that is not supporting the God concept. God made all humans in the likeness of God, and also endowed them with the power to co-create the universe. In this power comes the mundane obligation of working together and learning lessons that continually support the highest standards expressed on the path to Enlightenment.

One of those lessons is to learn to allow another the same freedom and expression of will that you enjoy; for it is in the completion of those lessons that one earns the right to higher states of Enlightenment.

If a soul does not learn to think for himself or herself, and blindly follows another's will, then that soul jeopardizes its own karmic debts and responsibilities. It cannot tolerate the lower negativity that occurs when another forces its free will over it. That soul then assumes the lower vibratory frequency just because of allowing another to convince it of a selected behavior.

In choosing to join with another, stronger force, one helps create another's dream. Even if this is a collective dream, if the level of energy that forms it is lower than the vibratory rate of the soul who participates in it, the heavier energy is always that which wins and lowers the frequency of the other.

This is an important principle to learn on the path to Enlightenment, for it is the basis for the truths that are hidden on the Earth today. The truths that one uses to conduct behavior in life are those which may be in conflict with the truths of the highest source of wisdom emanating from the Divine.

The choice of truths can only be made by the individual soul, because its progress on the path of Enlightenment can only be measured against itself. Even when decisions for thoughts and actions are based upon giving in to a lower force, but much stronger will, the choice is ultimately **ALWAYS** *that of the individual soul.*

With this explanation as the introduction, let us further explain what the Influx Setting of our Starship is. This is not actually an area of the Ship, but is, instead, a monitoring device that allows for each Being to experience and calculate the vibratory frequency it has achieved.

Since we are a civilization that purports mastery over our emotions, we use exterior devices to aid us in our evolutionary development. This monitoring device is one such instrument, used on an individual basis.

The results of these continual readings are shared with no one except the Elders. It is the Elders who give council and the reports that assist each on the journey.

We use this device on a regular, but not frequent, basis, for we have little need to monitor our physical and Light bodies more regularly than that. The reason this device was installed in the Starship was because when we are in "foreign" atmospheres, we have a need for regulation and feedback regarding our existence and well-being. This is just another way to assure that we stay on track with our mission and not let the Ascended and the God Light down.

The Influx Setting records our own earned vibratory frequency and compares it with our own reading. Only we are responsible for our own path, and we understand this without doubt. We have earned the right to total free will and to obedience. We share these traits with others in our civilization because we understand the differences between oneness and separateness. What makes the difference in the effectiveness of our two systems is not the understanding of good and evil, but the understanding of oneness. We know many Earthlings will not understand these words until they have mastered a certain vibratory frequency themselves. When this has occurred, then they will understand the power of these words.

THE INCREMENT LEARNING FACILITY FOR THE ELDERS

The last three areas of the Starship are designed for bringing Universal Law to civilizations that are entering the fifth dimensional frequency. The first of the three areas is called the Increment Learning Facility For The Elders.

This area of the Ship is reserved for the connection back to Divine Wisdom and Truth. It supports only that function and no one but the Elders and the Ascended Masters are allowed to enter. It is designed to support the life connection to the Liquid Light and also nourishment for the soul. It is what you call the holiest of places, and is likened to a temple on the Earth plane.

The word "increment" is used because each of the Elders is responsible for bringing into the reality of the plan one segment of information, and then measuring the success of its application through our activities by the increments that are accomplished.

As we have said, the beloved Terra is destined to enter the Seventh Golden Age, which is an era that will be unsurpassed in the records of your historical documents.

This will come to pass because of the planning and constant dedication of the Ascended Beings. This will also come to pass because it is the Divine Law and Will of God.

Each part of this plan must be monitored and completed in steps. Aboard our Starship only the Elders, the Commanders, and the Ascended Masters have access to the entire plan. And, of this group, only the Elders have the direct connection to the plan that is given to the others in smaller steps.

Therefore, they must be protected and nurtured in a sacred area, with no fear of energy contamination. It is this area of the Starship that protects them from this potential danger. We have situated this section of the Starship in the highest, most centered section of the vessel. As we explained earlier, the Commander's Bridge is situated on the lower area. Even the symbolism of positioning of these two areas is important. We honor the Divine Laws and Divine Will first and above all others. This is the protective frequency for the Beings that we care for. This is the protection that has raised and honored us to one of the highest positions of Enlightenment in the universe.

We call this area of the Ship "That which bestows the truth and the Light on all." Therefore, the positioning of this area extends its influence to the entire Ship, from the highest point down throughout the vessel. This is by design. This is the way to the truth.

DEBRIEFING ROOM FOR THE CHILDREN OF LIGHT FROM EARTH

This section of the Starship is not like the one described earlier. This area has a special function that is used to plan and reawaken the Earth-bound ambassadors to their missions and journeys on Earth. In the dream state we work continually with the messengers from the Ascended Masters and those who are on assignment to the planet Earth.

This is a special chamber for etheric conferences with souls who are completing their sections of the plan while serving out Earth embodiments. While many of these souls feel isolated on the planet, and wander with the feeling that they do not belong, we assure them in the sessions in this chamber that we are with them and have not deserted them.

The paths that some have taken on the Earth plane are not easy ones. It is not a simple task to change the consciousness of an entire world in the remaining time that is left. Many souls are unclear as to their connections between the higher forces and sources on the planet. As a result, many of them are floating aimlessly in the ocean of energy surrounding the planet, and uncertain as to how to find their way home.

This chamber is one which is used to restore these connections, as well as to bring into focus further development of the plan. This chamber supports the activity by providing children of Light with a process of recall. Many of them are presently moving into a space whereby they will have recall of some of their past lives and also will begin to see glimpses of the future. Time and space are barriers no longer, as they are opening up to newer frequencies. Much of this is made possible through our assistance to them in this chamber.

At first the planning sessions were not immediately revealed, not even to those who were in the sessions. Then, later, the opening up process began to unfold. With this increment of remembrance and discovery, the souls have slowly begun remembering why they are here. With this remembrance comes the slow recall of their missions.

For all children of Light, the mission is to bring wisdom of ancient truths and knowledge of the Divine back to the planet. To accomplish this, they will be positioned in different occupational areas in different countries. Victory will entail a collective effort by the many. It will be an army of forces, backed by the highest of Forces in the heavens, that will conduct this reawakening for the masses.

The legions of Light workers, as we call them here, will awaken the planet to a higher form of consciousness. They will hail from all over and will work to bring the connections of the many to a higher frequency. In this higher frequency will come Enlightenment and the peace for which the beloved Terra has so long yearned.

We are the life and support systems for these workers. We monitor, assist, and support them in many ways. We are an invisible umbilical cord and are referred to as their connection to the home from whence they came. They are the strongest of humans, and have a reserve of energy and heartfulness that most humans on the planet do not understand. They carry the sign of the Golden Star of Abraham above their foreheads and are marked with a distinction and a frequency unmatched by many. They serve the masses and carry many burdens of love. They are of the Divine.

We support them and carry their banners aboard our Ships, and rejoice at their progress when the ego of humans surrenders to the Christ-Self because of the work of one of our children of Light. For that is their mission. They are sent to the beloved Terra to help raise its vibrations from the negative masses. Whenever one soul is measured to be of purer heart, and is moving on the path of centeredness and alignment, then we know that we and the Mother Earth are one step closer to the destiny of peace and harmony in the New Age. There will be a time, though, when this period of self-initiated purification will no longer exist. It is at this time that the human form who is not centered in love and Light will have to vacate to search for a new home.

This chamber is the only home the children of Light know at this time. It is a chamber that supports them in their quest and on the troubled seas upon which they walk. In the dream state they wish to return to the home they remember as their permanent root structure, but in this assignment they understand they must complete their work. They are dutiful souls and Commanders in their own right. They are of the Highest, as was our beloved Jesus who walked the planes before us. We note what the masses did to Him in the name of justice, love, and mercy.

The coding in the souls of the children of Light is strong. The decoding, while taking a little longer, is equally as strong. Once information is unlocked within the heart and consciousness, the programming is irreversible.

To summarize briefly, then, this chamber of the Starship is reserved with love for those children of Light who are missionaries on a planet that is foreign to them. We honor this chamber and look forward to our sessions with them. While few of them remember their continued work with us, we can assure you that it continues on and makes an incredible impact on the planet.

CHAMBER FOR THE HOLISTIC CONCEPT OF UNIVERSAL LAW

We conclude our introduction to our home in the ethers with an explanation of the chamber that is the epitome of all that we have achieved. It is the chamber that represents the form and frequency of the Divine. You might liken it to a shrine or a museum, but to us it is the All. It represents the remembrance of our existence and the journey to the Great Central Sun. This shrine is the remembrance of the future-past and the present-future. It is the oneness of the All, and it is the void. It is difficult to describe this concept in any other terms without describing its form. So, let us take a moment and do so.

For one thing, there is a vibratory frequency and color display in this area that is above the third dimensional manifest plane. The colors and sound frequencies in this dimension are truly those which are ecstasy and joy for the Beings who participate in its beauty. It contains the range of highest honors to those who surpass the seventh level. It is the proudest of the emotions, and resonates Truth. It is the dimension that awaits the souls in Truth. Our shrine and chamber is a constant reminder of the purpose for which we serve.

There are no words spoken in this chamber. There is not even a need for telepathic communication. There are no dimensional forms manifested. There are only forms of light and sound and emotional frequencies of the highest Truths that are in existence in the universe. These are the Truths that Thoth tried to convey to the Initiates in Egypt. They are above the manifest plane of the mundane, but once mastered, can turn the human form into the co-creator of the universe of love and Light.

Once souls become this intensity of energy, there is nothing in the physical world that appeals to them any longer. That is one of the interpretations that our beloved Jesus tried to convey to the masses when He said that to come with Him they must leave all of their earthly attachments behind. For this form of brilliance and happiness cannot be matched in the third dimensional world.

This area of our Starship is thus dedicated to our origin. It is from whence we came and to whence we eventually shall return. It is the All, and the reminder that we are here to serve and to conquer. Our level of conquering is, however, to bring as many souls as possible, who wish to come, to this Nirvana. So, once again, our interpretation of a word does not quite match that in your language. Would you have defined "conquer" as such? As we suspected.

With this explanation now complete, let us end this discussion by expressing our sincere appreciation to you for your interest in our existence and life support systems. There are many on Earth who wonder and are curious, but are not unselfish enough to dedicate their time or energy to finding the answers that would nurture their inquisitive natures. Instead, they critique others, judge others' efforts, and find ways to disavow all that does not fit into their comfort zones. We suspect that you, also, have done so with some of the content. In spite of the fact this information might have been strange and caused you some discomfort, we applaud your dedication to the continuing investigation. For us, this could be a break-through in the barriers that keep our civilizations apart. But that decision is left to the readers of this information.

We hope that if they take our earlier advice and read these pages with their hearts, that they may find the answers to their questions. The reader will only find that comfort and those answers in their hearts. We say no more.

Thank you again for this invitation to discuss our Starship with you. We hope that you will find this technical information and instruction to be of benefit to you.

I AM Herdonitic, Elder of the Starship Athena, and trusted one to the Tribunal Council.

CHAPTER VIII:
THE TRAINING PROGRAM

VERY EARLY in our transcriptions from the Arcturians, at the end of the third session, they asked a question that surprised us.

May we ask one question also?

YES, PLEASE ASK.

We would like to know if we could ask you some questions and use this channel for a two-way communication, so that we also may gather more data from you.

If you agree, we will tell you how this may be done, and suggest to you that this might be the surprise that you have been waiting for. Please think about it.

Thank you again, and we do look for your appearances aboard our ship this evening.

I, Juluionno, do now sign off.

We did not quite understand what this question meant, and yet we were fascinated by it. This kind of intrigue was new to us. We had not been connected to this source for a long enough period of time to know that dialogue of this nature would be typical. Today we can say that the Arcturians seem to be "masters of psychology." They appear to know how to phrase things and just what to say to keep human interest and curiosity piqued.

We did not pursue this session any further that evening, for Norma's energy levels were running too low, but we were anxious to see what the next encounter would bring. To our surprise, the Arcturians did not mention their request in the opening of the fourth session. Instead, they began by saying that with our permission they were going to give us instructions, to help us in our opening to the Light. These instructions would help us expand our awareness and deepen our understanding of the divine order of the universe, as they relate to sound and Light vibrations and telepathic abilities. Little did we know, in consenting to undergo this experience, that it was also a beginning lesson in exchanging comments and information with the Arcturians.

The transcript is written as received, with comments from us as needed. Our comments are set off in brackets to help clarify the experience for the reader.

GREETINGS FROM CYNTHIA, BETTY, AND NORMA TO OUR SPACE BROTHERS AND SISTERS. WITH WHOM WILL WE BE SPEAKING THIS EVENING? WE LOOK FORWARD TO OUR EXCHANGE WITH THE ARCTURIANS TONIGHT, AND WE AGREE TO TRY TO ASSIST YOU IN THIS TWO-WAY COMMUNICATION.

Dearest sisters in the Light. We are with you this evening in the heat and Light of the north. There is a reason that we are placed in this position, but we prefer to explain that later. So, if you do not mind, let us begin this encounter with the introduction and tell you that Arturo will be the guide for you this evening.

He has been selected to take you on a journey that will delight and intrigue you. In this situation, you may be periodically surprised at the results and encounters that you experience. Can you not wait to get started on this journey?

YES, PLEASE TELL US MORE ABOUT WHAT IT IS THAT YOU WOULD LIKE TO DO THIS EVENING.

I will now begin, with your permission, and explain the instructions that will be necessary for this two-way dialogue. Let us now begin to entertain you and work with you as our true colleagues in the Light.

ARTURO, WE GLADLY GIVE YOU PERMISSION TO INSTRUCT US IN THIS TWO-WAY EXCHANGE. WE ARE READY FOR OUR INSTRUCTIONS.

Please begin by looking north and find a focal point behind your third eye. You will begin to feel an inward drawn pressure within your heads.

When you can feel this, you will know that you are in direct telepathic communication with us. Please proceed now with this instruction.

Now recite verbally the images that each of you saw. If you do not remember, then please repeat the experiment and tell each other of the pictures.

[We then gave our impressions to each other.]

CYNTHIA SAW A CIRCLE WITH A HOLE IN IT AND A LANDSCAPE OF CANYONS AND MESAS.

BETTY SAW A TELESCOPE GOING INWARD TO A POINT OF LIGHT WITHIN HER HEAD. SHE ALSO SAW PICTURES OF THE STARSHIP. SHE SAW THE INTERIOR AND NOT THE EXTERIOR.

NORMA SAW THE MESA AND CANYON AND A SUMMER SUNSET. SHE ALSO SAW THE COLORS OF SALMON AND VIOLET IN THE WHOLE PANORAMA.

Thank you for being such good students. The images, as you have already discovered, did have some commonalities, for we were projecting the one larger picture from our minds to each of you. Each of you responded to the image from personal points of references of many lifetimes, or embodiments.

Now, with this point of reference, please proceed with the next step. Take that image and draw it into the back of that energy vortex behind your third eyes—the area that you felt the pressure in when we gave you step one.

You might find that this will give you a slight headache, but do not be alarmed. Please proceed.

BETTY FELT PRESSURE IN THE THIRD EYE AND AROUND THE SIDES OF THE HEAD. SHE KEPT SEEING THE STARSHIP.

CYNTHIA FELT INTENSE PRESSURE IN THE THIRD EYE, BUT NO PAIN.

NORMA FELT INTENSE PRESSURE BEHIND THE THIRD EYE, AND WAS SURPRISED TO FIND THAT THE IMAGE OF THE CANYON IN THE SUMMERTIME TURNED INTO A WINTER SCENE WHEN IT WAS DRAWN INTO THE BACK OF HER HEAD.

Now begin to tone the color you associate with the scene that you each saw. Before you begin by sounding out loud the tone you feel, think of that tone in your head. Make certain you resonate inside your consciousness with the tone. Then, proceed with toning in a group, and try to do this all at the same moment, so as not to influence another's tone. Please continue.

THE THREE OF US TONED, AND TO OUR SURPRISE HARMONIZED BEAUTIFULLY.

Congratulations for such a success! We are proud of our kindergarten students. [We took this statement as an indication that we still had much to learn, and not as an insult.]

We began this evening by telling you our position in the north was critical for this evening's lesson. We would like to go back to that now, and begin to connect that position with this instruction. Are you ready for us to proceed?

PLEASE DO SO.

The northern energies are from where you will secure your power. That is why it is so important for one to meditate only facing the east or the northern directions. We tell you this, because you are connected with us in this direction.

We are ready to do some minor programming with each of you on a collective basis. We must tell you this first, before we proceed, for if we do not ask your permission and explain, we could be interfering with our karma and yours. May we have your permission to do so?

PLEASE CLARIFY WHAT YOU MEAN WHEN YOU SAY THAT YOU WILL DO MINOR PROGRAMMING ON EACH OF US ON A COLLECTIVE BASIS.

What we mean is that we will take each of your tones and tie them together with one another, on an energy frequency

level. *You do remember the differences between the frequency and wavelength, don't you?*

[We then had a discussion of our interpretation of frequency
and wavelength, as given to us in a previous session.]

*In this, we will be helping you to group your collective
thoughts and to tap into a more uniform picture in a
telepathic communication with us.*

*There is nothing more that we will do. There is nothing
more that we can do without your permission.*

*This connection can and will give you some collective powers
that you will be unable to tap on your own for many
years. Does this answer your question?*

YES, AND WE GIVE OUR PERMISSION, PROVIDED
THAT BOTH YOU AND WE, COLLECTIVELY, ARE
WORKING ONLY IN THE LIGHT AND LOVE OF GOD.

*I, Arturo, do give you my word from my heart connection
to yours, that it is so. So be it!*

WE HAVE BECOME AWARE OF INTENSE ENERGY
RADIATING FROM OUR HANDS. DOES THIS HAVE
ANYTHING TO DO WITH YOUR MINOR PROGRAM-
MING OF US?

*Yes, it does. It also has to do with the frequencies that
we are choosing to move in your direction. We are
submitting these energies to your hands for your approval.*

*If you believe that you can withstand them, then we will
proceed to transmit them to your third eyes. May we
proceed to do so?*

YES, PROVIDING THAT IT DOES NO PHYSICAL HARM TO ANY OF US OR ANY INDIVIDUALS WHO ARE WITHIN OUR ENERGY FIELDS.

You should begin to feel a cooling off. Does this energy relate to you?

WILL THIS PROGRAMMING HELP US TO BE OF BETTER SERVICE TO HUMANITY?

This programming will allow the highest of energies to flow through your consciousness and to serve all of humanity. As it is, each of you has a limited radius of effect as you allow the Ascended Masters to work through you. This programming will allow you to have the power it takes to affect more of your sisters and brothers.

ARE THESE OUR SPACE ORDERS, TO WHICH YOU REFERRED LAST WEEK?

No, they are not. This is in response to the two-way communication that we requested. You see, you began by asking all of the questions and receiving data from us. We asked if you would allow for more than a one-way mode of information processing.

Well, we are building with your permission, a two-way mode of communication, whereby you get what you need, and the Ascended Masters also get what they need to be more effective. Is this clear to you? If so, we will proceed with the treatment, for it is only half over.

YES. WE ARE HUMBLED BY YOUR ANSWER AND DO ALLOW YOU TO PROCEED.

The next step in the process is in the mastery of the breath. Please note this and go on with our instruction.

We see that all of you are shallow breathers. In this situation, you are not taking advantage of the Prana that is your life stream for consciousness.

We would like for you to know now that you have the beginning of a new power, and that in this power and beginning, you will see that the breath can help you become the oneness of the All. It is this oneness of the All that permits you to ride the pool of Liquid Light. It is in this pool of Liquid Light that you can connect to us at any time and in any space in the atmosphere.

What we wish for you to do is to practice the breathing from the lower stomach and take half as many breaths. Try this for about one of your minutes.

This is your second point of power. In this relaxed state, remember your tone. Remember the one of your vision. This combination is a dual key for tuning into our telepathic communications. These two are inseparable. These two are dual intensities, the breath and the tone, simultaneously worked.

With practice they can become one, and in that oneness will be synchronized with the Liquid Light. Does this make sense to you?

YES, WE THINK SO. IS THIS THE SAME AS OR SIMILAR TO CHANTING?

This is not chanting, but it is a form of that same technique. So, if you accept this, you will see that it is a form of chanting. Now that we have thoroughly confused you, we would like to add another, more definitive answer to your question.

So far we have only worked with the synchronization of two primal forces of the oneness of the All. Those are the Prana and the sound vibration or frequency. The one that is left is the light or the visual. We have not yet integrated that into this trio.

We are trying to get you to experience this holistic process in a step-by-step fashion.

SHOULD WE TONE MENTALLY OR OUT LOUD WHEN WE PRACTICE THIS, AND HOW FREQUENTLY EACH DAY SHOULD WE DO THIS?

In the beginning was the Word. This is how the universe was created. If you know that the Word is sound, then we would suggest that you try toning out loud with your frequency, while breathing from your lower abdomens. In this situation remember to take only half the breaths.

HOW OFTEN SHOULD WE DO THIS?

It is not so important how often you do this. What is important is the quality and the diligence of your activity. Also, it is VERY IMPORTANT to remember that if you set up a regular time each day, we will be able to assist you with your lessons. But it does not work that way if you do not begin to develop the habits and discipline to accomplish these masterful states.

At this moment, continue to do this and now note that the wave of the tone synchronizes itself with the heart beat. Since the heartbeat is the center of all love and all higher consciousness, please know that the higher the vibration of the frequency of the tones, the higher you can raise your own consciousness. This is the Truth.

It is for this reason that Masters tone. The toning done in the highest spiritual orders on your planet is done in synchronized fashion with us, for they cooperate and set up a regular schedule to rendezvous with us. It is in this relationship that we are able to help them reach high states of ecstasy quickly in their embodiments.

Remember, we said that visualization is the third aspect of this lesson. It is also the lesson that helps one to bring creation into the physical manifest world.

We will wait until next week for this lesson, and respectfully ask that you practice, for one week what we have given to you this evening, before we proceed with further instructions.

If this is permissible, let us sign off this evening.

I am Arturo, speaking for the Highest, Most Radiant One. On behalf of our Command, I bid you farewell for this evening.

THANK YOU ARTURO, FOR THIS INSTRUCTION TONIGHT. WE ALSO SIGN OFF AND SAY GOOD NIGHT TO ALL OF YOU.

Our training continued in the next transmission of August 2nd, 1988. Again, the transcript is recorded with our comments as needed for clarification. After we logged on the computer in our usual formal fashion, we received this response.

Our sincere greetings and affection to the three of you this evening.

We are in another position of your universe and space, to give you some additional instructions about visual communication this evening.

We thank you for continuing to keep this appointment with us every week. It is indeed a wonderful feeling and commitment to work with such devoted friends.

Let us continue with this evening's lessons. Are you ready to continue?

WITH WHOM ARE WE COMMUNICATING THIS EVENING?

I AM Juluionno, and I am here to guide you through this visualization.

I fear I have done you a dishonor, and hereby apologize to you for not making formal introductions. I hope this has not offended you.

WE ARE NOT OFFENDED, AND WE ARE READY TO CONTINUE.

Will one of you remember the instructions of the previous week?

[We had a general discussion and then a re-enactment of the exercise from that previous week, ending with toning together.]

The Lennon Sisters you may not be, but you are certainly heaven to our ears!

WHAT DOES THAT MEAN? ARE WE READY NOW TO PROCEED?

Yes.

The reason our ship is placed behind you this evening, and slightly to your left, is because this is where many of the images are in your brains. We are doing this only for the effect, for we know that the more the senses are involved in learning in Earthlings, the longer the memory retention.

Please understand, however, we really do not have to be positioned in that place to proceed with this instruction. It is only for the effect.

Now, what we suggest you do is look straight ahead, and then, while your eyes are fixed on one object, close them. In closing them, try to visualize the place on which you were concentrating without moving your eyes behind the eyelids.

In the back of your minds take the image that appears and try to hold that for at least 10 seconds. Most Earthlings, unless they are very advanced in meditative practices, are unable to do this. So do not get discouraged if you have difficulty doing this at first.

WE DID THIS TWICE. IN THE FIRST ATTEMPT, WE ALL SAW CROSSED LINES IN SOME FORM. CYNTHIA SAW THEM IN THE SHAPE OF A CROSS. NORMA SAW THEM AS TWO INTERSECTING LINES THAT FORMED AN X, AND BETTY SAW THEM AS ONE CURVED LINE WITH ANOTHER VERTICAL LINE ABOVE IT.

IN THE SECOND ATTEMPT, WE ALL SAW A SQUARE OF LIGHT WITH A DARK CENTER. NORMA SAW A POINT OF LIGHT EMANATING FROM BETWEEN

ROCKS. THERE WAS A FOG ALL AROUND AND THE MIST MOVED.

CYNTHIA SAW RECTANGLES, ONE POSITIONED VERTICALLY ABOVE ANOTHER.

BETTY SAW A YELLOW SQUARE WITH ANOTHER SQUARE UNDERNEATH IT. THEY WERE SEPARATED.

ALL OF US EXPERIENCED PRESSURE IN THE BACKS OF OUR HEADS WHEN WE TRANSFERRED THE IMAGES TO THE BACKS OF OUR MINDS.

You are excellent students and colleagues! Can you not see how many similarities are beginning to form?

In the next instruction we now suggest that you hold the image in the backs of your minds and combine it with the tone of the first color that you experienced. You may see how this toning will change the image in the backs of your minds.

Let us caution you that if you do not have the image positioned in the backs of your head areas, you may not have the effect of the image changing shape. Please note that we are guiding you in several things right now, and will explain later.

Please continue with this part of the experiment with your new found powers.

BETTY HAD AN IMAGE OF WAVES, AND WITH THE TONING THE WAVES BEGAN TO MOVE FASTER.

NORMA SAW A BUTTERFLY, AND WITH THE TONING IT BEGAN TO FLY.

CYNTHIA SAW A STAR IMAGE, BUT WAS UNABLE TO PUT IT IN THE BACK OF HER HEAD BEFORE THE OTHERS STARTED TONING.

ON THE SECOND TRY, CYNTHIA SAW AN ANGLE WHICH DISAPPEARED INTO A PURPLE-RED COLOR. WITH THE TONING, THE ELEMENTS OF THE RED AND PURPLE BROKE UP AND DANCED AROUND.

BETTY SAW THE MOON AND WITH THE TONING THE SUN, STARS, AND MOON ALL SHOWED UP TOGETHER LIKE THE UNIVERSE.

NORMA SAW THE BUTTERFLY AGAIN AND WITH THE TONING IT AGAIN BEGAN TO FLY, BUT ALSO MULTIPLIED INTO TEN BUTTERFLIES THAT DANCED AROUND.

What you are beginning to experience is the collective powers that you touched upon last week.

You are only beginning to reach up and tap the unlimited amount of energy that is available for you to use to develop your psychic powers. The key is the third eye.

You already know what it means to understand the energy of the aura around an individual. We would now like to instruct you to read the energy of the images that you are receiving telepathically.

Most of the images that you are receiving are coming from us, just as in last week's session. This is important to remember; for if you focus your intellect on us, it also will make it easier for you to manifest things, first in your minds and then in your reality.

You are aware that the two keys that you were using were the concentration of your mind and the tone. These are universal laws.

You read the energy of the image through your intuition. Intuition was what you used to sense the tone of the color that you saw last week. Now we will send you an image of us. Focus on it carefully. Pull it to the back of your minds, sense the color, and assign it a tone.

[We took a few moments in silence to follow these directions.]

CYNTHIA'S IMAGE LOOKED LIKE A PETROGLYPH FIGURE OF LIGHT, WITH A SQUARE BODY AND ARMS EXTENDING DOWNWARD. THE HEAD WAS ROUND. SHE COULD SEE NO FEATURES. THE BODY TAPERED OFF INTO NOTHING. SHE ASSIGNED IT THE COLOR YELLOW.

BETTY SAW AN IMAGE WITH A SMOOTH HEAD, BUT SHE COULD NOT DETERMINE IF IT HAD A COVERING. SHE COULD MAKE OUT NO FEATURES. SHE SAW ARMS, AND HANDS EXTENDED OUTWARD AND UP. SHE ASSIGNED IT THE COLOR LAVENDER BLUE.

NORMA SAW SMOOTH SKINNED BEINGS WITH HUGE, ALMOND SHAPED EYES. THEY HAD NO HAIR AND THEIR HEADS WERE SOMEWHAT ELONGATED, AND THEIR EYES WERE SIGNIFICANT BECAUSE THEY WERE VERY SAD. SHE ASSIGNED THEM THE COLOR GREEN.

[The tone we all sang was a perfect third chord. This surprised us all to hear how close we were to interpreting our images through sound.]

WE, THE ARCTURIANS

We wish to note first that the three of you zeroed in on the middle section of the energy vortexes within your own consciousnesses. [We all take this to mean the colors represented the three middle chakras—solar plexus, heart, and throat.]

We think that you should concentrate on this accomplishment. It truly is a testimony for how quickly you three are learning. Also, the significance of the like tones is another measurement of your success.

Now, what we would like for you to do is to try this one more time, and in this experience try to put an emotion to the image. It is in this step that you will combine the intuition with the visualization.

Please proceed.

DID NORMA BIAS THIS PART OF THE EXPERIMENT BY EXPLAINING THAT SHE FELT AN EMOTION WITH THE LAST IMAGE?

Masters are never biased. Please proceed.

[Again, each of us meditated for about two minutes in silence.]

BETTY SAW ONE BEING WITH A SERENE LOOK IN ITS EYES. THEY WERE EXPRESSING HAPPINESS, EVEN THOUGH SHE COULD NOT LOOK INTO THEM. THE FIRST COLOR SHE SAW WAS BROWN, AND IT CHANGED TO YELLOW.

CYNTHIA SAW A FUZZY BALL OF YELLOW LIGHT WHICH CHANGED TO PURPLE, WHICH BECAME THE TONE. THE TONE CHANGED THE COLOR BACK TO YELLOW.

231

NORMA SAW SEVERAL LITTLE BEINGS. THEY WERE
YELLOW-GREEN COLORED. THEY WERE EXPRESS-
ING GREAT JOY AND HAPPINESS.

[The tone we then sang was a three-part chord that was
in perfect harmony.]

WHAT DOES ALL OF THIS MEAN?

*We hear your concerns, and we tell you with sincerity
from our hearts to bear with us. We are giving you skills
that, if you practice them, will enable you to see long
distances through the use of our help from aboard the
Spacecraft.*

*You will be able to predict and get information on a much
more sophisticated wavelength than you have been able to
do in the past. Please recall the lesson on wavelength
and frequency during this coming week.*

*What this means is that you are taking your own power
back again by practicing these techniques; for it is in the
toning of your own frequencies, with our help, that you
will be able to do this.*

WE RECOGNIZE THAT THESE SKILLS WILL HELP
US OPEN UP PSYCHICALLY. THANK YOU FOR THIS
HELP AND FOR THIS INSTRUCTION. IS THIS IN-
STRUCTION NOW COMPLETE?

*The instruction is now complete for this evening, with the
exception of homework. In the next few days, may we
suggest that you reserve the same time each day to try
this. Then record what each of you saw.*

*You did not all practice your lessons in this last week at
the same time in your schedule each day. We do not*

232

mean to tattle on you, but we only serve to remind you that this is so important. [Surprisingly enough, this turned out to be true, even though we three had not discussed it earlier.]

If you practice this, then you will be able to compare notes, and we will be able to continue to give you weekly tips on how to improve. The instruction at that point will not be so concentrated on our imaging and lessons.

This ended the instructions given to us for that evening. There were several questions in the transmissions of later sessions that we felt should be included in this chapter, and the following contains some of the later transmissions that we had with the Arcturians.

IF LIQUID LIGHT IS USED AS A SOURCE OF PRO-PULSION, DOES THIS MEAN THAT YOU EXCEED THE SPEED OF LIGHT? IF SO, HOW IS THIS ACCOM-PLISHED?

The speed of light is only measured on your planet. In a wrinkling of the energy we can move the ship and our consciousness to any point we choose. We do this by focusing our emotions and energy on the object that we wish to manifest.

The material in our ship is propelled by the forces of the God Force of the universe, which is a part of the Liquid Light.

We move the ship a bit slower than we do our thoughts, for it is in the materialistic plane, and does not move at the speed our consciousness does. But we still can move to anywhere, at any time, that we please. Does this an-swer your question?

ARE YOU SAYING THAT WHATEVER YOU THINK,
YOU MANIFEST?

*Yes, to a certain extent. We also acknowledge that when
we are contained within a physical structure, such as our
Ship, we do not have the flexibility of moving it at the
same measured velocity that we do when we wish to move
our own consciousness.*

CAN YOU TEACH US HOW TO DO THIS ON THE
EARTH PLANE?

*Only a select few will earn the vibrational frequency and
increment that will allow them to do this. We can teach
anyone. The real question is, can they learn it?*

IS THERE ANYONE IN THIS ROOM CAPABLE OF
LEARNING THIS, AND IF SO, WHO?

*We do not waste our time with souls who already know
how to do this. We would not teach the three of you this,
for you already know this. Wait a few years, and you will
have all the proof that you need of our true statement
today.*

With the exception of some closing remarks, this concluded
the exchange of information for that evening. None of us
knew how to do what the Arcturians said we supposedly
could do, but they would not address the issue any further at this time.

The following is information that we requested about
diet to help with the cleansing of our bodies for spiritual
growth.

WHAT SHOULD WE EAT TO FEED OUR SPIRITS AND
RAISE OUR VIBRATIONAL LEVELS?

Since you are on a water-based planet, we suggest that you do not drink of the liquids as much as you should be doing.

We see a great consumption of the heaviest foods going into the digestive tracts of humans. We will not list the different foods that you should eat, but we can tell you that those foods that weigh less physically are those that are the best for you.

If you compare the weight of a cubic inch of meat to that of a cubic inch of lettuce, which do you believe is the item that weighs less? The lettuce, of course. It is because it is vibrating on the higher frequency, and can fly with the spirits. We say no more.

In the weeks following these sessions, Cynthia, Norma, and Betty began to notice an increase in psychic "coincidences" among the three of them. Betty and Norma began to read each other's minds quite frequently, and Cynthia's dreams became much more active. Betty and Cynthia found that they began to wear the same colors on certain days, even though they had not discussed this prior to meetings. This continues to happen in approximately 8 out of 10 instances.

Whether or not any of these experiences are related to this training program with the Arcturians, we cannot say. We only report what happened, and what continues to be an ongoing series of increased psychic experiences or "coincidences."

CHAPTER IX:
THE MISSION

CENTRAL TO the enigma of the extraterrestrials is their purpose in being here. Are they friends or foes, observers, villains, or angels?

There is, at this time, relatively widespread acceptance of the fact that there are space vehicles visiting Earth. Thousands of people have seen unidentified flying objects. Some have seen them at close range, some have seen occupants of these vehicles, a few even have claimed to have had personal experiences aboard the spacecraft.

Whether or not one assumes that these reports are true, there has been no clear account of the reasons why extraterrestrials are here. One school of thought is that they are here on a "scientific expedition," to study Earth in all its aspects. Some see the extraterrestrials as nefarious villains, intent upon controlling the Earth through secret agreements with our governments, while conducting vile and bloody experiments on unwilling Earthlings. There are those who believe the extraterrestrials are here to revitalize their own fragile bodies by a program of crossbreeding with human beings, thus introducing more hardy stock into their intellectually superior race. Many people see them as godlike saviors of the world, come to free the planet from the sorry mess we have made, while some see them as God itself.

The Arcturians, speaking through Norma as a channel, have sent Earthlings a gentle message regarding their purposes for being here. They claim that they are here to assist the Earth as it enters a New Age of spirituality. They cannot interfere with the free will or decision-making process of any Earthling. They are here to educate us and to help us raise the vibrations of all who choose to journey to the level of the new dimensions that we are about to enter.

They are here to help us understand the true nature of God, ourselves, and the universe. The impression they give is that this journey is a personal one. Each individual is important, and the Earth will reflect the sum of all its parts. Each personal journey is a part of the whole. In the words of Spar, the Arcturian:

"Each soul on the planet has a program stamped on his or her soul that is that soul's destiny. Each has a separate path or program, but in the combination of all the paths comes the oneness of the plan for the mission. Many souls are so lost on the planet today that they may never recover in this lifetime from their journey of forgetfulness. It will take many lifetimes for them to reach a level of enlightenment or consciousness whereby they will be able to access that coded document that is buried so deep within...the plan is to first raise one's own vibrations and consciousness, and then to raise the vibrations of those around. One cannot raise one's own without acknowledging and respecting the Godlike force within. One cannot raise the vibrations of the planet if he or she does not understand the concept of God being everywhere."

Each of the Beings who sent messages through Norma had something to say about the mission, each from a little different point of view. Some of the subjects overlapped, so it seemed best to organize this chapter on the mission by presenting the words of each Being individually. Not all who speak here are from Arcturus. Monka, for example, states that he is from Mars and is the head of the Tribunal Council of the Ashtar Command. Soltec, it appears, also comes from this higher level of the Masters.

Our most frequent communicator was Juluionno, Commander of the Starship Athena. Our first transmission on the subject of the mission was from Juluionno on July 5, 1988. We were concerned about a rumor that extraterrestrials have bases on Earth, one in New Mexico in fact; so we approached Juluionno about that subject in our usual, not-too-subtle way:

DO YOU HAVE PHYSICAL BASES ON EARTH, AND IF SO, WHAT IS YOUR PURPOSE FOR BEING HERE?

You ask why we are here on Earth?

We OWN the Earth. We have been here from the beginning of time.

We are in the fourth dimension of time/space right now, only because we are "leasing" the celestial body to many of our space brothers and sisters for work that needs to be done to further the advancement of all of our civilizations. We have been situated here for so long that we are within your realm of understanding or consciousness.

Our purpose for being here is for none other than the development of the higher consciousness in Earthlings, which, in turn, helps our species as well.

WHAT IS YOUR ROLE AS TRAINERS OR SUPERVISORS IN THIS MISSION?

We are the Beings who communicate through a means of Liquid Light, by sending information and thoughts of a higher nature to all of you on the Earth.

Those individuals who are evolved and perceptive enough are able to pick up on these higher thought waves; and in doing so become the transmitters of our messages on psychic, physical, emotional, and intellectual levels to the others.

It is a plan that does not interfere with the free will of humans, for each human has the right to accept or reject the information as he or she chooses. We are the transmitters of higher consciousness, and we take delight in sharing with you all of the wisdom that we have known for ages.

We welcome the opportunity to share this new knowledge and way of life with so many of our space brothers and sisters.

DO YOU EXIST ONLY IN THE FOURTH DIMENSION, OR DO YOU HAVE PHYSICAL BASES ON EARTH TOO?

The answer is "yes" to both of your questions. We are able to access both the fourth and fifth dimensions of time and space, and we can also lower our frequencies so that we become visible in your world, as well.

IF YOU OWN THE EARTH, HOW DO WE FIT INTO THE PATTERN OF EXISTENCE? DOES THAT MEAN THAT YOU OWN ALL EARTHLINGS TOO?

No, we do not own the humans that inhabit Earth or any other celestial body. We are in charge of the governing body that rules higher consciousness and intelligence that assists Beings on the paths to higher consciousness.

The Earth has been one of our training grounds for eons of time, and we have much responsibility on Earth.

We take our job very seriously. We can only tell you that we are in a position of watching and protecting, and have done so long before humans and other space Beings ever came to Earth and embodiment.

We claim the Earth only as the original Americans have claimed their territories: we were here first.

WHAT DOES AN EARTH BASE CONSIST OF, IF WE WERE TO ENCOUNTER ONE?

An Earth base has many forms.

We feel that you are imaging a section of land that is guarded and protected by forces, and one which has the power to access other worlds at a moment's notice.

Well, for some, our bases would resemble that, but they are inside many of the mineral structures that you call mountains or other land developments that are on your planet. When you can access other dimensions of time and space, you do not need to fear or plan around the physical.

In other situations, there are groups of souls in embodiment who are in tune with our communications, and these individuals also constitute a base, but of a different nature. These souls are always on our screens, and they are well protected, but with a power that is incomprehensible to most humans today. We watch and guard them.

The third kind of base that we establish, and perhaps the most important one of all, is the base and connecting point inside of each individual's heart that chooses to reach us and share with us the knowledge and consciousness of another and more glorified way of life. The base connection is in the heart, and is the one on which we choose to spend most of our time.

ARE YOUR BASES ALL OVER THE WORLD?

Our bases are all over the universe. We stand as the guardians and protectors of higher consciousness and that particular realm includes any point that is out of vision or perception from an observer's mind.

To speak more specifically, we are in every country on your planet, with star base operation two. We are referring with this statement to the groups of souls in embodiment, as described above. We are primarily located in your countries of power for plan one (bases in mountains or other landforms), and we choose all for the heart connection.

ARE THERE OTHER SPACESHIPS THAT ARE DESIGNED FOR BATTLE AND THAT DO HARM TO OTHERS IN THE UNIVERSE?

We weep to have to answer an affirmative to this question, but there are not so many of these around the beloved Terra today. While there are a few, there are so many of our Starships that they do not come very close to your planet, for they fear us just by numbers alone.

DO YOU SEE YOURSELVES AS OUR PROTECTORS?

We protect all Beings who are classified as our space brothers and sisters.

The great Karmic Board of the High Council is the governing body who determines the progress of souls to the Light. We are assigned to any group of Beings who warrant our protection, just on the basis of their earned vibratory rate, and the destiny of the star. We are here now, for it has been deemed this is a very special mission and that Earth is worth saving.

While it will never be we who will save it, it will indeed be the work of the souls who are in partnership with the Masters who serve God. We are only honored to be a part of this most glorious mission.

On another occasion, Soltec the historian, came through. We had evidenced concern and asked questions regarding rumors we had heard about previous contacts between extraterrestrials and our government. To answer our questions, Juluionno turned the transmission over to Soltec.

Soltec Speaks of the Mission:

First of all, we are here on a mission of peace. The real reason that we have arrived is to help Earth increase its vibrational frequency as it undergoes birthing into the New Age.

We are also here to awaken and protect the children of Light. We are here for the purpose of God and God's plan, and it is in this state of Being that we come in friendship.

In order to accomplish this mission, we have an agenda and activities to fulfill, which are designed to make our role and Terra's role easier. A part of this role involves education, which affects all of the planet's social institutions. This educational assignment has to do with the re-education of individuals as to their purposes in life, their powers, their health conditions, and even their destinies.

A mission as important as this one cannot be completed by increasing the vibrational frequency around the beloved Earth alone. One of the ways we accomplish this is by working with children of Light to change their vibrational frequencies. To do this in a lasting fashion, we have to educate them in areas that their souls already know.

In the past, we have tried many plans to communicate. What we find the most difficult to accomplish in this area is to penetrate the forces that control the average souls on the planet. Two of these forces are the government and the military of many countries.

We began to make our introductions to these institutions many years ago, and we did go to the social structures and individuals who were deemed to control the countries. That is the proper and fitting thing to do in societies of protocol, and we do honor and respect customs. In these introductions the doors were frequently closed, and we were met with hostile and sometimes deceitful behaviors.

These attempts to communicate have been witnessed for many decades of time. But in the transition of time, we have noticed that the power structures are slowly turning over from the highest in governments to the local control of the peoples. In this turn of events, we also have known many children of Light, who have been born and raised to be of that local control.

In this new relationship, we are now more free to attend to those who are not in the political and military realms. We are also in communication with many because we have been welcomed into their homes and hearts. One of the reasons is because the individuals with whom we communicate are not afraid. They are beyond the illusion of fear, and do not hesitate to see the glory of a multidimensional society that awaits the planet.

We love and appreciate our communicants for their openness and willingness to take us into their homes. We cannot and will not go where we are not welcome. That is a supreme rule and command that we must follow. We cannot interfere with the free will of individuals.

In the command and reign of the past many years, we have made contact with many souls who are deemed the highest. We have met with many Presidents and Premiers.

We do have much of importance to discuss, and find it very difficult sometimes to communicate using the terminology of energy and soul development with those in power. They are at the level of developing food for the physical and we are developing food for the soul. Our words and descriptions sometimes do not match, even though we are both in the business of producing more highly advanced human beings for the future.

We have been introduced to and turned down by many. In the closing of the doors, we have noted that they wanted our secrets or scientific advancements, but many did not wish to have information that would feed the spirit. This is a difficult situation. We have often found it somewhat difficult to deal with this compromising situation.

What we have done is to exchange some information on an equal basis, and this has been done mainly with the military. Interestingly enough, government officials have consistently turned us over to the military commands to discuss information whenever we have made a contact, which makes us ask the question, "Who really is in charge?"

It has not bothered us that much; however, we foresee that it may bother people at the local levels of your existence when this information reaches them. The ironic dilemma that has faced us has been that we are on a mission of love and peace, and we are sent to those who defend your borders against wars. Somehow this does not match the mission.

The instances whereby we have more prolonged contact with the individuals on your planet have been when we have been sought out by people themselves. In many cases, there is an openness and awareness on the part of many souls that actually have reached us before we had the opportunity to catch their vibrational quality on our screens. We have the ability to work with all souls on Earth, but in reality we work with fewer than one percent.

The number of countries in which we presently are working is 33. We also have had the privilege of establishing connections with the civilizations in Middle Earth, and we do much work with those individuals too.

Our mission is to raise the entire vibrational quality of the planet. What this means is that it is a united effort, and many souls all over and within the planet are being introduced to our work.

The gigantic problem with which you are faced in making the transition into the New Age indeed is underestimated by most souls in embodiment on Earth. There is no way that you could do this yourselves, in the present situation and state of mind that the planet is experiencing. There is no way that you could survive and bring the beloved Terra to her destiny in the dignity that she so deserves.

So, we are here to usher in the volumes of love and Light that are necessary to birth the soul of the New Age. In order to do this with all the proper respect, the Earth inhabitants must be reacquainted with their birthright. That right is knowing and experiencing the God-Self.

That is our curriculum. That is the plan.

The way we are managing to bring this new awareness to your planet is through education, medicine, healing, the arts and entertainment. These are just a few of the areas. For, just as your educational systems prepare you in many disciplines for a fulfilling, productive life; so must we re-educate the masses in a multidisciplinary fashion.

Therefore, the information is being received and shared by many, and it is the Earth inhabitants who are sharing and transforming the information. There is only one curriculum. That is the curriculum of God, and the understanding that this is the only force there is that sustains all of life.

As soon as more souls understand this, and truly anchor it into their consciousness, then the volume and intensity of Light on the planet will be raised.

So, with this brief introduction, I will now turn this communication over to you to ask more questions this evening.

IN WHAT FORM ARE THE CONTACTS BEING MADE TO OUR GOVERNMENT, MILITARY OFFICIALS, AND ORDINARY PEOPLE?

There are many forms being used that represent our contacts with select individuals in the world. One of the ways is to send information in written form. Often these documents, or "letters," if you will, have been manifested for the selected to read.

In many cases, we have found that the response to our requests has been met with curiosity and astonishment, but with little acceptance. It seems that the human mind is not easily impressed, even with an example of power that is beyond a soul's present capability.

There is a freedom in this kind of spirit, but one that must be watched carefully; for it is our observation that if one does not open up a mind to learning new things, or at least respecting them, that one can close down important avenues for the growth of a civilization.

In a second instance, we have appeared physically to our contactees.

There are always those who are indeed curious and heartfelt and wish the communications to continue. In many cases, those who make the decisions to continue communicating with us are not the same as those who welcome us from the heart. We see the vibrational frequency and disparity between the individuals whom we contact, and we can know from the inside level which are the ones to truly make the commitments and decisions.

Another form of communication involves transporting souls aboard our ships. We have done this upon numerous occasions. In this manner of communication, a soul is never taken aboard who has not first given us permission to do so, in its etheric state of existence. This is the purest form of communication and that is the one on which we rely the most. This is the true sense of telepathic communication, and this is also the form in which we can communicate on the highest levels of the soul's involvement.

Another form of communication involves those souls of alien origin on the planet Earth, who look predominantly like humans, and who live among the individuals from Earth. This is a form of communication that we readily rely upon, for these individuals are our primary contacts for the work that we have to do on an active level. We can see and hear these individuals on a moment-by-moment level, and we work with them in both the telepathic and the physical forms.

This is the channel for our deliverance.

Another form of communication involves only the telepathic. We can send messages and communicate to many, even though they are not linked directly to our souls' source of nourishment for our mission.

We can send messages, and are capable of receiving the total mass of consciousness that the inhabitants of Earth are collectively producing. We also know how to filter these messages and to take only that which we need for communication.

Another form of communication comes in the dream state of individuals. In this state we have access to the etheric forms of consciousness. This, again, is one of the purest forms of communication. This is also the form of communication from which no soul on Earth is exempt. So, in reality, it is important to note that all souls on Earth are in some form of communication with us.

In this dream form we have access to the oneness state, which is the reason that we are here. In this state of being, we also can help our sisters and brothers increase their own vibrational quality and see the direction of the future that awaits them. We are thanked the most in this form of communication. Therefore, we naturally do enjoy this state of communication somewhat more than the others.

We have other ways in which to communicate, but these are the most common.

DO YOU DO MEDICAL EXPERIMENTS ON THE PEOPLE WHO VISIT YOUR SPACESHIPS?

The answer to that question is very complex.

First, we do not do experiments in the same manner in which you define an experiment. Our medical maneuvers are done on an energy level, and they involve vibrational frequencies and consciousness of the individuals.

We have the capability of defining and measuring the frequencies of individuals by using a small sample of the tissue, the liquid, and the electromagnetic vibrational quality of these individuals. In each instance, the subject, in the etheric form, has given us permission to work with him or her in this state of consciousness.

What we have done is to give them instructions and the complete plan from us before they participate. It is only when they return to the physical form that their minds often block out this part of the remembrance. But while they are with the experts of vibrational frequency, they have participated fully and with full knowledge of what was happening to them.

Now, some of your inhabitants will not agree with this statement, for their physical embodiment remembrance will be one of fear, and this condition has blocked out the reality that this other is the truth.

Remember, only moments ago I mentioned that we are in direct contact with people primarily in the dream state and etheric forms. It is in this state that agreements are made. Often agreements are made long before the contact has come to pass. This is the truth.

Herdonitic and Juluionno communicated a long explanation, in several transmissions, of the more spiritual aspects of their mission.

Herdonitic and Juluionno Speak of the Mission:

WHY HAVE YOU COME TO EARTH AT THIS TIME?

We have come to Earth because we have been asked to assist in the planet Earth's birthing process into the New Age. The cry for assistance went forth into the universe from the Ascended Masters, Angels, and Celestial Beings, to come to this part of the galaxy to help our brothers and sisters of Earth to move through the window of space and into the fifth dimension.

This process is a most difficult one for any civilization that is increasing its vibrations to assume a speed closer to that of Light. We are here out of love and kinship for our celestial colleagues.

This transitional period through which the Earth is now passing is unlike any that has ever been experienced in the records of beloved Terra. It will be another 26,000 years before the planet again has the opportunity to assume the strength and position that it will soon experience in the New Age.

In this time of tremendous struggle, all of the old systems of a lower vibratory nature are crumbling and new systems of Light and higher sound vibrations are developing to replace them. What this means is that all structures that were built upon the work of mortals who had the desire to be separate or unloving will now come to an end. Replacing these structures will be only those systems that vibrate on the fifth ray and higher.

The fifth ray is the energy vortex of the throat area. It vibrates at the same frequency as the color blue. It represents the speaking of truth. This frequency will expose all of the individuals and institutions that have been established on the foundation of untruth, for these cannot be sustained in the higher frequency of light energy.

The White Light will assume the position of authority in this New Age, and through this frequency will come vibrations of truth, love, and surrender to the higher purpose of life and to the spirit of oneness and the all.

The fifth ray is the color of the rainbow that assumes the fifth position. It also is the same vibratory rate as the note of G. The two of these combined are a powerful tool for combatting the lies and the deceitfulness that have too long been sustained on the planet.

We have been channeling a frequency to Earth that is of this nature and higher. This higher frequency has been absorbed by individuals on the planet, and the consciousness of many souls has been affected by this frequency. Some of the results that have been experienced are:

1. *Many individuals are longing to expose the lies that have been smoldering and contaminating societies for centuries. Those characters who are harboring thoughts, emotions, and actions of a lower nature are being sought out and detected. In the process the exposure occurs.*

2. *Humankind is just beginning to feel a shift of consciousness resulting in a happier condition. This state of being is manifested in a "letting go" attitude or in the feeling of not being attached to negative emotions. Individuals of higher states of consciousness are beginning to separate themselves from those individuals of lower, more angry states. The vibrational frequencies of the two sets of individuals are beginning to clash. Let us tell you that as this higher frequency gets more prevalent, and more individuals absorb this frequency, this clash will become more obvious.*

What many souls do not yet know is that an individual who carries high vibrations is just as uncomfortable around the other of the lower nature as the latter is around the first. Often Earthlings tend to believe that those of higher vibrations sense more, have a higher intelligence, and know more than an individual with a lower vibration. We can assure you that intelligence is not a variable to be considered in this state of Beingness. This new state of consciousness deals only with the heart and the amount of love and Light that an individual carries.

The energy of the vibration is shown by the amount of openness and love that an individual channels. It is the energy of the Christ self.

3.   *Individuals are finding an increased hunger for the spirit. Many are beginning to look inward for answers and are rejoicing, for they are finally finding the answers to their long journey. What each needs to understand is that the physical, manifest world is truly an illusion, or the maya, as it is so aptly written in many of your great books. In this illusion, one wanders endlessly looking for the answers, turning to every object and individual and asking the question, "Will I find my peace and contentment here?" Alas, the wandering journey continues, without the peace of mind that one seeks, for the answers are never there.*

If we can leave you, our brothers and sisters of the universe, with any message of significance at all, allow us to state this one for your understanding:

"There is no truth or reality outside of yourself. You are the totality of the universe, and the oneness with God. It is all contained within, and the journey need

go no further than quieting the outer self for the purpose of discovering the wonders and the beauty from within."

The energy that is channeled to Earth by us is affecting the very inner consciousness of individuals on the planet. It is energy that can only be discovered by silencing the outer mind, and finding the connection to the inner sanctuaries of the mind. It is the universe within, that souls have longed to discover. It is the oneness that each strives to find on the journey of life.

Our role is to assist souls in finding the connection to this state of oneness and power. We are here to distribute this energy, but we do it with the aid of many of our space brothers and sisters.

4.   *Planet Earth is beginning to prepare for the cleansing of negative energy that surrounds her. You have already seen the signs with the violent weather changes, volcanos that have erupted and will continue to erupt, earthquakes, and the changing ozone layer, to name but a few significant occurrences. The energy of humankind has polluted beloved Terra long enough. It is up to higher forces to push against these negative vibrations in order to achieve the balance and harmony that is predestined for Earth. The cleansing will be complete. This can be completed either by humans or by forces which they perceive are beyond their control. It is your choice. But regardless of how this is accomplished, IT WILL COME TO PASS.*

We take our job seriously, and you have evidence that we do good work. We are truly here to assist those on higher realms who are waiting to join hands with humans who choose to rise above the needless negativity on the planet. We are here to work with as many souls as we can, who express an interest to journey with us.

Individuals, in order to survive in this New Age, must adorn themselves with the robes of this higher frequency. Should they decide to disregard this information and warning, they ultimately will make the decision of not going on with the rest to this Golden Age of peace and harmony. They will have to choose, but the choice will be theirs.

Those who do not choose to raise their vibrations must exit the Earth plane. Many souls will be exiting before the year 2000, as the decade of the 90s has been reserved for the cleansing.

It is not a negative statement we are making. IT IS WHAT IS. IT IS THE LAW. *Those souls who choose not to go on will be expressing their freedom of choice and will. They will actually be honored for their selection. Their souls will then reincarnate on a planet of their choosing that is more compatible with the frequency to which they are accustomed. In the reality of it all, they will be much happier, as will those of a higher vibratory rate who will inherit the Earth. There is an abundance of choices in the many universes from which to select one's next incarnation. Life will go on, for it is eternal.*

ARE THERE OTHER CELESTIALS FROM OTHER PLANETS HERE TO ASSIST, OR ARE THE ARCTURI- ANS THE ONLY BEINGS PRESENT AROUND EARTH AT THIS TIME?

The cry for help was heard throughout the universe. It would be false and egotistical to claim that we are the only ones who responded to the plea. There are other Beings from many other star systems here to assist in this transitional period.

WHY DID YOU, AND NOT THE BEINGS FROM AN-OTHER STAR SYSTEM, DECIDE TO CONTACT US? IS THIS EVEN A SIGNIFICANT QUESTION TO ASK?

If we may correct you once again, without sounding condescending, it was not we who contacted you, but it was you who contacted us. You see, there is a universal code which prohibits us from interfering with another's civilization or free will without permission. With all due respect, we never would do so because of the negative karma that we could accrue.

If you recall, it was you [Norma] who opened up the channel that evening one year ago, and invited any Being in the Light to respond to your light frequency. Naturally, we seized upon the opportunity to respond, but then you also had the right to close the channel at your own determina-tion. May we also remind you that you did close the channel, and that you were not contacted again by us until you once again chose to signal us for another com-munication. That was approximately nine months later, according to your Earth calendar. As a matter of inter-est, that precise time is the amount of time that Earth-lings need to give birth to a new life. The analogy that we are trying to make here is that you were provided the seed of this new discovery and understanding. Once the seed was planted, you gave it a full nine months to grow into maturity before giving birth to this new idea and to this book.

PLEASE TELL US MORE OF YOUR MISSION HERE ON EARTH.

Our mission is to educate the souls of the planet in the ways of survival for existence in the fifth dimensional frequency.

If we may repeat, the planet is moving into the New Age, which is the seventh Golden Age that the Earth will have the opportunity to experience. It will be a time of balance, harmony, and love that will raise beloved Terra's vibrations to the highest level ever experienced.

In order to accomplish this inevitable transition, human life on the planet must raise its own vibrations to reach the ecstasy that is predestined. Because of free will, the souls on the planet have a choice as to whether or not each will journey on the same path as Earth. Since each living organism on the planet is likened to a neuron in the great central nervous system of the planet, each soul must adjust its vibrations to match that of its Mother.

Each soul will choose its own destiny. There will be a massive cleansing on the planet over the next several years. This cleansing will be such that those who have the highest vibratory rate and light shining from their hearts will be those who will claim their inheritance—the Earth. The other souls will be taken away to rediscover their roots and other paths to the Great Central Sun. All will be perfect. All is as it should be. Before the newborn baby can grow and assume its new role and beauty, it must be cleansed.

Our mission is to educate as many souls as choose to listen as to how they might increase their own vibrational rates. The answer is to learn how to raise the light frequency of their souls, and the radiance generated from their hearts. To achieve this higher frequency, one must first:

◆   *learn the secrets of how to do this;*

◆   *maintain good physical health; and*

◆   *learn to provide for his or her welfare, in order that the peace and balance will endure.*

Thus, our mission once again is: To educate the souls on Earth on the health, education, and welfare issues that will affect their lives in the future and the fifth dimension.

IF THIS IS YOUR MISSION, WHAT IS THE MISSION OF OTHER CELESTIALS FROM OTHER STAR SYSTEMS?

The missions of all civilizations that have agreed to travel the universe to aid Earth at this time vary according to the special vibrational qualities of each star system. For example, the Orion star system is a very erratic system, meaning that they have the capability to polarize forces to obtain a balance and beauty that could not otherwise be created. You might call it havoc or chaos, but we call it another form of creation.

These sisters and brothers from space are bringing in souls who have an understanding of your recently formed theory of "cognitive dissonance." They are the ones who are working through the chaotic forces that surround them. By focusing their thoughts, emotions, words, and actions, they are able to transcend these same forces on Earth and to bring harmony to the volume of chaotic data with which they have to work. Thus, they create "systems."

In this process they actually have taken the skill of the highest quality on their home planet, transferred the application of it, applied it to the cultures and environment of Earth, and moved it into a theory of understanding that many can comprehend.

Even theories eventually do change. Allow us to prepare you for the eventual by telling you that even this theory will change one day in your future. As the Earth transcends its present stage of evolutionary development and the New Age dawns, Earth will have to discard this theory. When this day comes, it will be the souls from Lyra who will be sent to lead the discovery of a more advanced process of evolution and harmony which will be more appropriate for that moment of time.

For the purpose of clarification, then, let us state that the Orions are contributing their mental power for the development of smoothly running systems on the planet Earth. They ride on the color of yellow, and beam that frequency to Earth for the purpose of contributing to the stabilization of intuitive powers within human consciousness. They are the source of power for many of the organizational structures of government, business, and industry which have the main task of developing networks and linkages between data systems on the planet.

The Alpha Centaurians represent the band of violet. They are those who have scientific and technical knowledge that is of the highest quality in the universes. They are the theoreticians, and are here for the purpose of raising levels of knowledge to the higher realms of theory. Their difficulty is in finding ways to bring advanced concepts of the universe to the level of human understanding.

They bring a consciousness of processes to the planet. They are studying the scientific sites on Earth that have the reputation of being the most advanced, and are providing information through telepathic communication to the residents of those institutions. This information is to help speed the designs of new forms of technology that must be in place by the turn of the century.

We began by saying that the Alpha Centaurians ride the vibration of violet. The color band of violet is the highest vibrational frequency of the rainbow. It is through this frequency that connection to the universal intelligence and the Great Central Mind is made for all. This band is situated above the head area of the individual, and the information that passes through this part of the channel must be cleared to travel through all of the energy vortexes within the human. Only an individual who is vibrating at the highest of levels and in direct communication with his or her Higher Self has full access to this channel of communication. The Alpha Centaurians do have access to this channel of information in their natural state, which has provided them the abilities of being totally empathic and telepathic on their home planet.

It is because their intelligence rides so high in the ethers that it is often difficult for them to ground ideas on the Earth plane. That is one of the reasons why the souls from other star systems, such as Sirius, are here to help form the other part of the team for grounding the higher forms of information that are coming to Earth at this time.

The Beings from Sirius are here to help bridge the gaps between the theoretical levels of knowledge that are presently being brought to Earth and the practical application of those ideas. They are here to ground information and to make it usable for the inhabitants of the planet. They are the workers and the doers of the Earth.

It has been written, and correctly, we might add, that the civilization of Egypt was aided by the souls from Sirius who came to Earth at that time as god-men and god-women. They were the builders of the greatest pyramids and temples of the highest forms of knowledge that have been recorded in the historical records of the planet. They built the pathways and tunnels to inner worlds and to the stars, which allowed them to communicate above and below. They were the creators of the factors that provided for the grounding, applying, and integrating of all higher forms of knowledge into the physical manifest creations of Earth.

Creating this civilization was one of their greatest accomplishments. They excelled in the development and application of their knowledge. They ruled supreme for centuries.

It is the souls from Sirius who once again will help ground the information and build the Golden Age and its new shrines and temples in the future. But this time they will have help from all that are "hear" to orchestrate this overture. The response this time from other star systems is quite different from that former time, when few came to assist. In the future, honor, accomplishments, and rewards all will be shared equally among the teams that are "hear" to sing and orchestrate the song of Happy Birthday to the planet Earth.

Soon the secrets of the Great Pyramid will be uncovered, and many of the mysteries of life will be revealed. It will be our star sisters and brothers who will reveal the information once again to the planet, for, after all, it was they who sealed the mysteries in the first place.

The Beings from Hydra are those who excel at creating with their hands from the substances of the Earth. They are the agricultural experts, the archaeologists, and the Earth and clay people with the products they produce. They are the designers of the future who have excelled at

260

transforming the Earth's energy to new and usable forms of beautification. They love the common nature of human beings and they are expert at directing the love from their products and creations. They are the sensitives and the artistics. They are lovers of the land and labor.

The Beings from Lyra have brought a migratory quality and a freedom of spirit to Earth. These Beings are situated on the peak of experiences and have felt no attachments to the physical world of their home planets. They are the chameleons of the universe, and adapt their personalities to the conditions of those new environments in which they find themselves. They radiate much light from their head areas, but find it difficult to satisfy the heart centers while in the Earth's atmosphere. This is because they are not used to the lower vibrations of this planet. They are used to total freedom of expression and of movement. They do not confine themselves to systems or to movements on their home planet like we do on Arcturus. They are the independents of the universe.

This quality of independence is very much needed today. The independence of the souls who inhabit the Earth now is critical for movement into the New Age. We see this quality as a highly desirable one, and one which more souls on Earth need to acquire. The restrictions that Earthlings put upon themselves, because of the fears and illusions around them, almost prohibit them from experiencing any form of freedom, even when they are residents of free countries.

The Lyrians ride the frequency of multiband strata of color most of the time, but have been known to settle into select patterns when the occasion arises. They fluctuate in their own frequencies, but never in the consistency of the love that they channel. This is the foremost aspect of their characteristics.

The Pleiadians vibrate on the spectrum of blue. What this means is that they speak their truth and demand justice for all. The Pleiadians hail from a star system that is known for its incredible advancements in music and dance. The main contribution of their journey here is to change the rhythm of the planet with new forms of music that you are beginning to experience.

The new forms of music are those which contain higher vibrational frequencies that are designed to activate the higher energy vortexes within humans. By activating these higher chakra centers, the consciousness of the individual is transformed to a higher dimension. The higher dimensions automatically allow for more connections to the collective consciousness of the universe.

Sound and light frequencies are what comprise all of the order and manifestation of your world. The sound frequencies are also what activate the manifestation process. Visualization is not always enough to master manifestation.

Tones of the higher frequencies will open up the higher centers of wisdom contained within humans. When these centers are open, the mind has access to much more creativity and knowledge than when it is functioning at the sound and light frequency of lower natures.

The Pleiadians have conquered this understanding in their own evolutionary path and are considered to be experts at sound and light creations. Much of the hologram work and laser technology of the light frequencies and art works are due to the endless effort of the Pleiadians, who work with selected Earth souls who have opened to their frequency. The explosion of information and technology and the application of the knowledge of light and sound has opened many channels for advancements in science, art, medicine, and the humanities. Application of effort in these areas will only continue to produce incredible advancements. As you can see, each group of Beings is assisting in the areas in which they have excelled. We could go on and further define the contributions of other Beings from additional star systems, but it would seem pointless. The object of this lesson was to differentiate the missions between the various groups who are assisting the planet Earth at this time. We believe that we have accomplished this purpose. Do you have additional questions that you would like to ask?

YES. WE WOULD LIKE TO KNOW IF YOUR ACTIVITIES EVER HURT HUMAN BEINGS. THERE ARE SO MANY STORIES ABOUT INDIVIDUALS WHO HAVE BEEN ABDUCTED AND WHO HAVE REPORTED LAPSES OF MEMORIES DURING THESE TIMES. WE ASSUME THAT YOU ABDUCT THEM AND PERFORM TESTS OR EXPERIMENTS ON THEM. THESE ARE SOMETIMES DEFINED AS NEGATIVE, AGGRESSIVE ACTS AND SOME OF THE INDIVIDUALS ARE FEARFUL AND ANGRY. CAN YOU EXPLAIN THESE ACTIVITIES THAT WE PRESUME ARE YOUR RESPONSIBILITY?

If you mean "we" personally, allow me to correct you. We, the Arcturians, are not responsible for those actions that are taking place at this time. We will not take credit for this behavior. We will tell you that our sisters and brothers who ride on companion ships are those who are performing these activities, and the term that we give them is the "Physicians of the Universe."

If you mean "we" collectively, then I must say that we all participate in this action, just as do the souls from the planet Earth.

We have no need to defend these actions, for they are deeds that do not call for defense. In all cases, the individuals who have been taken aboard the ships of our colleagues are those who have agreed to this activity between embodiments. That is not an untruth. And that is not an explanation to lay the responsibility elsewhere. Let us explain.

In the present nature of the Earth, there is an aura around the beloved planet that spells out great danger for its survival. This encasement has developed through the centuries as a result of the negative acts of many humans who have inhabited the planet. The negativity that is so prevalent comprises a harsh veil around the planet, preventing the Light force of the Ascended Masters from penetrating the fields.

Individuals who are being "abducted" are those who have chosen to embody on Earth at this time, and to allow themselves to be brought aboard our ships to be studied. They are souls of the highest caliber and we honor them. They have come to Earth to assist in this transitional period by allowing these investigations to occur.

In order for humans to make the transition into the New Age, many things must come to pass. One of those things is that the physical body will have to assume a higher frequency, which will mean that the molecular structure of the body will actually change. For many souls who choose to go on into this new dimensional change and frequency, it will be difficult, because of physical changes and problems that they may experience.

Others may find that the loads they carry in this lifetime will not be suitable for the loads and responsibilities that they will assume in their new existence. In both cases, either a physical or a mental adjustment, or both, will be necessary to function at ultimate capacity. This is not an easy accomplishment to master, especially when the rules for survival in this new dimension will not be the same rules one followed in the third dimensional frequency.

We have been called to Earth at this time for a purpose much greater than to observe our sisters and brothers falter and stumble as they make their way into this new Golden Age. We have been called to assist, because we are already existing in the dimension that you are approaching. Therefore, we have a greater responsibility to all of humankind than to sit back and pass judgment, observe transitional pain without assisting, and allow the masses to make mistakes as they venture into the unknown.

We are here to help make this transition as easy as possible, and to assist all those who wish to come through this portal of time. But in order to do this, we also need data on your physical and emotional makeup. We need data on your acceptance and willingness for this change. We also need data on your Akashic records, which ultimately will allow you to pass through this time period with as little pain as possible.

The only data bank we have for collecting this information is you! If we appeared and asked you to volunteer to work with us, how many of you do you think would willingly volunteer to assist? How many of the governments on the planet do you think would run to assist us in this endeavor, if they knew we had to perform such a function?

You agree, as we suspected.

Therefore, we devised a plan with the incoming souls, who actually volunteered to assist us before they embodied into human form. *These souls do not understand or remember this agreement in their physical forms, for that is one of the conditions of an embodiment on Earth. The shields go up with the first breath of the infant, and from that moment on, the infant is on his or her own until he or she can once again make direct connection to the Divine mind of the universe. When this state of consciousness occurs, and when they once again unite with the vibration of the white Light, then fear is gone and the remembrances return. This is so. This is how it works. It always is perfect. Therefore, we wait for those who have worked with us to return to the vibrational frequency that will allow them to respond with the calmness that they once knew when we made the agreements together.*

Each soul who entered into this condition with us did so with total knowledge that an embodiment on the planet Earth can risk a karmic debt. The Earth is one of the most difficult planets in the universe, and is surrounded by an energy layer that is nearly impossible to penetrate with higher frequencies. Since one of the rules of embodiment is that the veils do prevent a soul from remembering the past lessons of previous lives, each soul understands that it is indeed taking a risk in coming to this planet. If a soul should get caught up in the illusion of the physical manifest world, or the maya, and not listen to the divine words of wisdom within the heart, it actually can lose ground in its evolutionary development.

These souls who are working with us at present, and who have done so in the past, are deeply honored and protected by all of us. We understand the delicate position they are in and the importance of the mission they have chosen.

Each soul on Earth does have a mission and a divine plan that was designed for each of them. The programming for these plans is all contained within the heart areas, and the only way to access this code is through one's Higher Self. Once an individual has re-established this connection, it is impossible to allow fear or illusion to direct one's life any longer. But very few souls understand this, and, therefore, do not take the appropriate steps to rediscover their paths on the Earth plane.

Perhaps this explanation will bring some relief and help to those who are in the emotional pain of doubt as to what is happening. We hope that these words allow them to regain the thoughts and attitudes of how important and special each of these space pioneers truly is. The information that is being obtained from them in the physical and emotional natures is extremely important for us to use to assist many on their journeys into the fifth dimensional frequency.

We call these souls "heroes." We hope that you honor them as such, as well, for it is because of their deeds that many of the masses will have a much easier transition in the future.

These souls need to be thanked and appreciated for volunteering to complete such a difficult mission. They are indeed sacrificing to serve the rest of humanity. This is not the only contribution that our sisters and brothers of the universe, who ride on companion ships, are providing to individuals on Earth. There is another form of service that is being conducted for humans who have desired contact with us, and who wish to move into the New Age.

The service to which we are referring is that of removing blockages that have allowed crystallization structures to form in the soul's consciousness. What this means is that often negative conditioning and programming from previous lifetimes is left, intact, on a soul's Akashic records. When this happens, individuals experience fears that do not relate to anything the individual can understand in his or her present lifetime. These programming activities can run so deep that they actually can interfere with a soul's progression to the Light and journey back to the Great Central Sun in this lifetime.

Our colleagues of the etheric planes are putting these individuals, who also have given their permission on the etheric levels of existence, through a series of treatments that can help remove these crystalline blockages. With the energy blockages removed, the recovery periods are then shortened, and each soul is in a state of mind that is equivalent to a higher vibration.

These treatments can be considered to occur in two forms:

> *The first kind of experience created for individuals is that of an actual Earth experience, established for the purpose of forcing individuals to face their fears and overcome the obstacles that are preventing them from seeing the Light.*

> *Or, some psychological suggestions are initiated into the human subconscious minds, which cause the individuals to face these events once again in their dream states. When this happens, the vivid dreams serve to work the illusions to a level of consciousness that can be dealt with on the higher levels of the etheric plane. When an individual truly knows that even the dreams are only the illusions of the manifest plane, and they are not of the god-like energy that is the oneness of the all, then that individual is free to face the world, the Light, and the path that is his or her own unique destiny for this journey on Earth.*

We hope this answers your questions once again, and that this information has given you another viewpoint as to what is actually happening on the Earth today.

IN THE PAST, WHY HAVEN'T YOU BECOME MORE VISIBLE TO MORE INDIVIDUALS ON EARTH? IT IS OBVIOUS TO US THAT YOU HAVE THE CAPABILITIES TO COME AND GO AS YOU PLEASE, BUT EVERYTHING SEEMS TO BE CONDUCTED IN SUCH SECRECY, WHICH ALLOWS PEOPLE TO BE SUSPECT OF YOUR MOTIVES. DO YOU HAVE PLANS TO COME FORWARD IN THE NEAR FUTURE, AND TO MEET WITH US OR LEADERS OF OUR GOVERNMENTS?

We order our thoughts through the use of rules and regulations. The reason that we have not appeared to more souls on the Earth plane before now is because it was not in the plan. We follow the rules and the game plan to a "T."

We are not responsible for the feelings or reactions of those who feel deprived that they have not yet made our acquaintance. We can only tell you that we are assuming the role and duty that we agreed to assume when we made our commitment to come to the planet Earth.

Yes, we are able to appear and disappear at will. Yes, we are in the midst of all of your activities. And, yes, we do have plans in your future to reach more souls with our communication and presence. We only operate this way now because it has been your governments and military that have kept us from all of you until this present moment of time.

We have made our statements and announcements to many in power on your Earth plane. In all of those attempts, the individuals have wanted to trade their statements for our military secrets and the information that reveals the mystery of the power. While we consider advanced technology to be an asset to any civilization, we also have more on our agenda than to discuss military and defense. In many ways we have more in common with the average human who walks on the face of the Earth than we do with those in control of running the governments.

Our agenda involves the concept of God and the oneness of the universe. Does it surprise you that the leaders approached by us did not have these on their minds when they wanted to talk? We spoke of energy and transformation of consciousness. We spoke of the state of the world and the evolutionary process to the Great Central Sun. They grew suspicious of our agenda and wanted to trade our rights to Earth, scientific data, and experimental information for the exchange of military secrets for what they called the defense of the world.

It is sad to see that the leaders of your world feel that its defense lies in weapons of the physical manifest plane. A civilization is ranked at its lowest when it describes survival using the comparison of creation against the capacity for total destruction. Therefore, we had little to negotiate and discuss. But we do keep on trying.

The incidents of our arrival and appearances have been sad experiences for us, because of the nature of the circumstances that have resulted ever since we began appearing in obvious formations. The stories that are just now surfacing, regarding the conditions of our Beings who crashed or were destroyed by humans, are but a small truth in the total picture. In reality, there are many of those episodes that are kept locked in the annals of your leaders' libraries and secret documents.

The results of those incidents are not pleasant for us to reveal. Is it any wonder we follow our plan with careful steps? What you would call secrecy, we call common sense. What you would call "taking a long time," we call an instant in time.

Humans are making much more out of our presence than we would ever think to acknowledge. We believe that is a part of human nature. What we take for granted as duty and commitment, humans seem to work hard to disbelieve or disallow. Perhaps one could call it a different perception of reality. For example, what you now take for granted as a weekly dialogue with us, another might perceive as an activity that is evil or insane. In an encounter with us of a third kind, you might believe us to be beautiful, and we might regard you as ugly. It is all in the perception. It is all in the reality that one chooses to embrace.

Our records will soon be brought again to the leaders of nations and we will want to renegotiate our position of strength in providing assistance to our sisters and brothers of the beloved Terra. We know that the day will come when we WILL be able to work with you in peace and harmony, and we will soon be sharing the common ground of the fifth dimensional frequency as our home.

Earthlings have a tendency to feel that we are the intruders, but if one opens the mind for a new interpretation, the opposite may be discovered. We are already in the fifth dimensional frequency and we are trying to welcome our colleagues on Earth to OUR home. That perspective, we hope, will bring a whole new light to the interpretation of what is happening.

One of the areas of confusion for us was the role that children of Light, star children, and extraterrestrials would have to play in the Earth's birthing process into the New Age. We were not even certain of the definitions of children of Light, star children, and extraterrestrials. To answer these questions, Monka, the "communicator of the technical," came through.

HELLO, MONKA. WE AWAIT YOUR WORDS OF WISDOM AND ARE HONORED TO HAVE YOU ADDRESS US THIS EVENING. WHAT CAN YOU TELL US ABOUT THE STAR CHILDREN PRESENTLY ON THE EARTH?

Greetings in the Light of the Most Radiant One. I am Monka, the communicator of the technical. I come here this evening to welcome all of you to the official Command, for in this regard you are among the honored ones.

To receive information on the topic that you have requested makes you privy to information that others do not have at this time. I can tell you that we are pleased to address your question and to give you information on those who are working to help bring enlightenment to the planet.

The star children on the planet today are among the finest of souls that this universe has known. They are of the color violet and they understand the direction to the white Light. I say this with caution, for it is in this information that the first part of the mission for all is revealed.

One of the things that is frustrating the children of Light today is that their missions are not being revealed to them at the rate that they would like for them to be. We can tell you that the plan is indeed on schedule and that the missions all come in two parts.

The first part for each mission assignment is that the children of Light are to open all of their energy systems so that each has direct access to us. Many do not understand this and, therefore, are not progressing as fast as they would like. We cannot do this for them. We can only measure their attempts, for the programming in their Akashic records is such that we cannot interfere with this part of the process. Once this is complete, the second part of the mission involves going into service to the planet Earth.

For both parts of the mission, each individual needs the coloring of the highest frequency. That is violet.

What we are doing on the Ascended Master level is channeling a new color, or frequency, to Earth, and the children of Light are our anchors. In this role, if they open, they are in a position to join with us to receive the many parts of the puzzle that is the plan.

We see that many of these children are responding, and they are beginning to have the sight of the fourth dimension of time and space. This sight is only opened to those who have the inner vision and to those who see this new color frequency. This new color vibrates at a higher frequency than ultraviolet light, and it is this condition that connects the children of the planet to the white Light and source of all power.

The children of Light are on every continent on the Earth plane. They are also in the oceans, and many are even in the territory known as middle Earth. They are anchored to us in such a way that they can do no one any harm. They are vibrating at such a speed that we can send direct energies and messages through their consciousnesses to those around them.

This is very important for those who need the Light, but cannot find it on their own. The presence of the children

273

of Light can suffice for the beginning paths for the many. They are of the highest, in that they serve the God and master of the universe well. They are of the highest when it comes to duty.

That is why the process of meditation and prayer can do more good than any single other action. It is because, when Beings are in this state, the energies can flow through and around them, and back up to us to use for the magnification of the moment.

It is the design of the Most Radiant One. But we need anchors to help us do the work. If it were not for the many children of Light on the planet, I am afraid the planet might not make it through the dismal energies that surround it today.

WE UNDERSTAND THE FUNCTIONS OF THE CHILDREN OF LIGHT AS YOU HAVE EXPLAINED THEM TO US. ARE THE CHILDREN OF LIGHT CONSIDERED TO BE EXTRATERRESTRIALS?

The children of Light are considered to be the finest of the extraterrestrial life that the planet Earth has ever known. In this role they have assumed the shape and form of humans, but that does not mean that they do not have the abilities and powers of other species from other star systems.

All of the Beings in the universe have access to the same powers and understanding. It is simply what is. We are with those who are dedicated to finding this, and are here assisting these beautiful souls to help them share this enlightenment with any soul who wishes it.

WHAT IS THE DIFFERENCE, THEN, BETWEEN THE STAR CHILDREN ON EARTH AND THE SPACE BROTHERS AND SISTERS WHO ARE VISITING US?

The differences are many. But before I go into this lengthy discussion, it is important to remind you that we are all one.

First, the star children are born into the human form. By comparison, the sisters and brothers, aliens, from other star systems are in the form that are native to those civilizations.

A second difference is that the species of different planets all focus their development on different lessons, so to speak. What humans do on the planet Earth is to learn certain customs, and what the aliens do on their planets is the same.

While there appears to be no common ground between these customs, there really is. The star children are here to bridge the gap between the enlightened paths of the home bases with those enlightened paths on the planet Earth.

If you recall, we stated in an earlier correspondence that the Earth must move on to the New Age with the dignity and mission that it is destined to achieve. This cannot happen if the inhabitants of the planet do not achieve the same stage of enlightenment.

The difference between the two species is that the lessons the star children are teaching to Earthlings are what comes naturally to those on the other planets. The star children are the filters of this knowledge, and they are acting as the funnels, so to speak.

The third difference is the ability to communicate on energy levels. While in human embodiment, a soul must relearn the powers of the fourth and fifth dimensions of communication. But the aliens have this focus automatically.

The fourth difference is that of the rescue. What we mean by this is that the star children will have to be "rescued" and taken back to their home planets, and will be indoctrinated back into their roles and forms when their missions are over. This will be quite a challenge for some. It will be quite an adjustment, for many do get attached to the physical world on Earth. But we are certain that the decision will be a quick one, and that the process will not be too difficult for the many who are serving the Command.

Does this give you enough of the differences for now, or do you wish for me to continue?

WHY ARE THE ALIENS HERE, THEN, AND WHAT IS THEIR FUNCTION?

Protection is their primary function on the Earth. They are interested in highlighting the spiritual path for Earthlings, and they are here to protect the children of Light.

They accomplish both of these well. They are in the mode of the adopted mother and father. They are here and working with all to ensure that the beloved Terra will achieve her destiny. This ensures that the inhabitants of the planet will receive the same attention and love that each of the aliens did when he or she went through their initiations on their home planets.

You see, each planet and star system goes through similar periods of trials and errors as the Earth is doing right now. We are here to help one of the most difficult birthing processes that has ever been the challenge to any of the Beings in the universe.

We are delighted at the response that we are getting from so many, but it is not enough. The moment for the quantum leap into the future is nearing the critical mass point, and we are hoping that the delay will not cause a retardation period for the beloved Terra.

WE BELIEVE THAT MANY INDIVIDUALS WHO READ THIS MATERIAL WILL HAVE A DIFFICULT TIME ACCEPTING THIS INFORMATION AS TRUTH. WHAT ADVICE CAN YOU GIVE TO INDIVIDUALS WHO ARE READING THIS KIND OF INFORMATION FOR THE FIRST TIME?

We are aware that many souls on Earth will not be ready for this new information. We are also aware that there is never, in the course of Earth events, a good time to bring in new information. Earthlings have a tendency to resist change and the new, and do not wish to progress into unknown realities and the beauty of other dimensions. Since we have acknowledged this condition, let us now move to the suggestions that might help ease the pain of interpreting and accepting the information that is being brought forth in this document.

We suggest that when this book is published you do one of two things. First, you allow the energies from our essence and that of the Ascended Masters to flow through this document, and give the responsibility of transformation to that level. If you give your permission for this to happen, then the true meaning of the document will be absorbed on the energy and intuitive levels of the readers. Thus, the transformation of consciousness will occur at that level.

The other thing that can be done to help ease the situations is for you to address this condition in the introductory pages of this manuscript. We have provided much of the information for the content here through the information that has been transmitted telepathically to you. In reality there is much of this content that should come from you as well. We have always called this a joint effort, and we see this information and process flowing. Since the three of you are of the human form, you understand the pain of transition for humans on your planet. It is appropriate that you address this issue from your hearts in the opening section of this book.

In the beginning, when we began to answer this question, we stated that you should do one of two things. In reality, you could do both. The choice is yours. And if you do not like either of these suggestions, stick around, and we can give you approximately 100 more.

DOES THIS MEAN THAT YOU HAVE NO ADVICE FOR THE READER OF THIS DOCUMENT?

No, it does not mean this. What it means is that your words will be honored more than ours will. It also means that we yield to the power of the Ascended Masters in this area, and choose not to take credit for the effects of this activity, should you follow our advice.

What we can tell the future reader of this document is to read this information with one's heart, and not with one's mind or eyes. If the reader takes this approach, then the real meaning of this information will come through, for in the heart is an acceptance of all.

We wish only to be accepted on the Earth plane for the gifts and benefits that we bring. We try to do our jobs with total dedication to the Light and to the sisters and brothers of Earth, whom we serve.

We would like for this document to be read as the comparison of two different worlds. We would be honored if some of the readers did find rejoicing in their hearts, in discovering the systems that we have designed. If this comes about, perhaps this will lead to the comparisons of even more advanced systems with yours. Before this can happen, this basic introductory information will have to be regarded with respect.

We look for ways to belong. We do not wish to be considered separate in a universe that is only one. We hurt at the misconceptions that Beings of your species propagate. We only wish for the truth to be revealed.

All truths are revealed through the heart. So, therefore, if the reader uses the heart as the primary organ for sensing truth, then we will be assured that our mission, through this document, will be accomplished.

HOW CAN THE PEOPLE OF EARTH ASSIST YOU IN ACHIEVING YOUR MISSION? PLEASE BE SPECIFIC.

The people of Earth are on a path that is irreversible. On this journey, they must realize that Light and love are the only two qualities that can be adhered to for advancement into the New Age. We are not speaking of the moment of time to accomplish this that is equivalent to a small day, month, or even year. We are talking about a transit of time, over the next several years, that will transform the energy of the beloved Earth to a Garden of Eden in the galaxy. The individuals on Earth need to have the tools and techniques for raising their vibrational levels higher than the Earth's manifest plane. They need to soar over the negativity on the planet, and to live in the world, but not be of the negative energy that changes their behavior so easily. They need a plan and program for advancing to this higher state of consciousness, and they need to take this responsibility seriously. They need to strive for cleansing within themselves and to assist in the cleansing of the Earth. They need to acknowledge God as the one, true Creator of the universe, and not honor their egos with the same intensification. This shift of attention must be made.

To answer your question as to how Earthlings can assist us: they need to help themselves, and the planet. If that becomes their first priority, then they are truly helping us with our mission, and we will be graded as being very successful.

WHAT CAN WE DO, AS A CIVILIZATION, TO HELP STOP THE DESTRUCTION OF EARTH'S ECOSYSTEMS AND HELP RESTORE ITS BALANCE?

The most important thing that your civilization must accomplish is to change its thinking. For each individual, in each of the areas that make up the parts of your systems, the critical element for survival is to understand the power of thought.

If this can be accomplished, then individuals can assume the posture of taking responsibility for cleaning up the untruths and injustices that have prevailed all over the planet in each of those systems. For each individual that accomplishes this, a contribution is made to healing the nervous system of Earth.

As a civilization, what you can accomplish is the moving of mountains. In the fifth dimensional frequency to which you are moving, you will find just how important this directive will be. For the powers of the mind will be so strong that powers of manifestation will be the highest forces that humans have yet experienced.

The Earth, to survive, must have the balance of energies, and each soul will walk the path of mastery over the governing of these energies. Therefore, if each soul does its part now, and begins to reclaim its power and rights on the path to the oneness, then the journey for the planet will be less painful.

WHAT CAN WE BE DOING NOW TO BEGIN THE CLEANSING OF OUR OWN BODIES AND MINDS?

The process is simple. You have four energy sources with which to work. You have your thoughts, words, emotions, and actions. Knowing this, what you need is to become aware of the power of each of these energy outlets. As humans you must begin to be masters over each of these areas. Do not let your energy be wasted. Do not let the negativity of others around you drain you of your valuable energy from a higher source. Do not allow your mind to wander. You are the master of your own temple and consciousness. Assume that role of leadership, within your mighty I AM Presence.

Another way in which you might accomplish mastery is to go through a purification of the physical. Any time that your body is distracted and is not allowed to function in its purest form, it too will drain vital energy from your heart center. The foods to avoid are sugars, bleached flours, caffeine and substances that dramatically alter the mind spectrum. Foods, such as red meats, are of the lowest vibration that the planet has produced.

By ridding your bodies of these foods, you will become a source of higher energy and power. In this higher source of energy you will find a state of consciousness that is clearer. In this higher state of consciousness, you will also find answers to the connections to the Higher Selves that reside above the body temples.

That energy source is such a pure form of electromagnetic energy that it can only be reunited with your body temple if the vibration rates are of a similar frequency. It is imperative that the body and mind be cleansed to such a degree that they can be reunited with the spirit on the same level.

The spirit will not compromise its frequency. There is no turning back once an essence has assumed that intense and beautiful radiance. It is up to the egos of humans now to raise their own consciousness levels to meet the presence on the higher intensity. That is the mission of the souls on the planet. That is the truth.

IS THERE OTHER INFORMATION ABOUT YOUR MISSION THAT YOU WOULD LIKE TO GIVE TO US?

Yes, there is one other piece of information that we believe is significant.

The fate of your world does not lie in our hands, our dear brothers and sisters of the universe. Instead, it lies in yours. We are here to assist you through the darkness that appears to be inevitable, because of the path you have thus far chosen to follow.

We honor your way and your freedom of will. We will not, however, sit back and watch you destroy yourselves, in the blindness of your own reality.

Our mission is to assist you to secure a foothold into this new world that is dawning. We will perform any function that is deemed necessary by the Ascended Masters to help you move through this portal of time, to join us on this higher dimensional frequency. We perform our work and duty with dedication and consider our work to be an act of love.

If you could sum up our mission with any other words, then, please choose these. Consider our journey to this far away land to be a journey of love and commitment to you. We honor and respect you for who and what you are. We only hope that someday you might reciprocate this attitude.

Adonai, our beloved sisters and brothers, in the Light of Our Most Radiant One.

There were several other transmissions from Juluionno which spoke of various aspects of the mission. In one, Juluionno speaks of the new energy, fragrance, and color coming to Earth at this time. In the second, he speaks of the Second Coming.

WHAT DID YOU MEAN WHEN YOU SAID, "WE HAVE THE POWER AND THE FRAGRANCE OF THE HIGHEST FORM OF ENERGY IN THIS UNIVERSE?"

What we meant by that is that we are of the few who have the ability to channel to the beloved Earth this new form of energy. We are the carriers and the creators, so to speak. We are the souls who can master this feat and bring this new occurrence to all of you. By the fragrance, we mean that we also carry with us an olfactory ability that is yet to be developed in many humans on Earth.

We have mastered the olfactory skills to a level of command that the sense of smell cannot comprehend in the present state of evolution on Earth. This is a state of existence that "feels" the energy with new senses and allows for the processing of this energy through emotional channels to assume a new path.

In this new path, one learns the powers of differentiation, and can control the senses more accurately. When one does not have this olfactory sense developed, there are many messages that get confused. When one masters this sense, then data and information presented from the energy sources automatically are perceived more accurately.

To tell you that we have the fragrance of few in the universe means that we have this power developed to an utmost factor, and that we are also on the horizon of teaching many Earthlings to develop this same sense within their own consciousnesses.

HAVE WE RECEIVED THIS NEW COLOR YET?

The color began to be channeled to Earth in the early part of 1988. It is being received in dosages, and it will not be complete until the end of 1989.

Out of this process will come two factors which will be renounced by scientists as new energy particles.

The color will not be seen by the human eye. Instead, it will be absorbed in the consciousness and the cellular structure in a manner which will foster new and added growth. In this way, the individual can process the effects in any way which is appropriate for that soul's development. This is the power of the unseen and hidden worlds that guide one's path to the Light.

It will be seen only as a new range of particles. It will be smaller than the dust particle, but larger than the neutrino. It will be the vastness of the Christ Consciousness. It will be as minute as a fleeting thought. It will be the All. It will be the Void. It is. So be it.

DO YOU MEAN THAT OUR SCIENTISTS WILL RENOUNCE THIS NEW COLOR AND FREQUENCY, OR THAT THEY WILL RECOGNIZE IT?

What we said, and what you typed, is accurate. The scientists will not understand this information or disturbance that is coming to the Earth.

Because it takes the human mind so long to accept anything new, they will renounce it and try to put it into a small box that is already defined with the data that already exists.

THE WAY THAT YOU DESCRIBE THIS, IT SOUNDS LIKE GOD. IS THE NEW ENERGY THE MANIFESTATION OF GOD?

Please refer to our communication on the subject of God.

THANK YOU. WE RECALL THAT BY YOUR DEFINITION GOD IS EVERYTHING. IS THERE SOMETHING MORE THAT YOU NEED TO TELL US ABOUT THIS NEW COLOR?

Not at this time, but it will be important when we get to the area of the human consciousness and the comparisons between your mode of thinking and ours.

For at that time, we would like to bring this subject up again, and would like for you to know that this new color becomes the central difference between the functioning on the third and fifth dimensions of time and space. We will proceed with this, then, at a later time. Is this permissible with you?

YES.

LAST WEEK YOU SUGGESTED THAT WE ASK ABOUT ENCOUNTERS WITH YOU OF THE "NINTH KIND." WOULD YOU PLEASE EXPLAIN WHAT THIS MEANS?

What we were referring to is the draft of the heavens that is among the three of you. Would you like for me to explain this concept further?

YES, PLEASE DO.

In the heavens we come from all directions. We have the power and the fragrance of the highest forms of energy that this universe has yet to observe in the third dimensional levels. In this coming we are more than the seven rays with which all of you are familiar.

The seven rays do make up your spectrum of white Light. We have promised that we would deliver to your planet a new frequency in the form of another color in this physical calendar year on Earth.

We have and are delivering this ray of the new spectrum to you all. We are also preparing and delivering a new frequency to the beloved Terra which will be heard only by a select few individuals, who have opened up their own frequencies and are able to accept and interact with this new ray. This is what we mean by the encounter of the ninth kind, and we are pleased to be the bearers of this good news to you.

Juluionno Speaks of the Second Coming As It Relates to the Mission.

WHAT EVENTS ON THIS PLANET WILL BEGIN TO MANIFEST THAT WE WILL RECOGNIZE AS BEING PART OF THIS PLAN OF THE SECOND COMING?

You will begin to see a strengthening of the bonds of the children of Light for the next few years of approximate Earth time. That is all the time that you will have left to develop your powers in the collective. On the soul's level, you will find that this will begin to unite many of the children of Light into final countdown sessions.

The second sign, related to this, will be the lost souls, who will begin to manifest another level of anger. On the cellular level, they will begin to see that hope for salvation in this period, or era of time, has been lost. They will begin to fight, experiencing an intense feeling of desertion. It is in this reaction that you will see the manifestation of the sadness of the dark side. This will become evident, even on the local level.

You will see this, but what we advise is that you throw the violet color and the white Light around yourselves first, and then to the others. Build your own protection first, and then you will be able to serve people better.

The third manifestation will be the countdown that you will see in words. Slowly you will see more and more of your media channels begin to speak of this as it is truly an event that needs to be recognized. It is in this media approach that you will begin to see sides lining up, and we advise you always to remain neutral.

In order to achieve mastery, you must be in this world, but not of it. To be in this state, you will have to rise above this battle, and you cannot afford to take sides.

See the perfection in the selection process and of God's work, and only that. Know that you will be put to work now for the final countdown, which is the Second Coming.

Be sure and concentrate your efforts on this. This major event is truly not for some time to come, but all of this other is in preparation for this event.

Let me pause here for a moment, and allow some contemplation of my words.

WHAT EVENTS WILL OCCUR AT THE TIME OF THE SECOND COMING?

The most significant event of all will be the appearance of the one most Radiant Soul, which is that of Sananda, Jesus the Christ. This has been promised, and it will be a reality.

This sighting of His radiance will be seen by all of the souls on the planet at the same time.

We can tell you this much also. This will occur on both the fourth and the third dimensions simultaneously, and we also can say with assurance, that many will tremble.

Many of the children of Light may also tremble, but they will do so only if they are not sure that they are of the chosen.

You also can count the sheep that will return to the Shepherd, for this will be a time of great rejoicing and the flock will surround this magnificent Being.

We know of no other soul who is more prominent in this mission than Sananda. He waits patiently to gather His sheep once more to the Light.

He has promised that his Father's house has many rooms. He is making preparations for each of you in the manner that your rank allows for the honors that will be bestowed.

The ceremonies will be most befitting of royalty. He will be there to wash the feet of all who pass through his house.

Not all will transcend to this home at the same time. Each will be greeted with the ceremony and accommodations that are appropriate when the time is right.

We prepare endlessly for this. We tell you that it is the event of the return to the Highest that the third root race has been awaiting for eons of time.

We welcome this new group with open arms to this new haven of honor, and we tell you that no greater glory awaits each of you than what we are preparing in the house of our Father.

WHAT IS THE ROLE OF JESUS OR SANANDA IN THE SECOND COMING AND THE MILLENNIUM?

Jesus, The Son of God and The Master of the Sixth Ray, is Head of the awakening of this planet for the dawning of the New Age. He is the glorious ray from the Great Central Sun that is the link between the souls on Earth and their destinies back to the All. He is the Being of magnificence who is selected to journey with all on Earth who have undertaken the path of the fifth ray. It is there that He is destined to meet each and every one of His

Lambs, and personally guide each through the door to the sixth ray and to His Father's Kingdom. His role is none other than the true position of leadership back to the Divine.

There is no punishment for those who choose not to enter this Kingdom, and it is clear that many souls on Earth today are not ready to make this journey with their magnificent Master. The only "punishment" is time, as you have defined it on Earth. Those who do not wish to take part in Jesus' hospitality, are those who must wait for the next appropriate time when the portal will again be opened. This portal in time will occur again approximately 26,000 years from this present moment.

This does not mean that there will be no opportunities for souls during this "frozen period" to be awakened and brought to the Kingdom. What this means is once this portal closes in this present opportunity, that the consciousness of individuals will be more independently governed, and it will be more difficult for a soul to understand the steps that lead one up the path to the Father's House.

The situation you are experiencing today on Earth is one where souls representing previous Root Races that were cast in the beginning of time, have awakened together and have the opportunity to learn from each other. They are also in the position to support one another. They will experience the journey together as they reach for spaces designated for the positions of the Lambs. They are the ones who will usher in this new and glorious Age of Aquarius, and will also be the ones who will surround their Leader with Love and Light as He rules for the next millennium.

Jesus is returned and is returning. He is among his children, sisters, and brothers, and is here with the love and gratitude that He showed over 2000 years ago. He has come to fulfill His promise. He has come because of His knowledge and great compassion, and is here for the duration of His reign.

PLEASE EXPLAIN WHAT YOU MEAN WHEN YOU SAY THAT JESUS IS RETURNED AND IS RETURNING.

Jesus has never left. He is returned in and through the Spirit, and is one with all of the children on the planet as well as in the universe. He is returning in the physical form and will be among you in that capacity. The time for this event is written in the books of Abraham, but is not in the books of your present documents. This date cannot be revealed until all of the points and conditions of Light are anchored on the planet. The forces of Light and the Angels that guard and surround this Master, are preparing the way for his return in this form. Only when the plan is complete, will you see Jesus in the form to which you can relate. He is the Master of all dimensions. He is the glorious of the glorious. He is the Son of God, who has taught all on Earth of the glory and magnificence that awaits every soul who follows His way. I speak the truth, Oh Daughters of the Light.

IS JESUS, THE COSMIC CHRIST CONSCIOUSNESS, SIMPLY RELEVANT TO CHRISTIANITY, OR DOES IT PERTAIN TO OTHER RELIGIONS AND TO THE WORLD AS A WHOLE?

God does not divide His children. It is humanity that guides and divides the people of the planet. Jesus taught that He was the way to and for All the children of the planet. But He also taught that many paths lead to the Kingdom of His Father. He taught that there was room for all of the children who practice purity of heart, by honoring the One, True Father and Mother, which is God.

Although our Master is often quoted as referring to God as the Father of Earth and the Universe, allow me to clarify this concept. The God Force encompasses both the masculine and feminine energy Force of the Universe. God is that which is contained in the All. God is the creation that made out of Itself the image and likeness of Itself. Jesus taught that all creatures, humans, and life, which are the universe, have an equal share in this creation, for everything is a part of this creation. Therefore, All of the Children on Earth will be welcomed in the Father's Higher Kingdom, but only if they want entrance into the Kingdom.

WHAT EFFECT WILL THE SECOND COMING OF JESUS HAVE ON THE NON-CHRISTIANS?

The effect of the Christ Consciousness energy that is preceding the Second Coming of this glorious Master is the same on all souls on Earth. The Christ consciousness is affecting each soul on an energy level that presents itself in the form that is best attuned for individualized integration into each soul's consciousness. What this means is this energy and higher frequency is presently being transmitted to Earth. It is designed to transform each soul in a very personal way, and only in the way that is directly connected to the individuals' paths. For both Christian and non-Christian souls this energy is requesting all to begin to re-examine their ways of life and to make decisions regarding their behaviors related to a more spiritual manner.

The rules of the universe are the same regardless of who or what one is. The rules affect each in the same way and they are unchangeable. When the rules of heart, mind, and spirit are followed with diligence and respect, the Creator of the All does not mind if a soul believes in a person or being. What is truly important is that the individual believes in the "Father within" that guides, loves and directs the individual paths. This is the key to eternal salvation. This is the key to the oneness of the reunion with the Creator. Honor first God and then obey the rules of the universe—those are the rules for salvation.

Can you not see how absurd it is that a poor, small child in a country foreign to your own, who has not heard the word Jesus uttered in his days and who leaves the Earth plane before he has had the chance to hear of this magnificent Leader, would "perish" because he had not? The example that I give you means that one is measured by the purity of the heart and the devotion to God. Jesus was the teacher of this message for his Father whom he loves with an intensity that few others have demonstrated. I am pleased to be able to bring you this explanation this evening.

The Master Kuthumi Addressed Our More Provocative Questions.

DID JESUS AND THE APOSTLES HOLD COUNCIL WITH ALIENS FROM OUTER SPACE?

The question you ask is the most serious question you have addressed thus far. It contains the energy of the answer to explode the electron and atom, and it also contains the secrets to the mysteries of Love and Light. It contains the success and failure of any soul as it spends years looking for the Holy Grail, and it contains the answer to the longing that each soul has for the union and re-union to the Father within.

Allow me to play the role of the Brother first, as I answer this question. I was one of the Brothers in embodiment to our Master, Jesus, as he took the challenge of taking on the sins of the World, by his dutiful fulfillment to His Father. I was one of the Apostles who came forth and journeyed with Him on the path to His Savior and salvation. I was John, the Disciple of the Heart, who loved my brother and Lord more than can ever be explained in a dialogue of this kind.

In this role I was in counsel with Him at all times, whenever there was an event of significance. I was the one who often cleared the path and made the vibrational frequency shift to the higher, whenever there was news of a Council meeting. When I was in embodiment, Jesus and His Council carried on a direct dialogue with the Brotherhood of the All. We took the commands very seriously, but before his death on the Cross, Jesus was the only one who could bring through the messages with clarity. We were challenged to have faith in our Savior and the Son of God. He took the role and responsibility very seriously, and so did we. All the events of that lifetime were very challenging to each of us in every way.

It was after the death of Jesus that we were given the gifts of communicating directly with the Command. It was later when we were able to make direct communication through our Beloved I AM Presence that we found the same magnificent power and love flowing through us. During the later years, I assumed the role of father and master to many, as I journeyed the countryside teaching and sharing this information with all who crossed my path.

Because of the direct communication we had with The Brotherhood of the All, I was able to reach clarity about the world in which I had been placed. I began to understand it for the illusion that it truly was. I began to make contact with the source of my power and with the source of the All. I then was able to love myself and the world in a way that I had not been able to achieve before this entire experience presented itself to me.

As a friend, father, teacher and Master, I now have a responsibility to all of you to take the same role seriously, only from the other side. Those who communicated to me from the other side of the reality are the ones to whom I now have an obligation. There are many who reside on this dimensional frequency and who take the care and responsibility seriously. The brothers and sisters who are willing to help those in need are those who are here because they have been sent by the Highest in the universe. We all work for God. You work for the same Master as we do on this dimensional frequency. Only the separation of the veil makes the difference in your perception of reality. That is the truth.

WHO ARE THE ASCENDED MASTERS OF THE UNIVERSE?

The Ascended realms contain the souls of all who have achieved the vibrational frequency equivalent to the seventh ray and higher. When a soul achieves only the vibrational frequency of a lower ray, that state of beingness does not in any way imply that the soul is of lesser quality. Once a soul has passed the tests of the seventh initiation on the Earth plane, then that soul is ready to exit the third dimensional frequency and journey into the Highest level that is known to humans—the seventh ray frequency.

There are many other dimensional frequencies available along the path back to God, but for the purpose of why Earth was created and what is accomplished in this area of time and space, this is the way of the path. This is a difficult concept to explain for the purposes of this dialogue, so perhaps you might like to ask this again when you are contemplating bringing through the transmissions for another document.

CAN YOU TELL US WHAT YOU MEAN BY THE VI-
BRATIONAL LEVEL OF THE SEVENTH RAY?

*As I have taught you in former communications, every-
thing in the universe is made up of vibrations. There are
millions of variances in the vibrational frequencies. Nothing, however, as you know it, vibrates higher than the
speed of Light.*

*Light is comprised of seven color bands, or frequencies,
that can be measured by your Earth scientists' measurements. Each color vibrates at a different speed. The color
of violet is the highest frequency before the color is consumed and becomes the white light which is the presence
of all color. This highest frequency is the vibration that
is equivalent to the seventh ray. It is that which stands
highest for you on the Earth plane, before one begins the
path of being consumed further by the Great Central Sun.*

SOME PEOPLE FEEL THAT THE END OF THE WORLD
MEANS THAT THE PLANET WILL BE DESTROYED.
WOULD YOU COMMENT ON WHAT THIS MEANS?

*Regarding the interpretation of the question, we can tell
you that it means different things to different individuals. To some it means that the planet will be physically
destroyed. To others, it means that the spiritual will be
destroyed. To others it simply means the poisoning of
energy and life, so that no other life forms will be allowed
to exist. This could occur through either chemicals, radiation, or both.*

*To us the interpretation of this question does not mean
any of these. To us it means that the physics of the
universe will no longer support the energy that surrounds
the planet and is one with it.*

It means that if the planet is destroyed, then there is no room for communication with the force of the all, which is God.

We can tell you that this Force will never be destroyed, regardless of what ever happens on the physical plane to this planet.

We can also tell you that the Force has an intelligence that is working right now to see that none of the other things ever happen.

We are proud of the efforts that the children of Light have made to save the beloved planet. We can tell you that we foresee a great destiny for this planet, but it will get more difficult before it gets better.

The outcome is totally up to the souls on the Earth. We will guarantee that we have been given the dispensation to interfere only if the planetary population chooses to blow the beloved Terra up.

WE WILL NOT PERMIT THIS TO HAPPEN. But that is the only choice of the interpretations that we are allowed to command. That is a given of which I can assure you this evening.

We are certain of this one thing only; the extent to which the Earth inhabitants have to clean up after the darkest of times yet to come is totally in your hands. So, GET TO WORK IN BRINGING IN THE COMMANDS THAT YOU KNOW ARE SO NECESSARY TO PREVENT THE WORST FROM HAPPENING.

CHAPTER X:
THE FUTURE

AFTER WE had organized the book, we asked the Arcturians to give us their opinion of the work we had done. We wanted to know whether they approved of the way in which we had organized the chapters and whether they had anything additional that they wanted to add. They replied:

We thank you for this opportunity to critique the document. We see the need for no major changes, for all that has been sent by us is significant in its own way. We have no ownership of what you choose to retain or to delete from the manuscript. It is all relative.

Each soul who reads this document will find a different truth in the messages. Therefore, no one script can suffice to meet with exactness the many needs and acceptance levels that humans have on planet Earth.

We would like, however, to summarize the book in a different way, if you would allow us to do so. The way in which we would like to finish this manuscript is to stress the importance of higher consciousness for humanity's survival in the future.

We have spoken a little of why we are here, which relates directly to the beloved Terra. The leap your planet will soon take into the future will demand that the souls on the planet interact with each other and with Mother Earth in a way that commands respect. It is this topic that we wish to address in the closing pages of this document.

This higher mode of living is what many have yearned for on Earth for several years. We observe that you weary of negativity and are waiting for redemption. We see that you toil long hours in the silence of your patience, as you wait for the return of your Savior. We have compassion for the length of time you have endured, waiting to inherit your "State of Beingness." Allow us to assure you that the day for your justice and redemption is coming. It is on the horizon of your future, and it will be the day when all those of higher consciousness will rejoice.

To be among the celebrants, all you humans have to do is to raise your eyes to the Divine. Hold the spark of hope, faith, and charity in your hearts, and watch the miracles unfold in front of your eyes. You are not leaderless in this quest for the Highest. Neither are we as we assist you on your quest; for we celebrate the same Leader as you do, our sisters and brothers of the Light.

A message sent to you centuries ago is still one of the most powerful tools you have to use for seeking guidance for this new day that is fast approaching. Allow us to recite it to you once again, and also to give you the interpretation of the message from our Elders back on Arcturus.

Psalm 23

The Lord is my shepherd; I shall not want:

> *All enlightened Beings address the same concept: there is only one God and Divine Being who is our Creator.*

299

This magnificent Being, whom you call God, takes care of all of the needs of the souls who are on the journey back to the Light. When these souls turn their attention to this Being, they do not want for anything, for their needs, on all levels, are met.

He maketh me to lie down in green pastures:

The color green is reserved for the fourth chakra within the human energy system. It represents the heart center. In humans, this center is the most powerful. It is also the one which is the most neglected by many. It is this center that hurts the easiest and is closed the fastest by many.

When one connects his or her consciousness with God consciousness, and truly behaves on a higher level, that is when the soul experiences operating from the heart center. In this state, the pastures then become very fertile and green, and contain all the ingredients of the power that will be bestowed upon the individual.

He leadeth me beside the still waters:

It is in acceptance of the heart center as the true source of wisdom, and the behaviors related to states of higher consciousness, that one acquires the calmness for which so many on the planet hunger. For it is the quieting of the mind that follows. The mind gets the soul and heart into trouble when the mind is not at rest. When an individual is in a peaceful state of mind, which is likened to the still waters, it is then that the individual can do no battle. It is at this moment that the second step of the power is given to the soul, for it is at this moment that the individual obtains his or her own mastery.

He restoreth my soul:

> With the above ingredients in place, the soul is then in the position to undo all karmic debts. In this undoing, it prepares for entrance into the kingdom of the Father.

He leadeth me in the paths of righteousness for His name's sake:

> When all karmic debts are released, the soul is free to be led on the path to higher kingdoms. On your planet you might call it Sainthood or the road of the Ascended Masters. We call it the fifth dimensional frequency, for it is in this state that individuals command the power to control the Liquid Light of the Great Central Sun.

Yea, though I walk through the valley of the shadow of death, I will fear no evil: For Thou art with me:

> The Earth is likened to a valley, for the consciousness of humans is so low. It is considered by many in the higher realms to be the valley of shadows and illusions.

> Death is an illusion. Death is only the crossing over from one state of consciousness to another. It is the passing of one karmic responsibility on to another. It is the connection back to the etheric body that is the soul. It is actually life.

> On Earth, another illusion is that evil exists. We observe that your negativity and terror are reality to you. What you do not understand is that you have created these processes through the powers of your own mind.

Therefore, when one walks on the higher planes with God, the Creator of all, evil and death are no longer feared. When one's consciousness transcends these illusions, there is no longer a need to retain them.

Since each creates his or her own reality through the power of the inner world, once negativity and fear are removed, those qualities will no longer manifest on the Earth plane or in an individual's environment. You really do have that much power, oh sisters and brothers of the universe.

Thou preparest a table before me in the presence of mine enemies:

The One Creator of all does not discriminate. God loves all souls with the equal intensity of a father and mother. Therefore, regardless of what one has done on the illusionary path, God does not punish, but actually prepares a feast table for all of the children.

Thou anointest my head with oil:

We are all the chosen children of God. We are all delivered from our weaknesses. It is only the ego that keeps you separate from the Father. God anoints us all with the mark of the Risen Savior; it is your ego and choice as to whether you will accept or reject the appointment.

My cup runneth over:

In the initiation from God, all children are offered abundance. That is truly one of the rewards from the deliverance of all karmic debts. The universe is actually one of abundance and not one of poverty. It is only the consciousness of the human form that has limited abundance. It is your minds, or knowledge, that keeps you in poverty.

Surely goodness and mercy shall follow me all the days of my life:

In this state of connectedness, the meek will inherit the Earth. Comfort, happiness, and peace are the rewards that will follow for all the children of Light who choose to raise their consciousness.

And I will dwell in the house of the Lord forever:

The Kingdom of God is eternal. There is no mistaking, the journey is an endless one.

As each civilization and species evolves, there are always new challenges, adventures, hopes, and states of ecstasy to experience. When the humans of Earth learn to transcend their basic fears and limitations, then they too will be free to explore other dimensions of reality.

The house of our Lord has many rooms. Each civilization and species is likened to another room. All are experiences and challenges just waiting in the future for the souls' next incarnations. All souls are on the path back to the Great Central Sun. It is only our experiences in the different areas of the universe that differ. In reality, all our journeys are one with the Creator of the ALL.

The day is coming for you, our sisters and brothers of the beloved Terra, to experience the other realities and rooms of the House of the Lord. We wait patiently for your new birth and the rebirth of the celestial body upon which you walk.

Let us now go in peace. We have appreciated the opportunity to get to know you in this fashion. Allow us to address you again in the future, with other words of wisdom and love.

We speak for the entire celestial gathering when we tell you that you are loved and admired for all that you are. Each of you is perfect in the State of Beingness that you are presently experiencing. You learn quickly, so we hope that the important information that you need to acquire for your "all too soon" future will not escape you in the pockets of your minds that you sometimes allow to stay closed.

Open up those areas and receive our words, for they sound the cry for the future.

The future is truly yours to create. We only hope that you choose the component of the future that will offer you the Garden of Eden you so deserve.

Adonai, our beloved children of Light.

We, the Arcturians, do bid you farewell from the northwest quadrant of the universe, and from the Most Radiant One.

GLOSSARY

ADONAI
Hebrew word for The Lord. The pronouncement of the Holy Name Jehovah (or the name of the God of Israel) is attributed the power of working miracles. The revealed absolute Deity, the Holy Creator, the Redeemer. Used by the Arcturians in farewell as a seal to the transmissions.

ARCTURUS
The brightest star in the Bootes Constellation, approximately 36 light years from Earth. It is called "Guardian of the Bear," because of its position behind the tail of Ursa Major.

ARTURO
Guide from the Starship Athena who directed the Light and sound training program with Cynthia, Betty, and Norma.

ASCENDED MASTERS
Particularly holy people who have reached a high degree of spirituality who have left the Earth plane and ascended into higher dimensions.

ASCHEANA
A feminine representative of the navigational crew on the Starship Athena from Arcturus.

ASHTAR

Supreme Commander of the Celestials, reported to sit at the right hand of Sananda, Jesus the Christ. Ashtar is said to come from Venus.

ATHENA

The name of the Starship from Arcturus which houses Beings with whom we are in contact.

AURA

See energy field.

BEINGS

A term used to denote the Arcturians or other species from other star systems. A life form, just as humans are the life forms on Earth.

BROTHERHOOD OF THE ALL

Confederation of Ascended Masters, also known as the Great White Brotherhood. The name does not imply any racial or gender discrimination. The term "White" refers to the White Light of the universe and the term "Brotherhood" includes females and males who are ascended and androgynous.

CHAKRAS

As defined by the Theosophical Society, the ethereal body's sense organs. They resemble energy vortices. There are ten in the body, visible to clairvoyants only. Of these ten, it is advisable to use only seven. Each vibrates at the frequency of one of the seven colors which the rainbow combines to create White Light.

CHILDREN OF LIGHT
This term refers to humans progressing on their paths of spirituality who seek the Light and are guided by it.

COSMIC BEINGS
Beings of other universes and galaxies.

ELDERS
Highly evolved Beings from Arcturus, who are revered by the others and who have earned positions of great respect through their wisdom and knowledge. They also are reported to have higher vibrational frequencies than many of the other representatives from their planet.

ENERGY FIELD
Area surrounding a being or object which is charged with electromagnetic energy, either positive or negative or both.

GALACTIC COMMAND
Constitutes the Brotherhood of the All and all the Masters helping Earth to enter the New Age that is upon us. They travel the universes in starships.

GREAT CENTRAL SUN
The source of all life. Another term for God.

GREAT WHITE BROTHERHOOD
See the Brotherhood of the All.

HERDONITIC
One of the Elders from Arcturus of the Starship Athena.

HOLISTIC

Emphasizing the whole and the interdependence of its parts. Each part, when separated from the hologram, contains all the essential characteristics of the whole.

JULUIONNO

Commander of the Starship Athena, from the planet Arcturus.

KUTHUMI

One of the ascended Masters, who serves Sananda, who is Jesus, the Christ. References cite Kuthumi's former embodiments as including Pythagoras, St. Francis of Assisi, John The Beloved, and the Master who built the Taj Mahal. According to the work of Alice Bailey, in his last embodiment he was known to have had the name of Koot Humi.

LIQUID LIGHT

The pool of electromagnetic energy that is the creator of everything that exists. It is called liquid because it moves continuously like a fluid, and it cannot be contained.

LOVE

A much used and widely abused term. As defined by the Arcturians, love is an electromagnetic force which encompasses the totality of the All. Another term for God and that which creates life.

MASTERS

Men and women who have evolved spiritually and who transcend their fellows and assist in ruling the world. Adepts.

MONKA
Head of the Tribunal Council for the Ashtar Command. Reported to be from Mars. Also self-identified as the "Communicator of the Technical."

NEW AGE
Deemed to be an age of spirituality and oneness. Some refer to this age as the millennium that is approaching in connection with the Second Coming of Christ.

PLANET (In reference to Arcturus)
Any heavenly body thought of as influencing human lives.

PRANA
Life support energy system of the universe. Also called the Liquid Light.

SANANDA
An Ascended Master who is reported to be Jesus, the Christ, the Supreme Commander of the Celestials who have come to Earth.

SOLTEC
Communicator from the Ashtar Command; son of Monka. Also reported to come from Alpha Centauri.

TERRA
Another name for planet Earth.

THIRD EYE
An area located in the center of the forehead between the eyebrows. A connection to spiritual energy that can be activated by meditation and awareness.

TONING
Soundings or tones which produce specific resonances that activate the chakras.

VIBRATIONAL FREQUENCY
The rate at which the atoms and subparticles of a Being or object vibrate. The higher the vibrational frequency, the closer to the frequency of the light.

Autobiography of Norma J. Milanovich

I WAS BORN and raised in the "cold spot of the nation"—International Falls, Minnesota. I am the second oldest in a family of four girls. My father was in the Border Patrol for several years, and later sold cars. I also remember a time when he owned and operated his own dry cleaning business. For all practical purposes our life was pretty normal.

My Mom was a homemaker for most of my younger years. Later, she got a job at the local movie theater. That was great, because my older sister and I got to see nearly every change of movie on the weekends! It was even more meaningful for my mother, as Hollywood became our occasional baby-sitter while she worked.

During the first five years of my education, I attended St. Thomas Catholic School and was literally raised by the Nuns. Those were memorable years, and I still cherish the fun times I had as a child. The Sisters were tough on us, but we did not seem to mind. It seems that even the wind chill factor of -60 degree temperatures did not keep us from attending Mass every morning or the classes during the winter.

In the middle of my fifth grade year, my family moved "south" to the Iron Range of Minnesota, where I eventually finished my schooling in the small community of Aurora-Hoyt Lakes. By this time my Dad was employed in the iron ore mines of northern Minnesota. Many tough times presented themselves to us, but we also had a life that was filled with clean living and hard work. We were poor, but we did not know it.

Throughout my childhood I was an active participant in most everything the community provided. New ideas, meeting people and working on projects added much excitement to my life. I found wonder and challenge in so many things around me. In those ways I have not changed much today.

After graduating from High School, I went to the University of Wisconsin—Stout Campus, and received a degree in Home Economics Education. Toward the end of my undergraduate days I married my husband, Rudy, a fellow Minnesotan whom I had met years before while participating in a speech contest at the college that he was attending. We have one child, Rudy Jr.

Two years after we were married, Rudy was transferred to Houston, TX to work on the NASA Apollo Projects, so we moved to Houston and enjoyed our nine years there.

In the early 1970's I was given a Teaching Fellowship at the University of Houston in the Home Economics Department. For nearly six years I taught there, while working on my Master's and Doctoral Degrees. In 1981 I finally completed my dissertation and was awarded my Doctor of Education degree. Looking back, those were some of the most important developmental years of my career, for I was also provided the opportunity to participate on several statewide educational teams and to work with a number of dynamic teacher educators from throughout the state of Texas and the surrounding five-state region.

It was difficult to leave Texas in 1975, but Rudy's career was calling him to Albuquerque. So, we packed again and headed further west.

Within a year I was employed in the College of Education at the University of New Mexico. I was the Project Director for selected educational programs during the first few years. The main focus for my developmental work was in the areas of professional development of teachers, sex and race equity issues, and vocational-technical certification. In the early 1980's I applied for and received the position of Assistant Professor in the College of Education. For the next six years, I combined this new position with the role of program developer and also became the Director of the New Mexico Consortium for Research and Development in Occupational Education, a position I held for my last three years at UNM.

In 1987 I resigned my position and started my own company in training and development. I decided, like so many of my colleagues, that it was time to gather my courage and try something on my own.

Approximately five years ago today I began to experience the events summarized in this book. They began after an automobile accident that shook me physically and left me with a whiplash from which I have never fully recovered. Soon after I began to experience puzzling psychic phenomena.

My whole understanding of the world around me has been altered by these events. It is like a huge gauntlet has been dropped in my life challenging me to re-examine all the traditional foundations that have provided safety around me in the past. But who is dropping this gauntlet and who are these Beings that have suddenly presented me with a curriculum more challenging than any I have ever encountered at two of our major universities?

All my life I have been taught that we must report to only one Creator, who is God, although each of us has a different perception of what God is. I was also taught that we should participate in influencing our own destinies and that we should pursue the path of our dreams and try to become all that we can be. Nothing will ever shake this belief system within me. On that I am clear.

What has been shaken, however, is my perception of reality. Suddenly there are real things happening to me that I cannot explain. I receive messages from a source that appears to be a highly evolved intelligence, which speaks only of God, Love, Light and energy, and yet I

313

cannot see the sender of these messages. Occasionally objects disappear or manifest around me, for no apparent reason. The unseen source tells of things to happen and I watch the events unfold. Clearly, I am not in charge of this reality—something else is; or that is how it appears to me. My continued, nagging questions are: "Is this only my experience, or is this happening to many others?" "If these experiences are real, what does all of this mean to us on Earth?" "Who is really in charge, anyway?"

At the universities, I promoted free thinking, research, and open mindedness to all ideas. I choose to approach this new "problem area" in my life with that same mental attitude.

My rational mind says that there is a possibility that something is out there and that this intelligence is affecting many individuals on the planet today. From the depths of my heart, I truly believe I am not the author of the messages that I receive telepathically. But then, "who is writing them?"

I ask God daily to provide me with the answers to the questions that I am seeking. I wish for only the truth to come through and to guide the way. While I do not have the full clarity and understanding that I hope to achieve, I also have faith that the answers will be revealed to me.

Autobiography of Betty Rice

IT IS VERY difficult to explain who we are and from where we come. For me, there is one place and time that I remember when I was born into the reality of this planet. Yet another part of me has always felt an attachment to a place in the universe far from planet Earth. So you could say that I really feel that I have had more than one birth. The knowledge and reality of my dual existence are something that I have always felt, yet I have few data around me to verify this feeling.

Since my journey to Earth I did all that was expected of a girl born and raised in Michigan, in a blue collar family. I married young, raised two children, and became a career woman after my sons were half-grown. The necessity of my starting to work resulted from an illness in the family; I applied at the telephone company and began my career.

In time I earned a position in the management structure of the organization. My retirement in 1983 marked the end of a 25-year career with the company. At the time of my retirement I was an assistant manager in the maintenance division of Mountain Bell.

Throughout my life I sought to improve myself and increase my knowledge of this world by taking classes at the University of Arizona and the University of New Mexico. I always have had an insatiable desire to read as many books as possible. The majority have been non-fiction; yet I also have enjoyed the classics, science fiction, novels, and the latest books dealing with metaphysics.

During the past several years I have continued to explore other realities including many aspects of metaphysics and different religious beliefs. Most of this was accomplished alone, without tying myself to any one group or ideology. My studies have brought me to a deep understanding of why we are here. They also have given me a knowledge of our interconnection to the Oneness of it all, as our unseen friends have taught us.

Cynthia and I became friends in 1984, after she had joined an art group with which I was affiliated. We met Norma through a mutual friend in 1987 and became friends shortly afterwards. It was through a telephone conversation I had with Norma in May of 1988 that we decided to put our heads together to see what we could bring through from the source to which she was connected; thus, this book was begun in July of 1988.

The information contained in this book has been a revelation to me, and also a welcomed confirmation of thoughts and ideas that have pushed me all my life. I am proud to be a part of this book, and hope that it will awaken those who are ready to learn where the true power may be.

Autobiography of Cynthia Ploski

I MUST HAVE been interested in art all my life. I have a photograph of myself at about the age of three in which I am drawing, totally engrossed. The other great loves of my life began early, too: nature, archeology, and spirituality. I think I was always on a spiritual path, but I did not realize it until the last several years.

My happiest childhood memories probably pointed the way. I was happy using colored rocks to draw pictures on pieces of gray slate, making pottery out of muddy clay and leaving it on the rocks to dry, climbing trees, and hiking through fields of flowers. These are summertime memories. My wintertime memories are of flights of fancy to other, ancient worlds through the National Geographic. In those pages I explored the ruins of ancient civilizations, dreaming private dreams of myths and gods and goddesses.

I grew up in an affluent suburb of New York City, advantaged but not rich. I was a member of every possible majority, caught without awareness in the lackluster roles that life in my environment in the 1940s and 1950s embraced. Looking back, however, I can see how many important decisions I made then, were the threads that would form the fabric of my later life.

I was only ten when I decided that there really must be a God, because there was so much beauty in nature that only something divine could have created it. My major in college (geography) included geology, earth sciences, and anthropology. I studied comparative religion, became an active Christian and spent as much of my time as possible in nature, which gave me a connection to something that I had been looking for all of my life.

317

Now, many years later, my early dreams have become my way of life. I live in New Mexico and move with love among the ancient ruins, the splendors of nature and the nurturing support of friendships with all people. I paint the ruins and try to portray the beautiful energies that remain there, finding expression for the awareness that dawns continually in my consciousness. I am no longer a member of any organized religion, and my beliefs are closely aligned with Native American spirituality.

Before I was able to come to New Mexico, however, I had to complete other lessons in life. I graduated from college in Vermont with a bachelor's degree, married, raised four children of my own and a few others who came into my life, and lived in many states to which my engineer husband was transferred in the course of his career. We were married for 20 years. During this time my father died, and I took over the reorganinzation and management of the two small companies he had owned. As I increased my knowledge and experience, stresses erupted in my life that eventually culminated in divorce.

I went back to school in Illinois, where I was then living. I majored in art this time, and was working on a Master's Degree when the divorce forced me to get a "real" job and set that goal aside. As a displaced homemaker, I obtained a CETA job which later led to a position as manager of a vocational assessment center. That job involved supervising two vocational assessment specialists and three clerical workers. I wrote proposals, developed budgets, managed the financial reporting necessary in government projects and acted as a liaison between the high school vocational education department and the community.

In 1982 I remarried, and early the next year my husband and I came to New Mexico to begin an entirely new and different phase of life. I began to earn a living as a professional artist and became a part of the art community in New Mexico.

Presently I am listed in *Who's Who in the West, Artists of New Mexico, American Artists, an Illustrated Survey of Leading Contemporaries—1989,* and the *Encyclopedia of Living Artists in America, Fourth Edition—1989.*

It was my friend Betty who first saw the spiritual and metaphysical aspects of my work. She and other friends encouraged me to read, and learn about, as well as to experience, the special vibrations that are here in New Mexico. I took workshops, met with other women who shared my interests in metaphysics and art, and gradually expanded my field of knowledge and increased my conviction.

When Betty and I first met Norma we were both impressed with her sincerity and her radiant beauty of body and soul. We met and conversed many times, and this book is an outgrowth of the excitement we began to generate as a group of three people: open, growing and learning.

To me, the most important result of working on this book has been the increased awareness of, and trust in, the beautiful flow of life energies that all three of us have experienced. Since these messages have produced this result in us, I feel that they may help others as well. I therefore offer this work in that same spirit of love and sharing that has blessed us in its formation.

For several years, Dr. Norma Milanovich has received numerous messages from Beings who identify themselves as Ascended Masters and Celestials from the Galactic Command. So much interest has been generated by these transmissions that she found it impossible to reply to inquires about them on a personal basis. Therefore, certain messages of special interest to the general public are selected and published periodically in the quarterly newsletter called *Celestial Voices.*

The first six newsletters cover a significant six-step process for guiding the people of Earth into the Fifth Dimension. These transmissions are received from Master Kuthumi.

To order your subscription of *Celestial Voices* newsletter, fill out and mail the coupon below.

- -

CELESTIAL VOICES

Please enter my name for a subscription to *Celestial Voices* Newsletter. Subscription rates (check your choice):

☐ 1 Year @ $12.00 ☐ 2 Years @ $22.00

Price outside the U.S and Canada: $18.00 per year

Name_____

Address_____

City _____ State _____ Zip _____

☐ MasterCard ☐ VISA (check one)

#_____ Exp. Date:_____

Signature _____

Send check or money order to
ATHENA PUBLISHING
Mossman Center, Suite 206, 7410 Montgomery Blvd. NE,
Albuquerque, NM 87109-1574 FAX (505)880-1623